WHERE WAS OPAL?

Teresa could no~~t~~  for
the phone to ring~~... She~~ to
take action. She wa~~nted~~ to
find her niece. She ~~pulled from~~
a chest and began ~~writing.~~

The picture of Opal snowed her in a black cowgirl
hat, a red vest with a sheriff's star on the left breast
over a stripped turtleneck shirt. Her small hands
clutched a black-and-white stick horse. Opal's dark
brown hair rested on her narrow shoulders; her
bangs covered her eyebrows and nearly obscured
her bright blue eyes. Opal's trademark grin was wide
and depicted a fun-loving, happy child. The photo
brought tears to Teresa's eyes and the ever present
question to her mind: where was Opal?

Teresa took a piece of paper and began writing:

*Opal Jo Jennings kidnapped about 5:30 on Friday, March
26 in Saginaw, Tx. Last seen being forced into dark purple,
almost black, car, may have tan or brown top. Late model
believed to be a Mercury sedan. A tall, white male with brown
hair in a ponytail with facial hair.*

*Age: 6 Hair: Brown Eyes: Blue About 4 feet tall Weight:
60 lbs. If you've seen or have any information about Opal
please call Saginaw Police . . .*

AND
NEVER SEE HER
AGAIN

PATRICIA SPRINGER

PINNACLE BOOKS
Kensington Publishing Corp.
http://www.kensingtonbooks.com

PINNACLE BOOKS are published by

Kensington Publishing Corp.
850 Third Avenue
New York, NY 10022

All Kensington Titles, Imprints, and Distributed Lines are available at special quantity discounts for bulk purchases for sales promotions, premiums, fund-raising, and educational or institutional use. Special book excerpts or customized printings can also be created to fit specific needs. For details, write or phone the office of the Kensington special sales manager: Kensington Publishing Corp., 850 Third Avenue, New York, NY 10022, attn: Special Sales Department, Phone: 1-800-221-2647.

Pinnacle and the P logo Reg. U.S. Pat. & TM Off.

First Printing: December 2006

10 9 8 7 6 5 4 3 2 1

Printed in the United States of America

This book is dedicated to the memory of Opal Jennings,
the other children who are honored in the Garden of Angels
in Euless, Texas, and the thousands of other children
who have been taken from loved ones prematurely.

CHAPTER 1

Six-year-old Opal Jennings crouched on her hands and knees in her grandmother's yard as she watched a colony of ants trudge through the dirt and over the occasional sprig of early-spring grass. It was 5:30 P.M., March 26, 1999. The sky was partly cloudy and the air was cool, perfect for active youngsters to be outdoors. The light easterly wind gently blew Opal's dark brown hair loosely secured in two "dog ear" ponytails. Spencer, Opal's four-year-old friend, sat beside her as Austin, her two-year-old cousin, amused himself in a nearby tree. The trio played cheerfully, free from fears and adult paranoia.

The children had just completed a make-believe sword fight, their sabers nothing more than fallen twigs from one of the large trees that bordered Robert and Audrey Sanderford's Saginaw, Texas, property. The three were imaginative children, adept at entertaining themselves for hours on end, and were great friends.

Teresa Sanderford periodically rose from her kitchen chair in the house she shared with her husband, Clay, mother, Audrey, brother-in-law and stepfather, Robert, grandson Austin, and niece Opal

Jennings to peer out the window and check on the children. Seeing that they were playing happily, Teresa returned to the book she was reading while waiting for her husband to arrive home. They would all be going to dinner at Opal's favorite Mexican restaurant, El Sombrero.

While Audrey rested on the sofa, Robert Sanderford, Opal's grandfather, walked to the small porch of his modest white-framed home and yelled at the children.

"Come on back closer this way," Robert hollered. "You're going too far."

The children appeared to be getting along well and having fun. Audrey Sanderford checked on the kids as well. She smiled as she watched Opal enthralled with the march of the ants. "Opal is a budding entomologist," she often told friends. "She loves bugs."

Between the doting grandparents, there were mere minutes when the children were unattended.

Audrey took one last look at Opal, Austin, and Spencer. Assured they were contentedly occupied, she again stretched out on the family sofa to rest before leaving for dinner. Robert sat in his recliner, watching the early news. Both of them could hear the voices of the children playing no more than twenty yards away.

Lemon Street is a short street off Saginaw Boulevard, the main thoroughfare through the small-bedroom community just nine miles north of downtown Fort Worth, Texas. The city, which tongue in cheek refers to itself as a "city on the right track," has a maze of railways running through the town. Home to some of the world's largest grain elevators, many of the trains from Saginaw carry grain from the agri-business center to much of the rest of the county.

Saginaw, predominately a blue-collar community, was rapidly growing with white-collar commuters who desired urban amenities and a small-town quality of life. The more than fifteen thousand residents enjoyed the slower pace of a tight-knit community, the luxury of good schools, and a feeling of safety from the high-crime levels of the larger more metropolitan cities of Dallas and Fort Worth. Crimes such as burglaries occurred occasionally, but by 1999, only three homicides and just one family-related abduction had happened in nineteen years. The town prided itself on its relatively crime-free, family-friendly atmosphere.

One block off Saginaw Boulevard, Lemon Street crosses North Hampshire Street. Near the corner of Lemon and North Hampshire, the trees where Opal, Spencer, and Austin played lined the open area of the lot where the Sanderfords lived. The houses along North Hampshire were small and unassuming, the front yards dotted with bicycles, plastic slides, and a variety of children's toys.

A dark-colored car moved slowly down Lemon. The man behind the tinted windows watched as the three youngsters amused themselves. The car turned at the end of the road, passed a couple of teenage boys throwing a ball across the street, rounded the block, and again passed the trio of distracted children. The slow-moving vehicle made the short circuit five or six times, finally pulling to a stop at the curb in front of Opal, Spencer, and Austin.

Unaware that anyone was watching, Opal continued to direct her full attention to the march of the ants to their colony.

"Hi," an unfamiliar man said as all three children looked up to see him standing in the yard. His long dark hair was secured in a ponytail and topped with a red ball cap.

Opal turned her head and naturally smiled, her blue eyes twinkling with innocence. Before she could speak, the man swept her up in his arms and dashed for his car parked only a few feet away. Opal screamed in fear, her fists striking against his strong grasp.

The man hastily shoved Opal into the front seat of his car. Frantic, the little girl's large eyes widened as she continued to scream in a shrill expression of panic. Her arms and legs thrashed about in the air as if she were drowning in a sea of terror. Opal's abductor knotted his fist and struck the struggling girl in the chest, knocking the wind from her small frame and sending her body back against the seat.

Before Austin and Spencer could react, the dark car sped down the street, taking Opal away.

Teresa Sanderford jumped to her feet the instant she heard Austin's cry. He was wailing like she had never heard before. It wasn't the shriek normally heard when the boy, not quite two years old, was hurt or the screech that said he wasn't getting his way. Austin's cry was filled with the sound of terror.

Teresa ran to the front porch. Austin was sitting in a small flower-patterned settee that occupied much of the narrow concrete slab. He was curled on the love seat, his short legs tucked into his body, his head down. His tiny body shook as he sobbed in obvious distress. Tears flowed steadily from his blue eyes, streaking the dirt that coated his cheeks.

Panicked, Teresa asked her grandson, "Austin, what's the matter? What's the matter?"

"Opal's gone," the towheaded boy howled.

"Gone where?" Teresa asked, confused by Austin's

statement. She glanced toward the trees where the children had been seen playing about three minutes earlier when Robert had last checked on them. The site was empty. Opal and Spencer were both gone.

"Opal went where?" Teresa questioned again, her anxiety growing. Robert and Audrey joined Teresa and Austin on the porch, their brows wrinkled in puzzlement.

Austin lifted his small hand and pointed a tiny finger toward Teresa's sister's house on the corner of Worthy Street and North Hampshire. "Opal gone bye-bye," the child said through his tears.

Teresa swiftly picked up her grandson and hurried toward her sister Patricia's house. From the absence of cars, she could see no one was home, but she continued on, hoping to find Opal there. Audrey followed closely behind.

"No. Car," Austin said. The grown-ups didn't understand.

Teresa saw no sign of Opal, but she noticed Trey Barnes and Michael Logan throwing a ball from one side of Worthy Street to the other. "Have you seen Opal?" Teresa frantically asked the boys as she pushed her long brown hair back from her face.

Twelve-year-old Michael shook his head in the negative, while thirteen-year-old Trey said, "No."

"Have you noticed anything unusual?" Teresa asked anxiously.

"There was a car circling the neighborhood two or three times, real slow," one of the boys replied.

Teresa turned to her mother who had just joined her and the boys. "Mom, go back and call nine-one-one. These kids saw a car come around two or three times," Teresa told her. Worry etched her face.

"You go over to Spencer's house to see if Opal might have gone over there," Audrey instructed as she started back to the house to make the emergency call. It had been less than twenty-four hours since Audrey had spoken to Opal about talking to strangers. Their discussion had been prompted by the disappearance of nine-year-old Fleisha Moore in Dallas. Opal had been curious about the AMBER Alert, which had been frequently heard on television. Because of their discussion, Audrey was almost certain Opal wouldn't have talked with any stranger who might have approached her. But she couldn't help wondering if Opal had been able to make that choice.

Less than five minutes had elapsed since Austin's first terrifying cries had been heard. Teresa rushed across the street toward the house where Spencer lived with his mother, grandmother Charlene Williams, and great-grandmother Dorothy Flora. Seeing Dorothy in the front yard, Teresa asked, "Have you seen Opal? We can't find her."

"Oh, my gosh!" Dorothy replied. "Spencer came in real excited. . . ."

Teresa didn't wait for Dorothy to say more, she went directly to the front door and knocked.

While Spencer had been playing with his friends across the street, Charlene had been enjoying a game of Free Cell on her home computer in the kitchen. Late in the afternoon Spencer had bolted into the house shouting.

"Grandma! Grandma!" Spencer had yelled only minutes before Teresa knocked on their door.

"What?" Charlene asked, a bit annoyed that her grandson had burst in the house screaming so loudly.

"Somebody took Opal!" the boy said excitedly.

Charlene looked at her grandson suspiciously.

"Spencer, go back outside and play. You're watching too much television."

"Somebody took Opal!" Spencer repeated stubbornly.

Charlene believed Spencer's four-year-old imagination had gotten the best of him. Spencer, like Opal, had watched recent events in Dallas involving Fleisha Moore's abduction in southeast Dallas. She'd later been released unharmed in Navarro County. Charlene was certain Spencer had just transferred that child's plight to his friend Opal.

"Oh, honey, just go out and play," Charlene prompted.

"I don't want to go in front," Spencer snapped sharply, perhaps fearing that he could be the next one snatched by the man with the ponytail and red ball cap.

"Then go in the backyard," Charlene said, still believing Spencer's fantasy had overtaken his reason. Reluctantly Spencer walked through the small kitchen and out the back door.

Two to three minutes later, Charlene heard Teresa's knock at the door.

"Have you seen Opal?" Teresa asked, fear making her voice sound breathless. "We can't find her." Charlene could tell from the tone of her neighbor's voice and the expression on her face that Teresa was bordering on panic.

"Oh, my God," Charlene said. "Spencer came and told us that Opal was kidnapped, but I thought he was being silly. I sent him outside. He's in the backyard."

"I have to talk to him," Teresa declared.

Charlene left Teresa in the house and hurriedly went through the back door to retrieve her grandson.

Four-year-old Spencer ran to where Teresa waited. The boy, his blond hair styled in a short crew cut, was shaking. Visibly upset, Spencer found it difficult to verbalize what had occurred to his playmate Opal.

"What happened?" Teresa asked. "What happened to Opal?"

"We were playing on the lot in the anthill and a car pulled up. A man got out of the car, picked Opal up, knocked her in the car, and took off!" the boy exclaimed. "Opal was crying. She was crying. She was crying!" Spencer babbled.

"Where did he go?" Teresa asked as calmly as she could, attempting to soothe the boy. "Which way did he go?"

"He started to head toward Worthy, but when he got to Pat's house, he pulled into the driveway, flipped around, and headed back," Spencer replied, sounding much older than his mere four years.

Teresa's initial worry quickly surged to panic.

"What did he look like?" Teresa questioned.

"He had little marks on his face," Spencer stated.

"Do you mean whiskers?" Teresa asked.

"No, they were just marks, like little pimples or things like that," Spencer stated.

Charlene's heart sank. Spencer had been telling her the truth. Opal had been kidnapped. Charlene felt awful—why hadn't she listened to her grandson? She believed he'd merely been repeating what he'd seen on television. She had lived in her house on North Hampshire for thirty years, had watched most of the neighborhood children play on the lot across the street. They would climb up and down the small trees, play ball on the grass, get into any kind of mischief they could. But nothing like this had ever happened before. She felt sick to her stomach.

"The man had long hair and a baseball cap," Spencer added, interrupting his grandmother's thoughts.

"What did the car look like?" Charlene asked,

attempting to help get as much information as she could from the four-year-old.

"It was a purpledy black car. He took Opal and put her in the car. It looked a little bit like Mommy's," Spencer said, referring to his mother's black Trans Am sports car. "But it's not just like Mommy's."

Teresa's mind was whirling. A purplish black car. Teresa remembered a black car with tinted windows moving extremely slowly up the street earlier in the day. She recalled it because the car was traveling no more than five miles per hour and had driven by two or three different times. Teresa had seen the car a couple of times before so she hadn't thought much about it at the time, but now she wondered if it could have been the same car, driven by the same person Spencer said had taken Opal. Teresa's heart filled with dread.

"Can Spencer come talk to the police?" Teresa asked Charlene.

"I'll bring him over," Charlene said as Teresa hurried back across to the Sanderford house, where police were already arriving.

Charlene's physical condition was poor. In the last seven years she'd been on medical disability as a result of three heart attacks, bypass surgery, diabetes, and the beginning of Parkinson's. She asked her next-door neighbor Colleen Vincent if she could take Spencer to the Sanderfords'.

After walking Spencer to the curb, where her neighbor met him to take him across North Hampshire, Charlene went into the house to fetch her car keys. She was in no physical condition to walk the neighborhood in search of Opal, but she was certainly able to drive.

While Teresa talked with Spencer, Audrey had made the 911 call to Saginaw police. Her hand had shaken as she took the receiver from the cradle and her fingers trembled as she punched the three numbers no parent ever wants to use to summon help for their child.

Speaking in a voice laced with traces of an Arkansas accent and the stress of a frantic grandparent, Audrey told the 911 operator that her granddaughter Opal had been kidnapped.

"My name is Audrey Sanderford," Opal's grandmother began, seemingly gulping for air. "My granddaughter was playing out in the yard and she disappeared and nobody can find her."

After urging from the 911 operator, Audrey gave the dispatcher Opal's description.

"My little grandson came in crying. He said Opal got in a car," Audrey said, struggling to maintain emotional control while desperately wanting to scream.

"One kid said there was a car driving around real slow in the neighborhood," Audrey stated. Then before disconnecting from the dispatcher, Audrey Sanderford repeated her street address.

Audrey's legs wobbled under the strain of Opal's disappearance. She reached for a chair to steady herself.

Within three minutes of Audrey's frenzied call, the familiar Saginaw black-and-white patrol cars pulled in front of the Sanderford home. In less then ten minutes officers had blocked off the streets surrounding the area. They immediately began scouting for dark-colored cars with children inside. Teresa's own son was detained by police. He was unable to leave until Teresa identified him and the kids riding in his vehicle.

Curious neighbors began to gather on the street in front of the house where Opal had been living for the past six months. They all knew the happy-faced little girl with the endearing smile. She had become a radiant light in their neighborhood. As each of the neighbors began to learn the news of Opal's abduction, their faces became drawn and creases of concern crossed their foreheads.

Saginaw Fire Department (SFD) trucks joined the police cars parked on North Hampshire. The firemen exited their units and immediately began to explore the Sanderford home. They searched every nook and cranny of the house, under beds, in closets, showers, and behind furniture. The men even delved into an old trunk in the attic in hopes Opal was playing a game, waiting for Spencer and Austin to find her. But Opal was nowhere inside the Sanderford home. It appeared her two young playmates had been correct; Opal had been abducted.

Charlene steered her car around Worthy, Western, and Lemon, then out to the highway. She made a pass by the playground, where kids frequently played on small rocking-type horses, the snow cone stand, the familiar red-and-white DQ sign of the local Dairy Queen, and Diamond's, the local grocery store. She pulled into the nearby convenience store. Charlene's eyes scanned the streets, the parking lots, the driveways. She was looking for any dark car with a child inside. She went down each of the blocks in her neighborhood from varying directions. She passed by a number of dark-colored vehicles, but none appeared to hold Opal Jennings. After a twenty- to twenty-five-minute search, Charlene returned home.

By the time Charlene turned her car back toward her house the police and fire department personnel were canvassing her street. Friends in the tight-knit neighborhood had learned of Opal's abduction and many had set out to search for the little girl themselves.

Together Trey Barnes and his mother went looking for the missing girl. Audrey, Robert, and Teresa nervously stayed by the phone in hopes of some word from Opal. Within an hour it was obvious the six-year-old was nowhere in the neighborhood.

The abduction of Opal Jennings was unlike any case Detective James Neal or the Saginaw Police Department (SPD) had ever handled. Neal spoke with each member of the Sanderford family, establishing the facts of Opal's abduction. He got a description of the child, including the clothing she'd been wearing. He would question the Sanderfords more intensely at the police station later, but right now, time was of the essence. Neal gave the order to sound the AMBER Alert. If lucky, someone would spot the dark-colored car with a small child inside and alert authorities. Or, as in the case of the Dallas abduction, the perpetrator would hear the alert, become frightened of apprehension, and let the girl go unharmed. Either way, the results should be positive. The detective didn't want to dwell on the negative statistics; he wanted Opal back safely.

Detective Neal also realized this was no time for egos or jurisdictional squabbling. He immediately notified the local branch of the Federal Bureau of Investigation (FBI).

"We have a missing girl," Neal began, providing the details of the abduction as he knew them. Although professional in his presentation, Neal was anxious inside. He knew the statistics, the possibilities of Opal Jennings's fate. He understood that quick action was possibly the only thing that could save the little girl from the clutches of an unknown perpetrator.

Neal continued with the description of Opal.

"She's six years old, has brown hair, blue eyes, is about four feet tall, and weighs about sixty pounds,"

Neal stated. "She was last seen wearing purple shorts, a purple shirt, and pink Barbie tennis shoes." Neal gave the location of Opal's abduction and the time frame from which they were working.

At the Sanderford house, Teresa and Audrey prayed for Opal's return. Teresa kept Austin close, insisting he remain in the house near her. She gazed out at the trees where only a short time ago Spencer, Austin, and Opal had been playing cheerfully. The beautiful cool afternoon had turned to a dreary, cold, wet night. Teresa continued to contemplate how Opal could be missing. They had kept a close eye on the children. They had talked to them about strangers. It all seemed impossible, but she knew it was real.

"She's out there," Teresa said to Clay as she stared out the window, her voice filled with concern. "She's probably cold and wet. She only had on shorts and a T-shirt. She must be cold."

Clay put his arms around Teresa to comfort her.

"I just don't understand," Teresa said, allowing tears to come to her eyes for the first time. "One minute she was out there playing with Spencer and Austin, and then she was gone."

CHAPTER 2

It was an atypical day for Investigator Danny Mc-Cormick. He was on his way home at four o'clock in the afternoon. More often than not he was late getting to the residence he shared with his wife, Paige, but Paige understood. A prosecutor in the Denton County District Attorney's Office, Paige too often arrived at their house well after nine-to-five workers were watching the evening news or in their kitchen preparing dinners. The McCormicks had accepted the unstructured hours of working in law enforcement long before they married.

McCormick had deliberately set his March 26 schedule to be out of downtown Fort Worth and well past Texas Motor Speedway before 5:00 P.M. It was the weekend of one of the biggest NASCAR races of the season. Nearly three hundred thousand people were expected to converge on the raceway north of Fort Worth's city limits on I-35. There would be 150,000 people in the stadium seats that rose high above the Texas plains; VIP campers would be parked in the infield, and other fans in designated camping areas adjacent to the stadium. A chosen few would be partying in one of the 194 luxury VIP skybox suites that looked down on the 1.51-mile quad-oval track.

One hundred thousand vehicles would be clogging up the roads, causing a number of challenges to working commuters. Danny McCormick didn't want to be one of those trapped for hours in raceway traffic. For all his forethought, McCormick had no way of knowing his stay at his North Texas residence that night wouldn't be for long.

Shortly after hanging his Stetson hat on an entry hook and sitting down in the living room, McCormick received a call between 5:30 and 6:00 P.M., informing him a six-year-old girl had apparently been abducted in front of her Saginaw home. As a member of the Tarrant County District Attorney's Special Crimes Unit, Investigator McCormick was instructed to make his way back to the Special Crimes office immediately. The traffic he had earlier avoided would be gridlocked by the time he was back on the highway headed south toward Fort Worth.

At 6:57 P.M., while en route, McCormick heard the disturbing, yet eerily familiar sound of the AMBER Alert. Three shrill blasts, then a radio announcer's voice declaring the frightening news that another North Texas youngster had been abducted. The child was Opal Jennings, of Saginaw.

McCormick listened carefully as the radio announcer described the suspect as a white male, forty to fifty years old, wrinkled face, long brown hair in a ponytail, and wearing a red baseball cap. The car was depicted as a dark purple or black two-door sedan, possibly a Mercury Cougar, with tinted windows, chrome wheels, antenna on the back of the car, and the front of the car set higher than the back. The abducted child was named Opal Jo Jennings, six years old, approximately sixty pounds, about four feet tall, her brown hair possibly in two pigtails. The announcer instructed anyone who had information on the suspect, the vehicle, or Opal Jennings to contact the Saginaw Police Department immediately.

The AMBER Alert concept had initiated in Arlington, Texas, after the January 1996 abduction of nine-year-old Amber Hagerman. Amber had been riding her bicycle when a neighbor heard her scream. The neighbor watched helplessly as a man pulled Amber from her bike, threw her in the front seat of his black pickup truck, and sped away. The neighbor urgently called police and gave a description of the vehicle and the long-haired driver. The local news stations covered the story on their regular broadcasts. Four days later, Amber's body was found in a drainage ditch, four miles from her home. Her throat had been cut. Her kidnapping and murder remain unsolved.

After hearing of Amber's abduction, a concerned citizen contacted a Dallas radio station suggesting that they and other area radio stations repeat news bulletins about abducted children just like they did with severe weather warnings. Local station managers agreed such a program would provide an important public service that might help save the lives of children and the AMBER Alert was born.

The Dallas/Fort Worth AMBER Alert plan commenced in 1997. Since that time, a number of cities, states, and regions have adopted the plan. Most North Texas law personnel were aware of the AMBER Alert and the criteria for which it was to be enacted. The child had to be seventeen or younger; the child was unwillingly taken from their environment without the permission of the child's parent or legal guardian; law enforcement personnel believed the child was in danger of serious bodily harm or death; and there was enough descriptive information about the child, the abductor, or the suspect's vehicle to make a broadcast alert to the public helpful.

As McCormick listened to the broadcast concerning the disappearance of Opal Jennings, he was aware that time was of the essence. The AMBER Alert first went out locally in the Dallas/Fort Worth area, then statewide, and within hours it had been nationally broadcast.

Frustratingly McCormick moved at a snail's pace along the crowded highway, back past the speedway, toward his downtown Fort Worth office. The Special Crimes Unit was located on Belknap Street, near the heart of the city. It was 8:00 P.M. before McCormick met with Assistant Chief Mike Adair and other members of the team to go over their individual responsibilities.

The Special Crimes Unit joined the thirty-five sworn officers of the Saginaw Police Department who had begun the initial investigation. The Fort Worth Bureau of the Federal Bureau of Investigation and other local agencies joined in to form a multi-agency task force.

Each officer, investigator, agent, and assistant district attorney (ADA) knew that time was critical. If Opal had been grabbed by a stranger, she was in immediate danger. They knew all too well the gruesome statistics. If they didn't find Opal soon, she could be gone forever.

Television trucks with tall antenna reaching upward toward the low-hanging dark clouds above North Hampshire Street in Saginaw provided technical support for the camera persons and reporters that scattered across the Sanderford lawn. Opal's photo flashed on the television screens of more than a million metroplex viewers watching the four local ten o'clock newscasts.

But while people sat in their warm living rooms or snuggled in their beds with only the illumination of the television screen delaying their sleep, Opal Jennings's whereabouts were still unknown.

Teresa Sanderford wrung her hands and paced the floor, often sidestepping other family members, who mirrored her actions. A haze of smoke hung just above their heads like an early-morning fog on nearby Eagle Mountain Lake as one cigarette after another was lit in an effort to calm their nerves. The interior haze provided a ghostly ambience to an already fearful household. Tears were kept at bay, but remained just below the surface, threatening to erupt whenever a prayer for Opal's safe return was uttered out loud.

Audrey Sanderford, Opal's stepgrandmother, rested when she could. Audrey had assumed the task of dealing with the media. Robert, a soft-spoken, timid man, and not only Opal's grandfather but also her legal guardian, had gratefully left the public family presence to his wife. But the stress of Opal's disappearance, combined with answering questions from the massive media contingent, had taken its toll on Audrey's physical strength, as well as her emotional stamina.

Opal had been gone for only a few hours, but it seemed like an eternity. Each time the phone rang, family members jumped and rushed eagerly to answer the call, hoping for the best, dreading the unthinkable.

At 2:00 A.M., the Sanderford family was seated in the Saginaw Police Station, awaiting their turns to be questioned by Detective Neal. Teresa, Audrey, Robert, and

Clay all gave statements to the facts of Opal's disappearance as they knew them. Each was fingerprinted.

Detective Neal had no doubt as to the real anguish, the obvious distress each of the Sanderfords was experiencing. But he had to question everyone, eliminate them as suspects, or continue to probe into their lives.

Two important people were missing from the interview: Opal's father, Randy Crawford, and her mother, Leola Sanderford. Neal learned that Crawford was living in Arkansas and Leola in North Dakota. He made a note to bring Crawford to Texas as soon as possible for questioning. Perhaps this was a relative abduction. It could be possible that Crawford, learning that his daughter had been sent to live with her grandparents, had become disturbed by the situation and picked Opal up. If lucky, Opal Jennings was in the neighboring state with her father, not in the clutches of a possible pedophile.

After the Sanderford family had left the station, Detective Neal made the calls to Arkansas and North Dakota. Unable to reach Leola Sanderford, Neal got in touch with the sheriff's office in her area and told them of the situation in Texas. They promised to get word to Leola that she needed to call her Texas family as soon as possible.

Leola "Lee" Sanderford was working the night shift at the Midtowner restaurant and lounge in Mandan, North Dakota. She hadn't talked to Opal in several weeks, the last time when she was able to scrape together enough money to buy a long-distance telephone card. Leola missed her oldest daughter and had hoped she would be able to join her shortly. But monetary difficulties, family problems, and a younger daughter at home had delayed Leola joining Opal in Texas, or having her daughter return to North Dakota.

When Leola was notified that she must contact her Texas family as soon as possible, she was frantic. Her first thoughts were of her daughter. Was Opal hurt? Was she okay? She called the Sanderford house in Saginaw as soon as she could.

Leola's heart ached as she digested the news that Opal had been snatched by a stranger and there was no clue as to her whereabouts. She sobbed for her child, and for her inability to be in Texas searching for Opal herself.

"I don't have enough money to get there now," Leola told her father. Her voice was faint, gripped by fear. "I want to come down, but I have to face my problems up here first."

Robert and Audrey were in no position to help Leola get to Texas, they got by on their meager incomes but couldn't offer any help in getting Leola home. Robert promised to keep his daughter informed of the progress of the search and advised his youngest daughter "to pray."

The morning after Opal's abduction, Audrey rose, took a cup of coffee in hand, and walked to the porch. She peered helplessly out at the spot where her granddaughter was last seen. She took in a quick breath and stared at the tree where she had last seen Opal playing.

Tied to outreached branches were yellow ribbons, their streamers softly caressed by the morning breeze. The trunk of the old tree was embraced by pink rabbits, brown bears, and cuddly white kittens, tokens of people's need to remember a lost little girl, expressions of hope that Opal would soon return. Tears burned Audrey's eyes. Everyone was being so supportive, so caring, but all she wanted was to see Opal's blue eyes dance with the excitement Audrey knew Opal would feel if she saw the stuffed animals. Just as she had done, time and again for the past terrifying hours, Audrey said a prayer for Opal to be found safe.

Along with the expressions of faith placed by the Sanderfords' tree, friends, family, and even strangers began to assemble on the lawn. They had come to help in the only way they knew how. They wanted to help find Opal. The volunteers were willing to do anything—march through mud, man phones, or cruise neighborhoods—but Nancy Wright, the SPD lieutenant directing the investigation, declined.

"We have to be able to know what's going on in order to coordinate this investigation," Wright told the media. "It's not like we're trying to run this on our own. We know our resources are limited. Right now, we're employing the best strategy we think is needed for this case."

Wright was fully aware that although volunteers can be helpful, using too many or bringing them in at the wrong time could actually impede the investigation. Police officers could easily lose command of a crime scene and untrained volunteers could inadvertently destroy evidence. The Saginaw Police Department, which had twenty-two members, including administrative staff, officers, and detectives, had few resources available to monitor outside help.

Wright's decision frustrated volunteers, who felt shut out by the police. After all, the community needed to feel useful, helpful in some way. But Wright's first duty was to preserve the scene and take command, so bright yellow police tape cordoned off the Sanderfords' home from even the closest family and friends.

Teresa walked slowly down the hall of the small house and stopped in front of Opal's room. She

wouldn't find comfort in holding on to any of Opal's
stuffed animals or touching the hems of any of her
clothing. The room had been sealed, a desolate reminder of the family's nightmarish loss.

Audrey sat in the warmth of her living room, staring at sheets of paper covered with the simple math
problems that Opal had been working on. At the
top of each one, scrawled in big purple marker, was
the name "Opal."

Outside, the chill winds whistled. Both Teresa and
Audrey feared that Opal was cold in her little purple
shorts and purple-and-white T-shirt, the same clothes
she had worn to participate in a Saginaw Elementary
"Fun Run" earlier the previous day. Purple and pink
were Opal's favorite colors, and her Barbie tennis
shoes would provide little warmth against the cold rain
that saturated the ground and dampened their hopes.

The family tried to remain positive, but the longer
Opal was gone, the more they worried. The frustration at being able to do nothing more than wait had
already begun to take its toll. Exhaustion was setting
in, but sleep was nearly impossible. The image of
Opal smiling, running, laughing, playing, continued
to fill the minds of all who loved her. Worry marred
their faces.

Teresa could no longer sit and wait, powerless for
the phone to ring with news of Opal. She wanted to
take action. She wanted to be involved in helping to
find her niece. She took a favorite photo of Opal from
a chest and began making notes.

The picture of Opal showed her in a black cowgirl
hat, a red vest with a sheriff's star on the left breast
over a striped turtleneck shirt. Her small hands
clutched a black-and-white stick horse. Opal's dark
brown hair rested on her narrow shoulders; her
bangs covered her eyebrows and nearly obscured

her bright blue eyes. Opal's trademark grin was wide
and depicted a fun-loving, happy child. The photo
brought tears to Teresa's eyes and the ever-present
question to her mind: where was Opal?

Teresa took a piece of paper and began writing:

*Opal Jo Jennings kidnapped about 5:30 on Friday,
March 26, 1999 in Saginaw, Tx. Last seen being
forced into dark purple, almost black, car, may have tan
or brown top. Late model believed to be a Mercury
sedan. A tall, white male with brown hair in a ponytail with facial hair.*
*Age: 6 Hair: Brown Eyes: Blue About 4 feet tall Weight:
60 lbs. If you've seen or have any information about
Opal please call Saginaw Police.*

A local Saginaw printer donated his time and materials to produce nearly ninety thousand flyers made
from the photo of Opal and the text written by Teresa.
Volunteers who had been ignored in the search effort
blanketed the area, tacking flyers to trees and telephone poles, taping them to stop signs and store-
fronts. They tucked them under windshield wipers
and stuck them on car antennas. It was impossible to
go anywhere in Saginaw without seeing the sweet,
happy face of the missing child. Flyers were distributed in Fort Worth and Dallas, sent to friends and relatives in other cities, other states, and eventually
other countries, to be circulated in hopes someone
somewhere may have seen Opal Jennings.

The efforts of the volunteers were acknowledged
and appreciated, but authorities knew that a study by
the Justice Department revealed that 44 percent of all
abducted children under the age of seventeen were
killed within an hour of their kidnapping. It had been
more than twenty-four hours since Opal had been

reported missing. Although they knew the statistics were against them, the men and women assigned to the Opal Jennings case continued to push for a positive resolution.

MARK 9, a Dallas canine search-and-rescue group, was called in, along with Fort Worth Police Department's (FWPD) mounted patrol, state police divers, and other authorities. A Fort Worth police helicopter equipped with an infrared device, which detects anything that emits heat, such as a person, searched for Opal. Lieutenant Wright, who had held off local volunteers, had amassed a group of more than two hundred searchers, all willing to look for Opal Jennings.

The commander of Arlington's Amber Hagerman Task Force was scheduled to meet with Saginaw police to share any information they gained during their search that might help with Saginaw's efforts to find Opal Jennings.

Saginaw police detective Mike Hughes spoke to a meeting of several hundred parents, asking them to share any pictures or videos they may have taken during the school "Fun Run" that Opal attended on the afternoon of her abduction. Checking the background of pictures for clues might help them identify any suspicious person or persons at the event.

"What is being done to protect our children during school hours?" one parent asked during the meeting. "How do we respond when our kids ask when Opal will return?" another questioned.

"You say you don't know. You say the truth," Becky Henton, the school counselor, replied. "Give them extra hugs."

The children were kept indoors for recess during the first week following the abduction while the massive search for their classmate took place outside the walls of their protected environment.

Police planned to use volunteer searchers when the time was right. Liability waiver forms were distributed to interested persons so that when it was determined their services were most needed, they would be ready to go into action. It was unsure exactly how the volunteers would be used. Some might take food to investigators; some might eventually be used in the hunt itself. During the first critical hours following the abduction, only certified law enforcement personnel would be allowed on the scene.

Although there were rumblings from those who most wanted to be a part of helping find Opal, the Sanderfords had no problem with the manner in which the Saginaw Police Department was handling the matter. They had faith in the officers. Opal's family could see in their faces, hear in their voices, that the officers were taking to heart their job of finding Opal. In only a few short hours, Opal had become part of them. She had become their little girl.

CHAPTER 3

In North Dakota, Leola Sanderford's mood was as chilled as the winter winds that blew outside her door. Far from Texas, she felt powerless to help find her daughter. Although she kept in phone contact with her father and stepmother, Leola longed to be in Saginaw, ached to be there when Opal returned home.

Leola's financial situation hadn't improved since the call came from home that Opal was missing. She worked long, hard hours at the restaurant, but tips were meager and she had another child to care for.

Nearly a week after learning of Opal's abduction, Leola received another call from Texas. Leola squeezed the phone tightly as she listened for news of Opal.

"Someone, an anonymous donor, has provided you a plane ticket to come here," Detective Neal told Leola. "We can get you on the next flight out."

Tears filled Leola's large brown eyes and spilled onto her pale cheeks. She was going to Texas. She'd be there when they brought Opal home. Her stomach dipped with excitement, but her mood quickly soured when she realized that she would have to leave Courtney behind. Courtney's father would take care of her, Leola was certain of that. But one daughter was already missing, she dreaded leaving the other. She also didn't look forward to facing Audrey Sanderford.

The Sanderfords were a multigenerational blended family. Audrey, the mother of eight, married Robert, the father of three, in 1985, and they set up house in Clarksville, Arkansas.

Leola, at age nine, was the youngest of the Sanderford girls. Her dark brunet hair, deep chocolate brown eyes, wistful smile, and shy manner gave her the illusion of spiritedness with an undertone of vulnerability. Leola was a good girl. She always did what she was told, and never talked back to her father.

The nine-year-old had missed out on the unique, if not occasionally volatile, relationship of a mother and daughter. She had no memory of her mother. She had never known her. Her father had become her whole world. Although strict, Robert was never abusive. For nine years they had coexisted in relative harmony, but then her father met Audrey, and Leola's life changed.

For the first time in years, Leola had to share her father, not only with her two older sisters, but with another woman in the house. For seven years the tension between the two Sanderford women grew. At sixteen, Leola began seeing Randy Crawford. Crawford, a friend of the Sanderford family, was twelve years Leola's senior, and old enough to provide Leola the chance to change her life. They quickly married and Leola gave birth to their only child, Opal, in 1992.

The couple bounced from city to city and from home to home. The marriage rapidly deteriorated. The attention Crawford heaped on Leola prior to their marriage faded and he showed little interest in either his wife or daughter. When Opal was only four months old, Leola decided to move to Corpus Christi, Texas. The Gulf Coast city was where Leola's grandmother and namesake, Leola Hartline, lived. Mrs. Hartline, along with other extended family, would help Leola provide a loving household for her daughter.

Leola wasn't disheartened at leaving Arkansas. Her husband really had never been a part of Opal's life, and Leola felt both she and her daughter could receive in Texas the love and nurturing they missed in Arkansas.

Opal thrived in Corpus Christi. She loved the beach, watching the boats motor up and down the coastline, and the seagulls in suspended flight. She had become the center of her extended family. She grew from an adorable infant to a precocious toddler, and her mother flourished as well.

While living in Corpus Christi, Leola met Chris Chase and fell in love. She eventually took four-year-old Opal with her and followed Chase to Mandan, North Dakota. Leola and Chase lived together, but never married. In 1996, they had a child, Leola's second daughter, Courtney. But their relationship didn't last and the couple eventually separated.

Undereducated and with little work experience behind her, the only job Leola was able to find was as a split-shift waitress at a truck stop in Mandan. The young mother found herself with little time and even less money to care for her two daughters. By the time Opal had turned five, Leola had made a heartbreaking decision.

Opal was unhappy in North Dakota. She missed her sunny days at the beach, her grandmother, and her aunts and uncles. As hard as Leola worked to make a home for herself, Opal, and Courtney, she continued to struggle. She knew what would be best for

Opal, and as much as it pained her, Leola thought the most sensible decision was to send Opal to live with her father and Audrey.

Robert and Audrey Sanderford had moved from Arkansas to Saginaw, Texas. They lived in an unpretentious home, along with Audrey's daughter Teresa and her husband, Clay, who also happened to be Robert's brother. Only a few houses down the street lived Robert's other daughter Pat. The family-filled neighborhood would provide Opal with all the love and attention that any five-year-old child would need. The thought of having Teresa and Pat close by comforted Leola. She knew Opal would be fine. And, after all, it was a short-term solution. She hoped she would be able to join her daughter shortly, just as soon as she got on her feet financially.

But sending Opal to Texas had been harder than Leola had imagined. Tears burned her eyes as she waved to Opal on the day Robert and Audrey walked her daughter to the plane, which would take her hundreds of miles away.

Opal immediately had made herself comfortable in a small corner bedroom of her grandparents' house. She quickly began to flourish.

Unlike her mother, Opal got along well with Audrey, who marveled in the child's perceptions.

"She loves beautiful things," Audrey had said. "She finds beauty in moss; she finds beauty in caterpillars. To have been so knocked around in her life, she just takes each day as she gets it."

Opal entered Saginaw Elementary School, where, in six months, she learned to write her name, read, work math problems, and tell time with a regular-faced clock. Six Flags Over Texas sponsored a reading program, providing any boy or girl who completed six hundred hours of reading in forty-five days with a free ticket to the amusement park. Opal had 780 hours before her grandmother tired of writing down her reading time. Opal had surpassed the goal. She had gotten the ticket. She looked forward to the rides, eating cotton candy, and walking the acres of park grounds.

But Opal never made the trip to Six Flags. She never rode the runaway mine train or got splashed on the log ride. She never saw the gunfight on Main Street or poked around in the souvenir shops. Opal was abducted from her grandparents' front yard before she could reap the benefits of her reward.

One week after Opal Jennings's abduction, Richard "Ricky" Lee Franks climbed the steps to the Romanesque Revival architectural-style Wise County Courthouse, some thirty miles north of Fort Worth. The nineteenth-century building, made of Texas granite in two colors and terra-cotta used extensively in the friezes, turrets, and dormers, housed the Wise County Adult Probation Department.

Franks made his way down the stone floor of contrasting colored tiles, along marbled walls, and past thick oak doors to a winding cast-iron staircase in the center of the building. He climbed the stairs toward the glass skylight above and to the office of Jesse Herrera.

Herrera was the last of several probation officers Franks had seen during his seven-year term of community supervision. Franks had a long history of arrests and convictions on sex-related crimes in Wise County. He was first arrested in January 1991 on two counts of aggravated sexual assault with a child in connection with incidents involving young female relatives. He pleaded guilty to the lesser offense of indecency with a child and received seven years' probation. Franks had been jailed twice during his probation for failure to attend required sex-offender-counseling sessions. His probation had been as much a struggle for the probation officer as it had been for Franks.

Herrera had been trying since Franks was assigned to his caseload to get him to "clean up his act." Each time Franks had arrived in Herrera's office, he wore unkempt clothes, his beard was shaggy, and his hair was long and dirty. Most often he wore his brown hair pulled back in a ponytail, often topped with his favorite red baseball cap. No words of encouragement or chastising had moved Franks to do better.

Sitting behind his desk when Franks arrived, Herrera's mouth gapped open in obvious surprise. Franks was dressed in clean jeans and shirt, was smooth shaven, and his hair was cropped short. Herrera wondered what could have possessed Franks to make the changes he had resisted for years.

Franks came from a poor family of native Texans. He was born in Decatur, and had lived in Chico, Newark, and Saginaw, Texas. Bessie Franks was a religious, overprotective mother to her three sons. Their father, Robert, worked as a trash collector. Robert was "slow." He had his son, Rodney, teach him how to write his own name. The Franks' marriage dissolved when Ricky was two years old. Robert Franks had little to do with his sons and later died in the late 1980s.

Bessie married Henry Hemphill Sr., a Saginaw barber. Hemphill was more of a father to Ricky and Rodney than their biological father had ever been.

Henry Hemphill's attempts to discipline Ricky were often hampered by Bessie's interference. She took up for her son, excusing his actions by saying, "He's a tenderhearted little boy."

When Ricky Franks would act up in school and his stepfather would leave the barbershop to pick him up, Bessie wouldn't allow the boy to be spanked. Or if Henry Hemphill raised his voice to Ricky, Bessie would counter with, "That's not how you treat him." Bessie and Henry Hemphill eventually divorced, but they remained friends.

Ricky Franks and his brothers were close, as he was with his stepbrother, Danny Doyle. Franks's natural brothers had watched out for Ricky most of his life. Slow in school, with an IQ of 65, in the range of borderline mental retardation, Ricky had been tagged a "retard" by his classmates and would complain, "They're calling me names. I'm an outcast."

"It just seems like the whole world picked on him," Bessie said.

Franks continued to attended special-education classes in Saginaw, eventually graduating from Northwest High School in nearby Justin.

Ricky Franks had held a number of minimum-wage jobs, including cashier at a Golden Fried Chicken, carnival ride operator, and motorcycle mechanic. He had shown mechanical aptitude early, fixing flat bike tires and broken chains for other children in his neighborhood. But as an adult, Franks never lasted at one job for any extended amount of time, preferring to roam the streets and hang out with his brothers and, later, his wife. Franks had been evaluated as a hard worker when he worked, but most of his employers recognized that he had no desire to hold full-time employment, often making excuses for missing work.

In 1993, Ricky Franks's half sister introduced him to Judy Magby, and on October 28, 1994, twenty-five-year-old Richard Lee Franks and thirty-five-year-old Magby were married. Judy stated they married, in part, because Ricky wanted to move out of his mother's house.

Judy took on the responsibility of caring for Ricky, along with her young daughter from a previous relationship. To outsiders, their relationship more closely resembled a mother-son situation than that of a husband-wife.

"I more or less watch over him," Judy Franks said. "He's not really growed up." She admitted she was "like a mother to him."

Judy refused to believe the reports that Ricky had sexually molested his nieces; therefore, she was unconcerned for her own daughter's safety.

But Franks had confessed to the Wise County Sheriff's Office in 1990 that he had molested a half-dozen children, starting when he was thirteen years old. Most victims were children of relatives or friends and ranged in age from four to ten years old. He also admitted sexual attacks on girls, starting when he was thirteen. Regardless whether his wife chose to ignore the truth, Ricky Franks was a sexual predator.

Judy enjoyed being with Ricky, and they spent most of their time together. Franks would often join his wife at her job as a school crossing guard and visit with her until the school bell rang and she picked up her red-and-white stop sign to assist the children across the street. The simple act of being within one thousand yards of a school was a violation of one of his terms of probation, but Franks obviously didn't care. He often ignored the directives of the court. Not only had he been jailed twice during his seven-year probation term for failure to attend required counseling sessions, he was now living with a child under the age of eighteen, and thumbing his nose at other sex-offender terms of probation.

On March 25, 1999, the evening before Opal Jennings's kidnapping, Franks had become enraged during his sex-offender-counseling session and had stormed out of the counseling center without explanation. No one knew what had set him off, or what repercussions would occur as a result of his anger.

Walking into Herrera's office, just behind her husband, was Judy Franks. Herrera cringed as he noticed her. She, too, often accompanied Ricky on his probation visits, frequently interfering with Herrera's officer-probationer discussions. Judy regularly made excuses for Ricky's lack of attendance at therapy or failure to perform community service. But as Herrera went through the usual inquiries about job, family, and counseling, a nagging thought in the back of his mind kept trying to push forward.

Once the Frankses had left his office, Herrera continued to ponder the reasons why Richard Lee Franks would pick now, after all these years, to change his appearance drastically. The small-framed Hispanic officer walked to the window, adjusted his glasses, and watched as Judy and Ricky Franks climbed into a black Mercury Cougar and drove off.

Herrera's eyes widened as he stood straight. Hurriedly he rummaged through the papers on his desk. Pulling the one he sought from the stack, he held it with trembling hands.

On the 8½-by-11-inch sheet of copy paper was the image of Opal Jennings, along with the brief description of her abductor. The depiction was familiar to Herrera. It fit the man who had just left his office. The car described in the flyer was eerily like the one driven by the Frankses to Herrera's office. He was certain the man authorities sought was Richard Lee Franks.

CHAPTER 4

A light mist fell on the hundreds of people who crowded the neighborhood street where little Opal Jennings had lived with her grandparents. They held hands, encircling the bewildered Sanderford family, while candlelight flickered, illuminating the tears that spilled down their cheeks. The sweet sound of "Jesus Loves the Little Children" brought painful sobs from Opal's family.

Donna Whitson, a tall, dark-haired woman, clung to Audrey Sanderford. Whitson, the mother of Amber Hagerman, was there to support the family, as were all the others who filled North Hampshire Street. Wearing a white sweatshirt with her daughter's image on the front, Whitson clung to Audrey Sanderford, holding her as she cried. Painful memories of Amber's abduction speared Whitson's heart, but she had felt compelled to be there for the family of this stolen child.

"A little girl is missing, Lord, and everyone is scared. A little girl is missing, Lord, and all we can do is pray," a resident read aloud. Everyone bowed their heads to pray for the safe return of Opal Jo Jennings.

Similar prayer services were taking place in

Arkansas, where Opal was born, and in Tennessee, where the Sanderfords lived for a time.

The events were meant to bolster the spirits of the family, who had slept little and worried ceaselessly since Opal's kidnapping. The outpouring of love and concern was overwhelming, but nothing would ease the pain of their loss, nothing but finding Opal.

Leola Sanderford wearily leaned against one of the two maroon posts that supported the tiny front porch of her father and stepmother's Saginaw house. It had been eight long days since her daughter's abduction. Leaving her two-year-old daughter back in North Dakota, Leola had flown to Texas, hoping she could help bring her older daughter back home.

Leola, her dark brown hair gently blown back by a mild westerly wind, straightened to address the press. The shy young woman didn't relish facing reporters and cameras. Unlike her stepmother, who seemed at home in front of the media, Leola was uncomfortable. She was there only to plea for Opal's return; then she would gladly fade back into the background to let others deal with the press.

Wearing a sleeveless flowered shirt in temperatures that hovered in the mid-seventies, Leola Sanderford spoke into a dozen black microphones set up to capture her words. She stated that she believed someone outside the family had taken Opal. "It had to be. There's nobody else who could have done it," Leola said softly.

The young mother of two was having difficulty speaking. Overcome with grief and fear, Leola said, "Please bring her home safe" before she broke down and was led inside the house. There, her grandmother Leola Hartline, who had traveled from Corpus Christi to Saginaw to help her family, consoled the younger Leola.

Outside, Audrey Sanderford stepped in front of the microphones and fielded questions from the massive media contingent.

"I don't want to think Opal is dead," her grandmother said. "I know she's alive. I know whoever's got her is moving around somewhere, somehow."

Audrey wanted desperately to believe Opal had not been harmed. She, as well as her stepdaughters and husband, wanted their lives back to normal, but life as the Sanderfords knew it prior to Opal's kidnapping would never be the same.

It would be changed forever for their neighbors as well. The students at Opal's elementary school were being kept inside for recess. Parents didn't allow their kids out of their sight. Some parents carried copies of the official list of registered area sex offenders with them. They would check and recheck the names, birth dates, descriptions, and streets where known sex offenders lived. Tensions were high. The laid-back residents of the small town had become prisoners in their own homes. Where, before, there had been kids playing football, riding bikes, and climbing trees, the Saginaw streets were now nearly deserted.

"It's kind of like it's raining all the time in Saginaw," one resident described. "The kids don't go outside to play. They're all cooped up inside."

Their children's mobility may have been severely restricted, but anxious adults finally were given official permission to get out and look for Opal. Divided into teams of five to ten, some volunteers searched on foot, others on horseback, while still others were led by dogs trained to detect human scent. Nearly 110 volunteers searched much of the thirteen-square-mile city, but found nothing.

While searchers combed the area in pursuit of

Opal, her family prepared for Easter. Opal had helped pick out a light blue dress she'd planned to wear on Easter Sunday. Her grandmother had been forced to hide it from the youngster, who had been handling it so much Audrey feared she would wear it out before she even had a chance to wear it.

Opal would have been beautiful in the dress, the color intensifying her deep blue eyes and accenting her dark brown hair. Audrey could envision Opal standing in the living room, posing for an Easter picture with a basket full of candy in one hand and a stuffed animal in the other.

Tears burned Teresa Sanderford's eyes, while at the same time a small smile crossed her lips. She watched grandson Austin scurry across the lawn in a frantic, fun-filled hunt for the brightly colored eggs hidden in the yard. It was Easter, little more than a week after Opal's abduction. Teresa's thoughts were of Opal, how cute she always looked dressed up in her Easter bonnet, a new dress, and shiny shoes, carrying her Easter basket filled with gooey treats left by that elusive Easter bunny.

But Easter 1999 was a time of emotional turmoil for Opal Jennings's family. It was a time to celebrate the resurrection of God's son and a time of mourning for the loss of their own child. Reverend Grady Brittian, pastor of the Davis Memorial United Methodist Church in North Richland Hills, Texas, not far from the Sanderfords' house, had offered to perform a sunrise Easter service in the backyard of the Sanderfords' home, but the family had declined.

During the crisis Brittian and the Sanderford family had bonded together as friends. The minister had made numerous visits to the family home, often taking along soft drinks, ice, or other supplies he thought they may have needed. He knew without a doubt that first and foremost the family wanted Opal back. Brittian also knew that Opal's Christian family wanted whoever had taken Opal to have a "life-changing experience." They hoped that if Opal had been killed, the person responsible would come clean and tell police where the young girl's body was hidden. Brittian knew the family not only wanted but needed relief from the enormous pain they were feeling. Telling them where Opal's body could be found would be the humane thing to do. But Audrey Sanderford wasn't prepared to accept her granddaughter was dead. In declining Reverend Brittian's offer of a private service, Audrey said, "I need to get out there (to church) and have that Easter service. I need to sing hymns, listen to the choir, and just get filled back up. Jesus is alive and in his heaven watching over Opal."

"It hurts and all, but we're going to get through it," Robert Sanderford remarked. "Opal's here with us."

The entire community had carried the heaviness of Opal's kidnapping with them for more than a week. Parents had kept their children closer, not allowing them to wander far from home, but Easter was a time for faith, a time to put their fears away. More than four hundred children turned out for the annual Easter egg hunt sponsored by the Saginaw Fire Department. Laughing and running under the bright blue sky dotted with puffy white clouds, the children scurried across the grassy fields of Willow Creek Park, gathering the prized colored eggs. For at least a short period of time, the people of Saginaw were leading regular lives again.

Saginaw police were doing all they could to find Opal Jennings. But with each passing day, the task became more intense, more overwhelming for the small-town department. The FBI and other local agencies were working closely with the Saginaw PD. However, with a week gone and no word of Opal's whereabouts, the decision was made to take the case to the national public.

John Walsh, the host of the immensely popular *America's Most Wanted*, was well known as a children's advocate. After the kidnapping and murder of his own son, Adam, from a Hollywood, Florida, shopping mall, Walsh had immersed himself in helping other grieving parents search for their missing children, as well as their abductors.

Walsh began his crusade by having the faces of missing children placed on milk cartons in an effort to raise national awareness. His actions sparked an international victims' rights movement, and his fight for change was felt among national policy makers. In 1988, Walsh became the host of *America's Most Wanted*. Through the national television program, Walsh had been able to help hundreds of families find closure and had helped expedite the capture of some of America's most dangerous fugitives. The program was a natural vehicle for a plea to help find Opal Jennings.

Walsh, a middle-aged attractive man with a face as serious as the crimes he reported, stood in a New York television studio as a photo of Opal Jennings appeared on television screens across America.

"There is a little girl who desperately needs our help tonight," Walsh said.

In the thirty-second feature Walsh briefly told the nation of the abduction of Opal Jennings and gave them a description of the suspect who had taken her.

"Let's find Opal Jennings tonight," Walsh said at the end of the segment.

The local Fox television channel aired the program

in Dallas/Fort Worth within mere days of the abuction.
A longer segment was planned for later, but Walsh
agreed with Texas authorities that the word of Opal's
kidnapping had to be reported immediately for para-
mount results.

The program aired at 9:00 P.M. Central time, and
by 9:30 P.M., the show's hotline had received nineteen
tips. More calls were expected after the show aired in
Mountain and Pacific time zones. Saginaw police
were relieved that six new phone lines had been in-
stalled prior to the show's airing to handle the magnitude of tips expected. One hundred fifty calls
poured in. Each lead would be checked out, no information disregarded. Every tip was fed into an FBI
computer system called "Rapid Start," which could
process huge amounts of information. The system
linked into the federal crime information databases
in Pocatello, Idaho, and Savannah, Georgia. More
than ever, authorities were determined to find the
missing six-year-old girl.

Help to find Opal came in many forms. Donors
gave more than $30,000 toward reward funds for infor-
mation leading to Opal's abductor. The fund had
been initiated by a $10,000 donation from Schepps
Dairy. A local industry, Schepps Dairy routinely offered
rewards for missing persons in the Dallas/Fort Worth
area. Anonymous benefactors also gave the Sanderfords
a fax machine and computer to help the family send
and receive information about Opal's disappearance.
Close neighbors began a fund to help Sanderford
family members who had to take off from work. A
proud family of modest means, Robert and Audrey
were grateful for all the assistance provided them.

The gifts of money and machines were appreciated, but, more than the tangible, the Sanderfords

were most grateful to the hundreds who searched for Opal.

As volunteers combed rain-swollen creeks, railroad tracks, saturated fields, construction sites, and residential developments for any clues leading to Opal's whereabouts, more than 750 Saginaw children lined up at a local grocery store to be fingerprinted, photographed, and measured. Their parents stood in line with them, many with arms draped around their child's shoulders, seemingly in fear of letting them go.

The assistant manager of Harvest Grocery Store on Saginaw Boulevard organized the event in conjunction with the Saginaw Police Department's Crime Prevention Unit. The goal was to provide parents with current photographs and fingerprints to give authorities if any child was to go missing. With Opal's abduction and the massive search for her abductor under way, local parents feared the kidnapper could strike again.

Search One and Children Education Search and Rescue, two trained volunteer search groups, joined local volunteers. Dressed in jeans, boots, bright orange vests, and carrying flashlights and walking sticks, they looked for clues that might lead them to Opal. They pushed back barren branches of bushes not yet covered with lush green leaves, which soon would be sprouting. They walked through dried grasses and smashed the random sprigs of green spring turf, which would blanket the area soon. They marched through gullies and combed the quarry shoreline. A Texas Department of Public Safety dive team searched the small lake in the quarry, but there was no sign of Opal.

Joining the ground hunt was Texas EquuSearch, a mounted exploration and recovery team. EquuSearch had begun with the purpose of providing volunteer horse-mounted searchers to recover missing persons. Launched by Tim Miller, the team was based in Galveston County, Texas, where a high incidence of missing persons occurred in a largely undeveloped area. Known as the "killing fields" after a number of bodies were found in the area, Miller had a personal interest in developing the search-and-recovery team. Miller's own daughter's body was one of those that had been dumped in the killing fields.

In 1984, Laura Miller was abducted and murdered. First thought by authorities to be a runaway, Tim Miller had disagreed and pressured authorities to investigate a particular area north of Lake City, but his appeals went unheeded. Nineteen months later, kids riding dirt bikes stumbled across Laura Miller's body in the same section of South Texas her father had requested searchers to explore.

"I remember that helpless feeling," Miller said. "I can't leave those families (who have lost children) alone. I know the feeling of despair."

Since Miller began the organization of dedicated, compassionate professionals, their membership has grown to more than 250, many of whom were trained in various rescue and lifesaving skills. They included business owners, medics, firefighters, housewives, electricians, and students. They are experienced riders, foot searchers, divers, and pilots. In 3½ years, Texas Equu-Search had conducted more than 330 searches and recovered more than forty bodies; out of nineteen Houston area alerts, they had saved six persons.

Watching as his troops climbed on their horses, Tim Miller hoped the group would be lucky in their search for Opal Jennings. He prayed that Opal, unlike his own child, would be found alive.

Sitting atop hundreds of pounds of horseflesh, the

EquuSearch team set off to explore a rock quarry area that included Marine Creek, south of Saginaw. They searched until nightfall, rubbed down their horses, and rested, waiting to return to the search on the following day.

Tim Miller knew from painful experience that the longer they went without finding Opal Jennings, the more likely the search would turn from one of rescue to recovery of the child's body.

As the hunt for Opal continued on the ground, authorities set up trap trace devices and recorders on the Sanderford family telephones. If the kidnapper was to contact the family for ransom, or hopefully, to let them know where Opal could be found, they would have a recording of the conversation and a way to trace the call in an effort to identify the abductor. Meanwhile, the tedious process of establishing alibis for the nineteen registered sex offenders residing in Saginaw began.

Tears pooled in Teresa Sanderford's eyes as she watched Opal's smile light up the television set. Her hair was slightly longer than in widely circulated photos, she clutched a white stuffed cat with black ears and tail and a doll wearing a blue dress and straw bonnet. Teresa remembered the day the video had been taken, during spring break only days prior to her abduction.

"And when she grins, it's clear that Opal is missing an upper front tooth," John Walsh, of *America's Most Wanted*, said. "That's important information."

It was the second time Opal Jennings's disappearance had been aired on the highly rated television program. The longer segment created more than twelve hundred leads, and authorities worked feverishly to prioritize and follow up on each tip.

On April 15, as thousands of Texans worked frantically over their income taxes before the midnight filing deadline, and hundreds of other Texans were spread out across the far reaches of northern Tarrant County looking for signs of Opal Jennings, Audrey and Robert Sanderford boarded a plane for New York City. Advice given to Audrey by others who had suffered similar losses was ever-present in her mind: "Keep Opal's picture and name in front of the public." She planned to do just that.

The following morning, Audrey and Robert sat in the ABC television studio of *Good Morning America.* The popular morning news program would be another vehicle Audrey would use to get Opal's photo and description out to millions of people across the country. The Sanderfords had already appeared on *Good Morning Texas,* the local ABC affiliate's answer to post-*GMA* programming each morning.

Audrey sat relatively calm while awaiting their turn to talk about Opal. It seemed to have become Audrey's purpose, what drove her every day to get up, and she appeared to thrive on it. Robert, on the other hand, was as nervous as a child in his first school play. He wanted no part of talking on TV. He left the public speaking to his wife.

After a few moments of lighthearted bantering between cohosts Diane Sawyer and Charles Gibson, Gibson's smile turned serious.

"Coming up this half hour, we are following a story that has gripped the entire Southwest section of the country. You may have read about it in other areas of the country, but it has been a focal point in the Southwest.

"A six-year-old girl, her name is Opal Jennings, is missing."

A few short minutes later, millions of people who had never heard of Opal Jennings or Saginaw, Texas, were aware that the precious child with the big eyes and engaging smile had been ripped from her family.

That same evening *Inside Edition* broadcast a similar segment. The family desperately hoped that the exposure of Opal Jennings to both national audiences would provide the break needed to find her.

CHAPTER 5

Two fishermen cast their lines into the murky waters of the Elm Fork of the Trinity River in Irving, Texas, some twenty miles from Saginaw. They waited for a strike and a catch they could take home. Neither man ever expected to see the deteriorating body of a small child.

The anglers scrambled up the bank of the river and flagged down a Dallas police officer. Shaking from the sight, the two frantically told the officer of their grim discovery.

Within an hour a small boat from the Irving Fire Department (IFD) was in the water. Divers carefully lifted the remains into the craft while news crews sped to the site, hoping to learn if the body was that of Opal Jennings, missing for twenty-six days, or that of three-year-old Cristy Ryno, a toddler abducted from her parents' Irving apartment only three days earlier.

As the Rynos huddled around their television set in Irving, Leola Sanderford and friends stared at a television provided by a TV station on the lawn of the Sanderfords' Saginaw residence. Leola's eyes were mere slits as she strained to see any sign of familiarity

from the small covered body. Her lips pressed tightly
in fear, her neck tensed from anxiety. The white T-shirt
Leola wore left no doubt that her thoughts were of her
daughter. HAVE YOU SEEN OPAL was in large block letters
with a prominent photo of the smiling six-year-old in
the center.

Teresa Sanderford was confident the body wasn't
that of Opal.

"Anytime that there's talk about a kid's body, you
get concerned," Teresa said. "But my heart and everybody else's heart says she's still with us."

At the same time the Sanderfords concentrated on
news reports, Karl Johnson, a Saginaw police
spokesman, watched with the same intense interest. He
also waited to hear from the Saginaw officer who had
been sent to Irving in case a connection was made between the body and Opal's abduction. Although the
name of the child wasn't released immediately, awaiting positive identification, Johnson soon learned from
his inside source that it was the body of Cristy Ryno,
not that of Opal Jennings, that had been pulled from
the Trinity River.

Audrey Sanderford nervously faced a studio audience and thousands of at-home viewers from the
stage of *The Montel Williams Show*. She sat between
Williams and psychic Sylvia Browne. Browne, a frequent visitor to Williams's show, often answered questions from the audience and guests concerning
missing or deceased persons. Browne had expressed
an interest in Opal's case and the show's staff had
flown Audrey to New York to appear on the nationally televised program.

The family kept reports of a child's body found in
nearby Irving from Audrey. There was no need to

upset her until a positive identification had been made, since Audrey was two thousand miles away in New York, hoping to gain information on the whereabouts of her granddaughter. Unsure of her feelings about the paranormal, Audrey was willing to try anything to find Opal.

Browne's red hair blazed under the bright studio lights. She spoke to Audrey in a serious, somber tone, telling her that Opal was alive, but had been sold into white slavery in Japan. The idea seemed far-fetched but gave Audrey a ray of hope that Opal would be found alive.

Audrey also met with Texas congressman Martin Frost in Washington, DC. Frost presented Audrey with a picture of Opal that would be featured on his constituent services envelopes in an effort to present Opal's picture to as many people as possible who might have information.

"I wanted to come to Washington to meet with the people who may be able to prevent this experience from happening to other families," Audrey told reporters. "Communities need to do more to keep our children safe. Expanding the AMBER Plan and tracking the people who prey on kids can help do this."

Frost planned to meet with members of the Arlington, Texas, Police Department, who had devised the AMBER Alert, later in the week. He had invited them to speak to members of the U.S. Congress about the tremendous effectiveness of the program and how to expand it to other media markets throughout the country.

Believing whoever took Opal probably had committed a similar crime previously, Frost also proposed stiffer penalties for child predators. He hoped to mandate life sentences for two-time child sex offenders.

Opal's case had gained national prominence and

some positive steps to protect children would eventually come from it, but the Sanderfords' focus remained on getting Opal back. Alive.

Leola Sanderford had remained back in Texas while her stepmother appeared on national programs asking for help to find her daughter. More than anyone else, Leola wanted her daughter back, but the shy mother of two hurt too much. She knew she wouldn't be able to control her emotions if she were to beg the American people for help.

There was still an undercurrent of tension between the two Sanderford women. The friction that developed between Audrey and Leola when Audrey married Leola's father apparently hadn't eased with the passage of time. Audrey couldn't seem to recognize Leola as an adult, instructing her not to smoke outside in public, chastising her for having a drink. Leola, in turn, still appeared to resent her father's marriage to a woman she'd barely known. But the two women had one common bond: Opal. They both desperately wanted Opal back and agreed to do anything in their power to bring her home again.

On April 23, 1999, twenty-two days after arriving in Texas, Leola Sanderford returned to North Dakota. She had another daughter to look after, and she had no idea how long it would take for Opal to be found. She felt it was best to wait for word of Opal at home.

Back in Texas, Audrey Sanderford's optimism began to fade as exhaustion set in and she bent under the strain of waiting for Opal's reunion.

"Everyone keeps asking me how I feel," Sanderford sobbed into a pillow on her sofa. "How do they think I feel?"

Teresa tenderly put her hand on Audrey's shoulder. She understood the strain, the frustration her mother was feeling. She, too, was tired of the often repeated questions as to their own well-being. All they were interested in was Opal's welfare. Teresa and Clay had celebrated their twelfth wedding anniversary during the turbulent days following Opal's abduction, but their thoughts were constantly with the missing child.

"The best present would be to get Opal back," Teresa told reporters.

May 19, 1999, nearly two months after Opal Jennings's kidnapping, the FBI's National Center for the Analysis of Violent Crime (NCAVC) profiled Opal's abductor in hopes of generating new leads.

The FBI profile detailed ten major characteristics of the abductor, believed to be a white or Hispanic male. It was believed he was familiar with the Saginaw area and had a propensity for impulsive and violent behavior. The kidnapper was also believed to have changed his appearance since the abduction by cutting or coloring his hair and removing or growing facial hair. He may have sold the vehicle used in the abduction, changed its appearance, or displayed an unusual interest in cleaning it. Authorities thought the man was living alone at the time of the abduction and that he would have found reasons for being absent from work or for missing other scheduled appointments or social functions during that time. The profile concluded that the man may have found an apparently legitimate reason for leaving the area after the abduction, that he may have moved or changed jobs. He probably also had changed his eating and sleeping habits and become more nervous, irritable, preoccupied, and withdrawn.

"Hopefully, there's someone out there who can put this together and will know the person who did this and give us a call," Agent Craig Olson stated, following the announcement of the FBI's profile. Only time would tell if someone knew a person that fit the general description and displayed any or all of the characteristics mentioned.

There had been someone who had recognized the description of Opal's abductor, even before the FBI released the scientific profile. Jesse Herrera, Wise County probation officer, believed the man who took Opal Jennings was his probationer, thirty-year-old Richard Lee Franks. After watching Franks leave the probation office, six days after Opal's kidnapping, Herrera had telephoned his friend Sergeant Harlon Wright, the sex offender registrar for the Wise County Sheriff's Office. It was another ten days before Wright called a church friend, Fort Worth police lieutenant Mark Krey. Krey, supervisor of Fort Worth's violent personal crimes division, passed the information on to the FBI.

Herrera's tip sat in a box among more than twenty-five hundred information sheets that contained possible leads in the Opal Jennings abduction. Investigators were busy running the leads, as well as locating and interviewing about two thousand registered sex offenders residing in Dallas and Fort Worth. There hadn't been time to expand inquiries to neighboring counties, such as Wise County.

At the time of Opal's abduction, there were 17,235 sex offenders in the Texas Department of Public Safety database. Registration requirements for convicted sex offenders were more stringent after the 1993 killing of seven-year-old Ashley Estelle, of Plano, and the 1996 slaying of nine-year-old Amber Hagerman. And state lawmakers had agreed to make registration even more severe with public newspaper notices published to let residents know where sex offenders lived and would include the offender's specific address and photograph. Offenders were required to register within seven days of moving into a new neighborhood, and those convicted of sex-related crimes would be evaluated as to their risk of committing another sex offense. Their risk level would determine how intensely they would be supervised. But with all the safeguards built into the system, no one could know when a sex offender would reoffend, or whom he would choose as his victim.

For the next four months the search continued for Opal Jennings and her abductor. The leads that had been fed to the FBI were systematically researched, and anyone suspected of the heinous crime had been eliminated. Frustrations were mounting within the Saginaw community, as well as the law enforcement population.

In late July 1999, Assistant Chief Mike Adair, a twenty-year veteran investigator with the Tarrant County District Attorney's Office, assisted the task force by taking some of the leads, one of which was a person known to be Richard Lee Franks.

After talking to Jesse Herrera at length and making several inquiries concerning Franks, the assistant chief investigator drove to Franks's residence in South Fort Worth on August 3, 1999. Ricky Franks was not at home, but Adair had an opportunity to speak with his wife.

Adair simply told Judy Franks that he needed to talk to Ricky, with no explanation of why. Adair left his business card, requesting Franks call him to set up an appointment. Within forty minutes Adair's phone at the Tarrant County District Attorney's Special

Crimes Unit rang. It was Franks. He agreed to meet Adair at his house the following day.

As Adair approached the simple reddish brick house Franks shared with his wife and in-laws on Sheridan Street, Adair noticed a black Mercury Cougar and a white Chevrolet parked in the driveway.

The Franks lived in a working-class neighborhood where vehicles were parked on the street and in the yards, rather than in the one-car garages attached to the houses.

The yard of the Frankses' house was scattered with white metal lawn chairs, a wood and iron bench, and a concrete birdbath adorned with a terra-cotta squirrel. The large sprawling tree in the center of the front yard held a white iron birdcage. Adair suppressed a grin as he noticed the wooden yard art displayed near a front window. One was of a man bent over, the other of a woman, her ruffled panties showing.

The veteran cop stepped on the front porch of the house, walked past empty flowerpots, and knocked on the screen door.

Adair, slightly taller than Franks with a heavier frame than the thin suspect, took a mild-mannered approach. Franks wasn't under arrest and at no obligation to speak to Adair. The investigator's relaxed style immediately put Franks at ease.

"Are you familiar with the Saginaw area?" Adair asked without explanation of the reason for his inquiry.

"Yes. I'm familiar with Indian Creek and Jacksboro Highway," Franks responded.

Adair considered Franks's answer. Although adjacent to the City of Saginaw, neither Indian Creek nor the Jacksboro Highway were within the city limits, giving Adair reason to believe Franks was unfamiliar with the area in question.

"Ricky," Adair said, noticing the short haircut

described by Jesse Herrera, "have you ever worn your hair long, perhaps in a ponytail?"

"I've worn it long enough to pull it back in a ponytail at times," Franks responded.

"How long ago was that?" Adair questioned.

"I cut it about four or five months ago," Franks replied.

Adair concluded his interview with Franks without mentioning the purpose of his visit to either Ricky or Judy Franks. He didn't say he was investigating the Opal Jennings abduction or that Franks was a possible suspect. Adair left the Frankses' residence without incident but with the determination to continue to investigate the convicted sex offender.

Surveillance of Franks began almost immediately. Between Mike Adair and Danny McCormick, the two observed Franks's habits and behaviors for nearly two weeks. The two investigators spoke with Franks's brothers, known associates, and followed him as he went about his daily routine. One thing that both investigators noted, Ricky Franks was rarely without his wife.

Other DA investigators were busy researching Franks as well. Kathy Manning, a former Fort Worth police officer who had been with the DA's Special Crimes Unit for seven years, checked with the municipal court liaison officer and learned that Richard Lee Franks was wanted for an outstanding traffic ticket. It was a simple failure to wear a seat belt, but Franks's failure to pay the ticket had resulted in a warrant for his arrest. Four days later, August 17, 1999, Manning double-checked with the court officer to make certain the outstanding warrant was still in effect.

At 7:30 A.M., August 17, Kathy Manning and Danny McCormick were parked outside Ricky Franks's home. As they sipped their coffee, they watched for any movement, any indication that Franks was leaving the residence, just as they had done the day before.

In an effort to avoid detection, the investigators' car was parked down the street from Franks's home. Manning's blond hair gleamed as the sun streamed through the car window. McCormick's familiar Western hat was perched atop his cleanly shaven head. The two had been on many stakeouts, and although they chatted to pass the time, the seasoned investigators never took their eyes off the target.

Franks emerged from his residence, along with his wife. Dressed in blue jeans, a white T-shirt, and sneakers, Ricky drove away with Judy in a black Mercury Cougar. Following close behind the Frankses, the investigators observed the couple as they ran several errands. They made no attempt to apprehend Ricky. They simply waited. At last, early that evening, investigators had the opportunity they had been hoping for. Franks, who had been with his wife throughout the day, dropped Judy off in front of her parents' house on Sheridan and drove to a convenience store at Altamesa and I-35 for a pack of cigarettes. He was finally alone.

Franks, unaware that his every movement for the past few days had been scrutinized, stepped from his car.

Suddenly a car with Gary Philibert, Celeste Rogers, and Charlie Johnson, all DA investigators, pulled in behind Franks and blocked his vehicle. The three investigators jumped from their unmarked car, ordered Franks to put his hands on his vehicle, and placed him under arrest.

Franks appeared stunned and confused. He offered no resistance to the three plainclothes officers. Within seconds, Mike Adair, along with Danny McCormick and Kathy Manning, had joined the others.

Franks's hands were swiftly placed behind his back. The distinct click of the steel handcuffs secured around his wrists rang in Franks's ears. Patrons of the convenience store gawked.

Ricky Franks was quickly led to Charlie Johnson's county-issued vehicle and carefully put in the backseat. Accompanied by Johnson and Manning, he was taken to downtown Fort Worth and the offices of the Special Crimes Unit. Housed in the old district attorney's offices, the Crime Unit occupied one entire floor of the old Tarrant County Courthouse. It wasn't a jail but a place where Franks could be interviewed without interruption.

At Franks's Fort Worth home, Judy Franks fretted over her husband's unexplained absence. He had only gone down the street for a pack of smokes—why hadn't he returned? She had no idea her husband of five years had been taken to an interview room in downtown Fort Worth and was awaiting interrogation by one of the area's top interviewers.

Ricky Franks was placed in a small corner room furnished with a desk and chair. The handcuffs were removed for his comfort.

"Are you okay?" Danny McCormick asked Franks.

"Yes," Franks stated.

"Do you need anything?" McCormick inquired.

"I'd like a Dr Pepper and a cigarette," Franks replied.

"Do you want anything to eat?" McCormick asked.

"No."

"Ricky, we want to talk to you about Opal Jennings," McCormick explained.

"I don't even know how to get to Saginaw," Franks blurted out. McCormick stared at the suspect questioningly. He had never mentioned Saginaw. Franks's outburst was totally unprompted.

"We need you to take a polygraph," McCormick stated.

"Okay," Franks responded.

"And we'd like to search your car. Will you give us consent to do that?" Kathy Manning asked.

Franks agreed. Within minutes McCormick returned to the small room with a consent-to-search order. Franks scrawled his name across the bottom, and the signature was witnessed by Mike Adair.

Kathy Manning left the office where Franks was sitting to make a photocopy of the Miranda warning. The small 4-by-6-inch green card was often difficult to read, therefore Manning enlarged it for Franks's benefit. When she returned with the larger-sized Miranda, McCormick slowly read each of the suspect's rights, having Franks initial after each one to show that he understood. Franks also gave verbal acknowledgment of his understanding of each warning, signed at the bottom of the page, and dated the form.

McCormick left momentarily to get the suspect a Dr Pepper.

"Would you like to call your wife?" McCormick asked.

With Franks responding that he would, McCormick made a phone available and Franks telephoned Judy. She had no idea where he was being held. No idea how long it would be before she would be allowed to see him, post bond, and take him home. All Judy Franks could do was wait for further word from her husband.

McCormick explained that someone was on his way to talk with him, and asked Franks if there was anything else he needed. For the next hour and a half, Ricky Franks remained alone in the small office. Periodically

McCormick would inquire if he wanted anything to eat or drink or needed to use the bathroom.

The door leading to the room where Franks waited was left partially open. McCormick could see the suspect fidget with his cigarettes, play with the ring top of the Dr Pepper can, and twist nervously in his seat.

"Hey, what is this guy going to ask me?" Franks questioned McCormick. "What do you know about all this?" The wait was beginning to get to Franks. His nerves were fraying, his confidence wavering.

McCormick, too, felt the strain of waiting for the interviewer's arrival. He knew it was best not to question Franks. They wanted the interviewer to take control of the examination. They needed Franks to give him his first reactions to the questioning, but it was difficult for McCormick to stay away. For the most part, Ricky Franks sat in isolation, smoking cigarettes and drinking Dr Pepper. He wasn't interviewed or questioned by anyone from Special Crimes.

Eric Holden, a well-known and highly respected specialist in interrogation, had been called in by Mike Adair to assist in the interview of Ricky Franks.

Holden had begun his career as a psychologist with the Texas Department of Corrections, then with the Texas Rehabilitation Commission, where he was a specialist in making diagnoses and evaluations on the basis of testing and test results. The licensed professional counselor was now in private practice. On thousands of occasions he had interviewed people that were perhaps involved in crimes, for both law enforcement agencies and defense attorneys.

Holden, who resides in Dallas, didn't arrive at the Fort Worth offices of the Special Crimes Unit until about 10:30 P.M. After being briefed about Franks and his possible connection to the Opal Jennings kidnapping, Holden entered the room where Franks was being held at about 11:30.

Holden wasn't in a rush. He took his time to make certain Ricky Franks was not only willing to be interviewed but that he understood what the interview was about. Holden needed to determine if Franks was in good condition both physically and emotionally, especially considering the lateness of the night. The psychologist talked with Franks at some length about the issues that would be brought up during the interview process. He then had Franks sign a release, agreeing to speak with Holden. A Miranda warning was part of Holden's release form, the second one Franks had been read that night.

Prior to meeting Franks, Holden had been told the suspect was a slow learner. However, in their conversations prior to the interview itself, Holden had determined Ricky Franks capable of conversing normally. He talked smartly, and didn't appear to be disadvantaged in his ability to communicate, understand, and deal with Holden on any issue. In fact, Franks had rather impressed Holden.

His preliminary assessment completed, the release signed and dated, Eric Holden was ready to commence with the formal interrogation. His goal was clear. He was to learn what happened to Opal Jennings and what part Richard Franks had played in her disappearance.

CHAPTER 6

Eric Holden emerged from the 5½-hour session with Ricky Franks about 5:00 A.M. The expert interrogator looked exhausted. His eyes drooped and dark circles underscored his lower lids. He reeked of the smoke that had flooded the small room where he and Franks had smoked cigarettes and talked into the wee hours of the morning.

Holden held a yellow tablet filled with scrawled notes. Franks had admitted that he had picked up Opal Jennings in front of her house, but he insisted he had let the child go shortly after she had climbed into his car. Wearily Holden handed his notes to Kathy Manning.

Manning's nose crinkled and she squinted her eyes. Holden might be one of the best in his field of interrogation, but his handwriting left Manning distressed. She handed the notes to McCormick with a shrug.

After visiting with Holden for about a half hour, McCormick and Manning entered the room where Ricky Franks had been held all night.

"Because Mr. Holden's handwriting is hard to read, we're going to type it up to make it a little easier," McCormick told Franks. "It'll be just a little longer. Do you mind if we put this on a typed form? We'll be back and read it to you to make certain it's what you wanted to say."

"That's fine," Franks replied. Like Holden, Franks looked extremely tired. He hadn't slept, hadn't eaten, and had been drinking Dr Pepper and smoking cigarettes for more than ten hours.

Charlie Johnson was given the notes and asked to type up the written account. Several times Johnson asked Holden to interpret his handwriting, finally having Holden read the notes as he typed. When completed, the statement was given to McCormick, who read Franks's declaration to him:

> *I, Richard Lee Franks, prior to making any statement, having been duly warned by Investigator Danny Mc-Cormick, the person to whom this statement is made; that I have the right to remain silent and not make any statement at all and that any statement I make may be used in evidence against me in court; that I have the right to have a lawyer present to advise me prior to and during any questioning; that if I am unable to employ a lawyer, I have the right to have a lawyer appointed to advise me prior to and during any questioning; and that I have the right to terminate the interview at any time. Having been informed of these, my rights, and understand same, I hereby freely, intelligently, voluntarily, and knowingly waive these rights and not desiring a lawyer, voluntarily choose to make the following statement:*
>
> *My name is Richard Lee Franks, my date of birth is 8/4/69. I live at [address blacked out] Sheridan in Fort Worth, Texas. I have completed twelve years of school, and I can read and write the English language.*
>
> *On March 26, 1999, I went to Saginaw, Texas, to*

*see my brother Danny when I saw Opal Jennings and
two other kids playing in a field beside a house. This
was about 4:00 p.m. in the afternoon or a little later.
I was driving a Ford Cougar, and was by myself. I went
by Danny's house, saw the girls and a boy outside
playing in the field. I stopped to talk to them and Opal
said, "Where are you going?" I was in the car and Opal
was talking to me through the fence, she asked where I
was going, and I told her that I was going to see if my
brother was home so I could go visit with him. I told
Opal, "If he's not there, I'm going home." She said,
"They might be at work," and I then asked her how she
was doing and she said she was doing good in school.
She said that she was getting good grades. She came up
to the car on the driver's side, the driver's door was open,
she came up to the door, gave me a hug, and shook my
hand. I asked her if she was passing and she said, "I
hope so." I then told her that if she was doing good in
school, then she would. I said, "I hope you pass." The
other kids wanted her to hurry up so she could play with
them. I said, "You need to get back and finish playing
what you all are playing." They were playing some
kind of ball. She reached in the car, I thought she was
going to try and grab me, I didn't know what she was
going to try to do, so I pushed her back and said,
"What are you trying to do, I'm not the one to be doing
it with." I didn't want to do nothing that would get me
in trouble, she was just a kid. I don't see myself doing
nothing like that. I was afraid she was going to make
a pass at me or get me to take her somewhere. She was
wanting me to take her to the store, she went around the
front of the car to get in the passenger side. I was
afraid she wanted me to take her to have sex with her
or something. I took her to the store, she got in the passenger side, the other two kids were outside playing. I
told her I was going to bring her back so she could finish*

playing with the other two kids. I took her to the convenience store a block from the house, I sat in the car, and she got something to drink.

She bought a Coke, then she came back to the car, she said, "Thank you for bringing me up here," but I said, "I won't do it again." Opal tried to move over toward me, I didn't know what she tried to do. She tried to grab me between the legs, she grabbed my dick. She wanted me to fuck her, I told her no. She said, "Fuck me." She tried to take her pants off, I told her, "No." She asked me why and I said, "Because I don't do that." She asked me why and I said, "Because you're too young and I could get in trouble for it." She unzipped my pants, took my dick out, she had it in her hand, she went down like she was going to go down on it. I pushed her back, I put my dick back in my pants. She was sitting beside me, when she went to bend over I pushed her back. I said, "I'm not going to have sex with someone younger than I am." I told her that she needed to get out of the car, this happened on the way back from the store. I took her to her house, and left her off the same place where I talked to her at. I don't know if she went in the house or not. I just wanted to get away from her. When I dropped her off, she gave me a hug, and I left, the other two kids were in the field playing.

Everything in this statement is true and correct and I said it in my own words. I stopped the interview at my request, when I got tired. I was treated good tonight, and everything I said is in my own words.

The document was signed "Richard Franks," dated 08-18-99, at 8:00 A.M., and witnessed by Danny McCormick.

Ricky Franks made one correction to the document. He changed his brother's first name, incorrectly typed as "Donny," to "Danny." He initialed each paragraph "R.L.F."

McCormick stared at Richard Franks, hiding the disdain he felt for the suspected kidnapper. No six-year-old child would make sexual advances to an adult male. It was the typical response of a depraved pedophile. They frequently blamed their victims for their own sick sexual desires, but McCormick was a professional. He made no comment to Franks, he showed no personal feelings.

In addition to the written statement, Franks had also submitted to a polygraph exam. Four questions were asked Franks—all connected to the disappearance of Opal Jennings and the location of her whereabouts. Franks's answers all showed deception. As suspected, Franks had first-hand knowledge of Opal Jennings's kidnapping.

At 11:30 A.M., after Franks had signed his statement and after Eric Holden had returned to his Dallas residence, Danny McCormick and Special Agent Lori Keefer, with the Fort Worth FBI office, conducted an interview with Richard Lee Franks. Keefer and McCormick were about as opposite in status as any two persons could be. McCormick was tall, muscular, and an imposing figure; Keefer was petite, with soft brown hair and delicate features. But the two law enforcement professionals had one thing in common: they wanted to find out what had happened to Opal Jennings.

For the third time in some seventeen hours, Franks was read his Miranda rights. And for the third time in as many hours, he signed them, acknowledging that he understood and waived his right to legal counsel.

McCormick and Keefer had Ricky Franks begin

by talking about his family. He had been married to Judy for five years, and although they had no children, Judy had a fifteen-year-old daughter named Kimberly. Ricky's voice softened as he spoke of his father dying four years earlier of a heart attack and of his mother, who lived in Cisco, Texas.

Franks's features hardened when he told of his mother's three marriages and his three stepfathers, and when he spoke of his first stepfather's physical abuse of him. Franks stated he had one blood brother and six half brothers and two half sisters. He had depended on his family most of his life to take care of him.

Franks seemed proud of the fact that he had graduated from Justin Northwest High School, admitting he had been in the special-education program.

It was when Franks began to talk about his past crimes that he exhibited some discomfort at being in the room with Agent Keefer. He fidgeted in his chair and focused his attention on McCormick.

Franks started by telling McCormick and Keefer that there was only one victim in his past, his half brother Dale's eight-year-old stepdaughter. Franks's eyes nervously darted toward Keefer, then back to his hands folded in front of him on the table. It was obvious he was uncomfortable speaking in front of the female FBI agent.

Noticing Franks's reluctance to elaborate on his past crime, McCormick brought Franks's focus back to him and away from Keefer. Franks then began an uncensored, and rather arrogant, account of the molestation of his niece.

"I don't feel like it was my fault," Franks stated. "Dale and his wife had gone out to the bars partying and left me there to babysit. They left some marijuana at the house and I smoked it. I was feeling real strange and couldn't hardly stand up. She wanted to watch some dirty movies and I started watching one with her. She started kissing me and then we went into the bedroom, where I tried to have sex with her, but I couldn't get my dick in her because she was too small."

McCormick stared blankly at the suspect. He talked of having sex with an eight-year-old child as though it were a normal act. Keefer felt distress at hearing the words the convicted pedophile spoke so casually.

"Ricky, you admitted to your probation officer that you were finally able to penetrate her. Right?" McCormick pushed.

"Yes, I did have intercourse with her," Franks admitted.

Franks explained that when his brother had gotten home, the girl had told her father what Ricky had done and he and Dale had had it out in the front yard of Dale's house.

"But that's the only time that it happened. It was because I had smoked marijuana and she told me she wanted me to do it," Franks insisted.

Franks announced that he had spent eight years on probation for the sexual assault and had made his final probation payment of $400 on April 1, 1999. His final payment had enabled him to get off probation.

"Didn't you tell your probation officer and sex counselor about other victims?" McCormick prodded.

Franks took a long breath, his eyes avoiding both McCormick and Keefer. He admitted to other victims and said that there were two named Amber and one named Lori. He wasn't sure of the last names of the girls but stated they were both relatives.

"I was set up by Lori," Franks contended. "She was ten years old and I was fourteen or fifteen at the time. Lori lived in Newark, Texas."

Just as he blamed marijuana for his violation of Dale's daughter, Franks blamed alcohol for the other incidents. He added that he and Lori were both young and she had initiated the contact.

Attempting to avoid any further discussion of his sex crimes, Franks changed the subject to his martial arts training.

"I began karate at age fifteen and took karate until I was twenty-eight," Franks boasted.

He bragged of having a black belt in karate, advising that his hands were lethal weapons.

"But I don't like to fight," he stated. "And with all my brothers taking up for me, I don't have to fight."

Franks explained that his real brother Rodney often took up for him, and if he had trouble with anyone, he would simply tell Rodney and he would fight his fights for him.

"Do you and Judy have fights or arguments?" Keefer asked.

"We argue, but I don't hit her," Franks said quickly without looking at Keefer. "I'll just leave or go out in the backyard and stay until I calm down."

The investigators then approached the subject of the black Mercury Cougar that Franks had been driving when apprehended by the Special Crimes Unit. Franks stated he and Judy had bought the car sometime the previous year. He claimed he drove the car occasionally, but Judy most frequently drove the vehicle.

"Ricky, I need to talk to you about your statement. You said you had Opal Jennings in your car on March 26, 1999," McCormick said.

"No," Franks quickly responded, denying that he had made any statements. "I wasn't telling the truth when I made that statement."

McCormick reminded Franks that he was the person who took his statement and read it to him again. His head dropping slightly, Franks finally admitted what he had previously stated wasn't true, that he had been confused. He hadn't let Opal in his car. He even denied being in Saginaw until after he had seen the reports of the kidnapping on the news. Franks then claimed that he and Judy had driven to Saginaw, just to see where Opal lived.

Frustrated but determined to get a clear picture of Franks's knowledge of Opal's disappearance, McCormick again read Franks the statement he had made to Eric Holden.

"What parts are true and what parts are false?" McCormick questioned.

"I don't even know my way around Saginaw," Franks claimed. "I haven't been in Saginaw for years, other than to travel through on my way to Indian Creek, where Rodney lives."

But when pressed by McCormick and Keefer, Franks again admitted to being in Saginaw on March 26, 1999. He claimed to have been looking for a man named Ray, who occasionally employed him for odd jobs. He couldn't recall Ray's last name.

"What job did you do for Ray that day?" Keefer questioned.

Franks couldn't remember if Ray had been home, so he wasn't sure if he did any work or not. He continued to deny seeing Opal, but he did admit that he probably went to North Hampshire Street, but only to visit his brother Danny, who also lived on North Hampshire.

"Ricky, Danny moved off of North Hampshire in December 1998," McCormick stated.

Franks was unresponsive but appeared anxious, lighting another cigarette and tapping his thumb against the table.

McCormick pressed on by asking Franks about the possibility that he had been seen talking to Opal. Squirming in his chair, Franks finally admitted that he had seen Opal and two smaller children playing. He claimed Opal had waved at him and asked him to stop. He acknowledged that he did stop and alleged Opal asked him to take her to the store.

"I knew I would get in trouble because I was on probation. I told Opal that I had to get to my brother's house and that I couldn't take her to the store," Franks stated.

He asserted that while he was talking to Opal, the other kids were yelling for her to go back in the yard and play with them. He said they were playing with some type of ball.

"I told her that she needed to get back to playing with the other kids," Franks stated. "Then she started begging me to take her to the store. I think the car door was open while I was talking to Opal. She shook my hand and gave me a hug. Finally I agreed to take her to the store to get her a Coke."

Franks reported Opal went around to the passenger side of his car and got in.

"What car were you driving?" McCormick asked.

"I was driving Judy's black Cougar," Franks responded.

"What happened next?" McCormick asked, encouraging Franks to go on.

"I drove her to the store beside the motel on Main Street, I can't remember the name of the store because it's had several different names," Franks began. "I told Opal that she had to hurry because I didn't have time to be waiting around while she was in the store. I waited in the car while Opal got out and went in the store and got a Coke. When she got back in the car, I took her back home and let her out in the same place I picked her up. She started playing with the other kids again and I drove off."

McCormick and Keefer exchanged glances. There were a number of discrepancies in Franks's story.

He was lying, holding back the truth as to what really had happened to six-year-old Opal.

"Ricky, there are some problems with your story. Opal never made it home," McCormick stated.

Franks looked from McCormick to Keefer. "Opal had seemed upset. I think she might have run away from home," Franks said.

"Did Opal tell you she was going to run away?" McCormick prodded.

"I don't remember," Franks said, taking another drag on his cigarette.

"But I do remember her saying she didn't like school," Franks offered. "I told her she needed to study hard if she wanted to do good in school."

McCormick took a long, deep breath. "Ricky, I have a hard time believing anything you're telling me now, because of all the changes in your story."

Franks's eyes again darted to Keefer, then to the cigarette he held between his fingers. It had become obvious Ricky Franks was intimidated by Agent Keefer. Perhaps because she was with the FBI, perhaps because she was a woman with power—the power to take him down. McCormick nodded slightly toward the door and Agent Keefer left the room. She remained just outside the interview office and listened to the remainder of Franks's discussion with McCormick.

Tears welled in Franks's eyes and began to run down his pimpled face.

"I'm not a bad person," Franks cried.

"What are you talking about, Ricky?" McCormick asked.

"I took Opal to the store, but I left her there because I was afraid I would get in trouble, because I was on probation," Franks sniveled.

McCormick straightened in his chair, frustration beginning to sound in his voice. "Are you telling me now that you didn't take Opal home? That you left her at the store? That someone else took her from the store?"

"I think that's what happened to her," Franks gulped.

"The police have been to all the stores in Saginaw after Opal was abducted," McCormick said, "and she was not at any of them."

Franks again began saying he hadn't been in Saginaw that day, he didn't know Opal, and he hadn't seen any of the kids playing. The convicted sex offender contended that McCormick was putting words in his mouth—words he hadn't said.

McCormick snapped back at Franks, reminding him that the words were Franks's own, that the detective had merely been listening while he spoke.

Agent Keefer reentered the room and spoke directly to Franks, asking him about a girl named Jessica, who lived in Keller, Texas, a child who also had been abducted about the same time Opal was taken. Unknown to Franks, Keefer had concocted the story. It was a test for Franks, a test to see if the simpleminded man knew right from wrong.

Ricky Franks sat up straighter, showing a newfound confidence, a strong voice, and an insistence that he had nothing to do with that crime.

"I'll be blamed for every missing kid because of what happened to Opal!" Franks shouted.

"That's not true," Keefer said. "Those things have to be proven in court."

Franks sat back and appeared to feel assured by Keefer's words. McCormick and Keefer were certain Richard Lee Franks knew right from wrong. They believed he was not easily led and would not confess to crimes he didn't commit.

The two investigators returned to a discussion of Opal and Franks's involvement in her disappearance. They told him his car had been processed while he was being held at the office of the Special Crimes Unit. Keefer informed him that the stain found in his car was human blood.

"That's probably because I was a mechanic and I was always cutting my hands and arms," Franks explained.

Franks was employed at the time by the Motorcycle Performance Center (MPC), a motorcycle shop in Fort Worth.

"The blood will be checked to see if it matches Opal's blood type," McCormick informed Franks.

Franks said nothing, but looked as if he were seriously contemplating the words McCormick spoke.

"We'll also be testing hairs and fingerprints found in the car," Keefer advised.

Franks stated that Opal had probably left her fingerprints in the car when she reached in to give him a hug, but that prints could also belong to Judy or Kimberly, Judy's daughter.

"That might be right," McCormick stated. "But all fingerprints are different, and if Opal's prints are in the car, we'll find them."

For several moments Franks sat silently, as though thinking about what McCormick had just said. He then addressed McCormick directly: "If Opal's fingerprints are in the car, they got there while she was hugging me or when I took her to the store."

McCormick's voice rose, "We're not going to go back to that story. We all know you never took Opal to the store."

"You're right," Franks acknowledged after a few moments. "I never took her to the store. I took her to the park on Longhorn Street. Opal wanted to go to the park and play, so I took her to the park. I left her at the park and drove off. She might have run away from home."

McCormick was growing tired of Franks's changing

story. The Special Crimes investigator had been awake for more than twenty-four hours and the interview was seemingly going backward. Franks had made a statement to Eric Holden and had signed it. Now he was changing key elements that McCormick knew were inconsistent with the original statement and not true. McCormick took a deep breath and began flushing out Franks's latest rendition of the events of March 26, 1999.

"What happened on the way to the park?" McCormick asked.

Franks at first stated he and Opal just talked, but when asked what they talked about, Franks said about how the young girl was doing in school.

"Did anything sexual happen?" McCormick questioned.

"Do you mean did we have sex?" Franks asked.

"Did you talk about it or did something more than just talk happen?" McCormick pushed.

As before, Franks claimed that six-year-old Opal wanted him to have sex with her, and again he declared he told her he couldn't have sex with someone younger than he was because he was on probation and would get into trouble.

"Opal kept asking me to fuck her, but I said no," Franks reiterated.

He once more alleged Opal unzipped his pants and took his dick out and acted like she was going to go down on him. Franks stated he made her stop and put his dick back in his pants. He then stated Opal started removing her shorts.

"I told her to stop, she'd get me in trouble," Franks claimed.

"What happened next?" McCormick asked.

"I just drove her to the park. Opal got out and I left," Franks stated.

"Well, if Opal's fingerprints are in the car, that will explain how they got there," McCormick remarked.

Franks said nothing, but a slight smile crossed his weary face.

"If Opal's hairs are found in the car, we need to find out how they got there," McCormick said.

"I never pulled her hair," Franks quickly declared.

McCormick explained that hair can fall out easily and they can blow out and end up in the car.

"That's probably what happened because my car didn't have air-conditioning and the windows were rolled down. Her hair probably blew out in the car." Franks quickly offered that as an explanation.

"That's possible, but there's still a problem if the blood in the car is Opal's," McCormick said.

Franks sat quietly, as if forming an explanation for any of Opal's blood that might be found in his car, just as he had offered a clarification for the possible presence of Opal's hair.

"Did Opal have any cuts or scratches on her that might have caused her to bleed in the car?" McCormick asked, as if offering Franks an easy clarification.

But Franks said he didn't see any cuts or scratches on Opal.

"Think about it for a minute," McCormick offered.

After a few minutes Franks said he thought he might know how Opal's blood got in his car. "When she ran from the car, she fell in the street," Franks offered.

"Where was she bleeding from?" McCormick continued.

"From her nose."

"I have a problem with your explanation," McCormick said accusingly. "If she fell after running *from* the car, and you didn't see her again, how did the blood get in your car?"

Franks stared at McCormick, not speaking for several seconds.

"Oh, I remember," Franks began, "she came back to the car, reached in, and gave me a hug for taking her to the park. She said, 'Thank you for taking me to the park.'"

McCormick watched Franks without speaking. This was no simpleminded man. When faced with possible unexplained facts, even if fictitious, Franks was readily able to devise an explanation.

Franks stated he drove off but returned to the park to check on Opal because it was getting dark and it may have started raining. He claimed the last place he saw the girl was on the other side of the fence, by the creek.

"Where's the quarry?" Keefer injected.

"It's across the street from the park. I've only been to the quarry a couple of times," Franks stated. "I drove back to that area and parked on Longhorn Street. I'm not sure exactly where, it was where some trailers were parked. I walked back down to the creek area and yelled Opal's name, but she never answered, so I drove home."

Franks continued by saying that when he got home, Judy told him about the AMBER alert on television and she wanted him to drive her over there so she could see where Opal lived. He said they drove by the house and saw all the cameras and newspeople at the house.

"Did you tell Judy about taking Opal to the park?" McCormick questioned.

"No. She probably would have been mad because of my probation," Franks answered.

The suspect continued to insist that the last time he saw Opal she was bleeding from her nose, but otherwise was all right.

Attempting to push Franks into more specific details concerning the location of where Opal ran from the car, Franks turned and again started saying that he didn't remember Opal at all.

"Ricky, you aren't able to tell the truth. We can't believe you when you say you last saw her alive, then say you don't remember her at all," McCormick said flatly.

And again Franks told the investigators that Opal did get in his car on her own, that he didn't force her, that she was making the moves on him, and that she wanted to have sex with him.

Agent Keefer again left the room, and once again Ricky Franks started crying and shaking uncontrollably.

McCormick leaned forward, hands flat on the desk, where Franks sat, and asked Franks what was the matter.

Without saying a word, Franks grabbed the ink pen from McCormick's pocket and started drawing on a napkin. It appeared to be a map.

"Describe for me what you're drawing," McCormick instructed.

Franks stopped his drawing and looked up at McCormick.

"My family is going to think I'm some kind of 'sicko,' but I want you to understand that it was a terrible accident," Franks said, tears still wetting his eyes.

"What happened, Ricky?" McCormick asked in a soft tone.

Franks said he had put Opal in the water under some trees, where he used to fish for crawdads when he was a kid. He told McCormick it was by the rodeo grounds in Saginaw, where two tunnels went under the highway. Franks said there was a cable that kept people from driving all the way to the tunnels, but he parked his car at the cable fence and that is where he put Opal in the water.

"Was Opal moving, or was she hurt bad?" McCormick asked.

Franks couldn't speak. He was crying harder than before. Once he caught his breath, Franks expressed his fear about what his brother Rodney and the rest of his family would think about him.

"How bad was Opal hurt?" McCormick pressed.

"Pretty bad," Franks responded through his tears.

"Will you take us out to where you put Opal in the water?" McCormick asked.

"Yes, if I don't have to see you get her out of the water," Franks said.

"If you show me where it is, I'll get her out of the water and you won't have to watch," McCormick assured Franks.

"I will," Franks stated. "But you know she might not be there anymore."

"What are you talking about?"

"The water there gets to flowing pretty high when it rains and she might have washed away," Franks explained.

"We'll go see," McCormick responded.

Leaving Franks in the interview room, McCormick went into another room and phoned Special Agent Andy Farrell, of the FBI. He informed Farrell of what Franks had said about leaving Opal in the water and asked Farrell to meet them at the location Franks had given them.

Franks left the Special Crimes office with McCormick and Tarrant County Sheriff's deputies Beckham and Ramirez. Assistant Chief Mike Adair and Agent Keefer followed in Keefer's car.

As the caravan reached Main Street in Saginaw, McCormick asked Franks how to get to the location where he had left Opal. Franks directed them to make a left at the road that led to the rodeo grounds. As they drove through the gate, several media vans and trucks were parked across the rodeo grounds, waiting for them. Franks appeared nervous at the sight of the reporters. His demeanor changed. He instructed McCormick to drive toward several large mounds of dirt. Franks pointed out the cable fence and showed McCormick where he had parked the day he claimed he had taken Opal to the location.

Leaving the car at the mouth of the two tunnels, Franks and the officers walked down to take a look.

Glancing around, McCormick asked, "Where are the trees that you put Opal under?"

"This place doesn't look right. I'm not sure if this is the place or not," Franks said. "Can we go over closer to the park that has the Stop-n-Go store?"

The deputies, investigators, Agent Keefer, and Franks got back in the cars and drove over to the park on Longhorn Street.

"Make a right at the park," Franks instructed.

The deputy turned the car on Thompson Street toward Bryan Swingler Park.

"Stop here," Franks said. "This is where Opal fell down and busted her nose."

McCormick shook his head. Franks was back to telling the story that Opal had run from his car and down to the bank of the creek, where he had seen her for the last time.

"What about putting her in the water by the trees?" McCormick said with a degree of irritation.

"Those are the trees right there," Franks said, pointing at some trees in the creek.

But Franks now said Opal ran into the creek, that he hadn't put her there.

"Where is the quarry from here?" McCormick asked.

"That's it," Franks said, pointing to the creek.

McCormick decided to take a different direction. "Will you take us to Opal's house?" he asked.

Franks agreed. As McCormick drove down Main Street, Franks was quiet, but as McCormick was about to make a turn, he spoke up.

"No. No, not here. Go down to the next street," Franks said. It was Lemon Street, which intersects with North Hampshire, at the northwest corner of the Sanderfords' property.

Franks identified the location as the place where he had stopped and talked to Opal. He also pointed out the Sanderfords' vacant lot as the site where the other children had been playing when he first talked to Opal. Finally, after driving on what seemed to be a wild-goose chase, Franks had correctly identified the scene of Opal Jennings's abduction.

Following the path Franks gave them as his exit from the Sanderfords' neighborhood, they took a right on North Hampshire to Northern Street, a right on Main, and eventually a right on Longhorn to the park, where he had taken McCormick earlier. Finally they returned to the Special Crimes office in downtown Fort Worth.

"Will you call Rodney for me?" Franks asked McCormick.

"What do you want me to tell him?"

"I want to make sure Rodney knows that what happened was an accident and that I didn't do it on purpose," Franks stated.

A few minutes passed before Franks asked McCormick another question. "Do you think I could take another polygraph? I think I could beat this one."

"I'll check and see," McCormick said, "but I don't

think you'll pass it." The detective knew Franks had shown deception on all four questions asked him concerning Opal's disappearance.

"I always do better when I get a second chance," Franks admitted.

"I'll check, but what will you do for me if you take it and fail?" McCormick asked.

"If I fail, I'll tell you the truth."

"I'll check," McCormick said as he left the room to speak to Special Agents Farrell and Keefer, and to Assistant Chief Adair. They all agreed to call the polygraph examiner.

McCormick returned to the room where Franks waited, informed him he would let him take another polygraph, and reminded him what he said he would do for McCormick if he failed the test a second time.

"I'll give you good news. You'll be happy, but I think I can beat this one," Franks said with confidence.

"Are you tired? Are you ready to stop the interview?" McCormick asked.

"I'm not really tired, but if you are, we can stop until tomorrow," Franks answered.

The next morning, Ricky Franks was brought back to the Special Crimes office for a continuation of the interview. Before they could begin, McCormick received a phone call from Tarrant County chief deputy district attorney Greg Miller. Attorneys Leon Haley and Edward Jones had been retained to represent Ricky Franks. Miller instructed McCormick that he needed to call the attorneys and let them know where their client was. He provided McCormick with the attorneys' phone numbers. Miller also instructed McCormick to tell Franks that two attorneys had been retained to represent him and to ask if he still wanted to take the polygraph.

McCormick, along with Kathy Manning, gave

Franks the information that his family had hired an attorney to represent him and asked him he still wanted to take the polygraph, or if he wanted to talk to his attorney first. Franks told McCormick he wanted to take the polygraph first, then talk to the attorney.

Following Miller's directives, McCormick then phoned Ed Jones, telling him where his client was being held and giving him directions to the Special Crimes office. Ed Jones said Leon Haley was in his office and they were on their way. He instructed McCormick to cease interviewing Ricky Franks until they were present.

McCormick didn't return to the interview room where Franks waited. Franks never took the second polygraph.

CHAPTER 7

While Ricky Franks was smoking cigarettes, drinking Dr Peppers, and talking with Eric Holden, then with Danny McCormick and Lori Keefer, FBI agents were diligently and thoroughly dismantling Franks's car. The black Mercury Cougar, with black landau half roof, showed years of rough wear. A pair of fuzzy dice hanging from the rearview mirror was reminiscent of the 1950s. The back left panel above the rear tire was deeply dented and the back bumper severely marred. A piece of metal hung loosely from the left side of the broken rear license plate holder. The plate itself displayed a small Texas flag, just to the right of the state's name, and a white star on blue background with broad white-and-red stripes.

Inside the trunk, agents found normal paraphernalia such as a tire iron, jumper cables, and a dusty toolbox. A large red-and-white school stop sign was stored in the trunk—a shocking item to belong to a convicted child molester. Although Franks's wife, Judy, was a paid school crossing guard, agents could only imagine the threat of such an authoritative tool in the hands of someone as dangerous as Ricky Franks.

Overall, the unkempt condition of the vehicle reflected the owner's known image.

Once the initial run-through of the exterior and interior of the vehicle was complete, the FBI agents began a more thorough exploration. The Cougar was carefully vacuumed inside to catch any fibers, hairs, or tiny objects that might have been missed in the first examination. Before removing the seats, as well as the dashboard and console, the entire interior was sprayed for any sign of blood or semen. Latent fingerprints were lifted. By the time the agents had finished their two-day extensive scrutiny of the vehicle, they had removed the door panels, seats, and carpet, leaving no more than an interior shell of a car.

All evidence, no matter how minute, was transported to Lab Corps in Raleigh-Durham, North Carolina, for testing. If Opal Jennings had been in Ricky Franks's car, the agents would find any telltale signs that may have been left behind. But, as dirty and unkempt as Franks's vehicle appeared, investigators knew that he'd had nearly five months to clean the car extensively any number of times. And, in Texas's hot—often 100 degree or more—summer weather, it was very possible that any DNA, fingerprints, or other organic materials could have been destroyed by the elements.

In addition to the Cougar, investigators obtained a search warrant to explore Franks's residence for tools that could have been used in disposing of a body, clothing that Opal was wearing the day she disappeared, a red baseball-style cap reportedly worn by Opal's abductor, and any type of container that could have been used to transport or store the girl's body.

While investigators searched for those items at Franks's residence, they found a pair of bloody car mats in the single-car garage. Judy Franks was quick to offer an explanation, stating she believed the blood was hers, the result of a December 1997 motor scooter accident that cut her arm and caused her husband to rush her to the hospital. She explained she had received stitches as a result of the incident. "The doctor said it was so deep, he could put his finger down in it," Judy told investigators.

Along with the floor mats, fifteen pieces of evidence, including a hair clip, red bead, a sledgehammer, a lawn mower blade, a toy helicopter, a partial roll of duct tape, a rug, a spare tire, cables, a box of tools, a crowbar, a tire jack base, and an empty bottle of lighter fluid were collected at Franks's home, along with a doll that Mrs. Franks claimed belonged to her daughter. All pieces of evidence were sealed and sent to the FBI lab for testing. The items would be tested for fibers, DNA, or blood linked to Opal Jennings.

As FBI agents moved from room to room in the modest, small brick home, one agent noticed a stack of spiral notebooks casually lying to one side. Flipping through the books, he paid special attention to the March 1999 entries. Not a part of the search warrant affidavit, the notebooks were not seized; however, the judicious FBI agent snapped photos of the pages marked March 25, 1999, and March 26, 1999. No one knew how important any snippet of information might be later, or how it might be linked with other known intelligence.

With Franks's statement in hand, the Special Crimes Unit presented their evidence to a Tarrant County judge and obtained an official arrest warrant for Richard Lee Franks. The suspect hadn't left the Special Crimes office since his apprehension for the seat belt violation; however, it was imperative that procedures be followed to the letter.

Once the news broke that a suspect was in custody

for the kidnapping of Opal Jennings, the media frenzy became as intense as when Opal was first abducted. Throngs of newspeople crowded the steps of the Tarrant County Justice Center, all wanting every detail of the arrest and the identity of the alleged perpetrator. They soon learned the name of Richard Lee Franks, a name that would be on their lips for months, even years to come.

For most of the eighteen hours that Franks had been held at the downtown Fort Worth location, Judy Franks and her in-laws had been frantic. When Ricky had called Judy and told her he was being held for questioning in the Opal Jennings case, Judy was both shocked and dismayed. She notified her husband's family and they, in turn, contacted local defense attorney Ed Jones to represent Franks. Judy immediately went on the offensive in defending him.

Judy Franks revealed to the media that her husband confessed, not because he was guilty of the unthinkable crime, but because he was scared and confused by the investigators' relentless questioning. She claimed that same fear as the reason for his poor performance during a polygraph examination.

"I know he didn't do what he is accused of, or is getting framed with, because I go everywhere he goes," Judy Franks stated. "He says things he don't mean to say."

Judy claimed she and her husband were together at their South Fort Worth home most of March 26, miles away from Saginaw.

Tears pooled in Judy Franks's eyes, mascara blackening the skin below her lower lids as she insisted authorities had the wrong man.

"If he didn't do it," Judy said tearfully, "they need to let him out."

But Ricky Franks wouldn't be let go. Franks had been taken to a Tarrant County magistrate and arraigned for the kidnapping of Opal Jennings. Bail had been set at $1,000,000, an amount that assured Franks wouldn't be able to make bond and be released from custody.

The large bond amount and the intense scrutiny of Ricky Franks didn't dampen the resolve of Ed Jones, or Leon Haley, whom Jones recruited to help with the Franks case. Haley, to serve as lead defense attorney, had been practicing criminal law since 1982 and had more experience than Ed Jones with murder cases. Jones had moved to Fort Worth only three years earlier. He had been hired by the Franks family because he had represented another family member in an unrelated case. Both attorneys publicly supported their client.

"From what they (investigators) have said so far, I don't think they'll have anything to present," Leon Haley remarked to local reporters in a positioning declaration anticipating a grand jury hearing. "They're reaching for straws."

Greg Miller, chief deputy district attorney, disagreed. He felt his investigators, as well as the FBI agents, had given the DA's office sufficient evidence to take before the grand jury and request an indictment of Richard Franks for the kidnapping of Opal Jennings.

Greg Miller was known for his expertise in winning cases short on physical evidence. Hence, Miller was often given those cases deemed most difficult to win.

"One day I'd love to have a case with a smoking gun and a full confession," Miller said, tongue in cheek, but his tenacity and ability to wage a winnable prosecution was the reason Miller had been assigned to Richard Franks.

Miller began his career with the Fort Worth Police Department in January 1971 when he joined the cadet program, primarily working traffic detail. The police department wanted the cadets in college, so Miller took advantage of the Law Enforcement Assistance Program (LEAP). Sort of the "GI Bill for cops," Miller's college tuition was paid by the government in exchange for four years of police service. He graduated from Texas Christian University in 1976 with a degree in business administration. He had planned on going on to law school, but he found he enjoyed police work and was good at it. In the meantime, Miller worked on his master's degree in criminal justice at the University of Texas in Arlington.

For two years Miller patrolled the streets of Fort Worth before moving on to the Crime Search Unit. There Miller found himself embroiled in one of the highest-profile cases in Fort Worth history.

On August 2, 1976, a man dressed in black entered the Fort Worth mansion of Cullen Davis, shooting Davis's estranged wife, Priscilla, and killing her twelve-year-old daughter and her current love interest, Stan Farr. Greg Miller was called to the home and served as the primary crime scene investigator.

Cullen Davis was arrested and a year later was on trial in Amarillo, Texas, for the double homicide. Miller, who was on his honeymoon at the time, was summoned to the Texas Panhandle city to testify.

After six days of questioning by the district attorney and cross-examination by Richard "Racehorse" Haynes, one of Texas's most notorious defense attorneys, Miller had had an opportunity to see great lawyers in action. *I can do this,* Miller thought. He loved testifying and had many opportunities while in the Crime Search Unit to do just that. After two years in crime scene investigation, Miller was promoted to detective. At age twenty-seven, Miller became the youngest homicide detective in Fort Worth.

Through his police work Miller had gotten to know many of the ADAs personally and knew he wanted to be on the prosecution team. Miller's desire to pursue his original plan of attending law school was renewed, but he loved police work and waited until 1984, after receiving his master's degree, to enter the Southern Methodist School of Law in Dallas.

Miller joined the Tarrant County District Attorney's Office right out of law school and soon was consulted by other ADAs on police procedures and crime scene analysis. He knew those subjects well and felt confident in helping with any case that dealt with physical evidence.

It didn't take long for Miller to gain the respect of his peers and earn him the reputation of making difficult cases work. He moved up quickly within the district attorney ranks, and was promoted to Court Chief in 1991. Thus, Miller was the natural choice to try Richard Franks. No body. No physical evidence. No reliable eyewitness. If anyone could make the case against Richard Franks, it was Greg Miller.

McCormick, Manning, and Adair, of the Special Crimes Unit, along with Lori Keefer and Andy Farrell, of the FBI, provided Greg Miller with all the information they had on Richard Franks and the abduction of Opal Jennings. It was up to Miller and his team to take the case to the grand jury and secure an indictment.

Miller was not comfortable with presenting the evidence to the grand jury so soon. Franks had been in custody less than two weeks.

"We're doing it primarily in response to the defense attorneys wanting their side out, so to speak," Miller told reporters. "But that doesn't mean we aren't going to be thorough with this case. I would have rather waited another week or two, but I can deal with this."

"We're glad it's going on," Ed Jones, of the defense team, responded. "If Ricky's not indicted, hopefully the public will see him as an exonerated man. If he is indicted, that doesn't mean he's guilty of the offense. It just says that there's enough [evidence] to make him come to court and answer these charges. Then we could go from there with discovery on the evidence and go about the business of showing our client is not guilty."

There were some law enforcement officials who were beginning to agree with Jones, to have doubts that Franks's statement admitting responsibility in the crime was true. The lack of physical evidence connecting Franks to the crime seemed to be a huge stumbling block for many.

Meanwhile, as some investigators toiled at gathering evidence, others continued to interview Franks's friends and relatives about the case. Among those questioned was twenty-four-year-old Harold Hemphill, one of Franks's half brothers. Detectives had run a routine background check on Hemphill prior to attempting to question him. They found Hemphill was in the Wise County Jail for failure to appear in court in connection with a charge not related to the Opal Jennings case—aggravated assault with a deadly weapon.

Hemphill's wife, Katie, disputed the statement that there was no connection between her husband's arrest and the Opal Jennings case. She believed authorities were "just messing" with the family. She also believed investigators were merely grasping at straws.

Franks's neighbors in South Fort Worth had mixed feelings after hearing the news that one of their neighbors had been arrested for Jennings's abduction.

A plumbing contractor who lived two doors down from Franks, and who had employed Franks for about a month, expressed his shock upon hearing of Franks's arrest.

"He was a hard worker, but I had an odd feeling about him," the plumber said. "I could never put my finger on it. But to think he's involved in a case that has all of Fort Worth's hearts bleeding, I just can't believe it."

Several blocks away, at MPC, a shop where Franks occasionally worked changing carburetors and performing general maintenance work, the owner was startled at the news of Franks's arrest.

"Several times I tried to put him on full time," the burly owner stated. "He'd work about a week, then miss a day. He was sick. His mom was sick. Always something. But I used him part-time, off and on, for three years. Any girl around, he'd just stare them down, big time. More than one mentioned it to me. My girlfriend's daughter came up to me and said, 'He's weird, very weird.'"

But Franks also had his supporters. A neighbor whose son was friends with Franks dismissed the allegations: "He didn't seem like the type who could do something like this. And I wouldn't believe a word anyone in this neighborhood would say about Ricky."

Meanwhile, FBI agents combed a forty-acre tract of land two blocks from the Frankses' house, but found no trace of Opal. They had been acting on a tip that Franks had been seen walking through the neighborhood covered with mud and carrying a shovel after Opal's abduction. Franks's brother Rodney dismissed the incident, stating that his brother had been in the muddy field trying to free a pickup that had gotten stuck and that the occurrence had nothing to do with Opal.

This Fort Worth acreage was covered with grassy fields dotted by groves of trees and rimmed by a creek and a railroad track. Agents walked the land in a straight line, searching among the trees and even turning earth in some spots. They utilized trained dogs to aid in the search, but their efforts proved futile. No sign of Opal was found.

When news of Ricky Franks was personally delivered to the Sanderford family, Audrey Sanderford had only one question: "Where's Opal?"

The ailing grandmother pulled out the multitude of media contacts she had made during the past five months and began calling radio and television stations telling the news that someone had been arrested in Opal's case.

Immediately reports began to be broadcast. Soon the small kitchen at the Sanderford house was turned into a war room. Scraps of paper covered the kitchen table; phones rang off the hook. Media outlets across the county clamored to get the first interview with the Sanderford family, anxious to get their reaction to the promising news that Opal's abductor had been caught.

"Mom, pick up the phone. It's CBS radio news," Teresa Sanderford urged.

As Audrey spoke with countless callers, Robert Sanderford watched images of Opal on the living-room TV. Seeing a shot of his beloved Opal playing with her stuffed animals, the heartbroken grandfather broke down and wept.

Throughout the day Audrey's blood pressure soared, causing her niece, Barbara Wallace, a licensed vocational nurse, to administer pills from the cobalt blue vial never far away.

"I'm going to be fine, y'all," Audrey insisted. "I can handle this."

But with all the media attention, the roller-coaster

ride of emotions, gladness at the news of Franks's arrest, and the ultimate distress of still not knowing where Opal was, the Sanderfords were most stunned by surprise visitors in the late-afternoon hours.

As the door of the Sanderford home opened, the family expected another local reporter to be standing on their porch. Instead, Rodney Franks, Ricky's older brother, and his girlfriend, Tina Crowley, waited along with Franks's half brother, Danny Doyle.

The trio entered the Sanderford home, still decorated with pink ribbons and photos of the smiling first grader. The family's television continued to play updates on Franks's capture.

Danny Doyle tightly clutched Barbara Wallace. Speechless, with eyes squeezed shut, they clinched in an embrace and the unlikely duo sank to the floor.

Wallace comforted Doyle, saying, "It took a lot of courage for y'all to walk up to that door." Then, lowering her voice in a soothing, almost motherly tone, she added, "We're not mad at y'all."

The Franks family was devastated by the arrest of Ricky for Opal's kidnapping. They hurt in much the same way the Sanderfords felt pain.

Rodney Franks and his girlfriend of eight years sat teary-eyed on the living-room sofa.

"I've known him all my life," Rodney said, tears blurring his eyes. "I keep thinking, did we do something as kids that messed him up in the head?"

Rodney hadn't seen his younger brother in a couple of months, not since a June family reunion. He hadn't been able to talk to Ricky since his arrest.

Rodney confessed he had yet to tell his mother, who was living in Cisco, Texas, of Ricky's arrest, fearing that she would be devastated.

"She's not going to handle it," Tina interjected.

Before they left, the family of the missing girl and

the family of her alleged abductor joined hands, forming a circle of mutual despair. They all prayed with Reverend Grady Brittian, of Davis Memorial United Methodist Church.

When Rodney, Tina, and Danny walked to their car, Teresa Sanderford looked after them pensively. "They're victims, too," she said with empathy.

Keeping the story of Ricky Franks's arrest for the kidnapping of Opal Jennings alive, Dallas/Fort Worth news outlets probed into every aspect of the alleged kidnapper's life, as well as the facts leading up to his arrest for Opal's disappearance.

They learned that questions concerning Franks's mental condition had surfaced in January 1991, when a court-ordered mental evaluation was performed after he was indicted in Wise County on charges of indecency with a child. Franks's attorney at the time, Ross Simpson, filed a motion that stated Franks appeared to be insane. He described Franks as having a long history of behavioral instability that previously required treatment at a mental-heath center.

The court-ordered psychological examination concluded that Franks was a pedophile with mild mental retardation. The report added that Franks fantasized about his sexual impulses, and described him as an impulsive and sad young man who was at risk for acting out. The psychologist recommended that Franks be placed somewhere that provided structure and supervision for the long term.

On April 4, 1991, Franks pleaded guilty to a lesser charge of indecency with one child. The other case was dismissed. He could have been sentenced to two to twenty years in prison, but Judge John Lindsey sentenced Franks to seven years' probation.

In July, August, September, October, November, and December 1993, Franks failed to pay his probation fees and also failed to report to his probation officer in December. District attorney Barry Green filed a motion to revoke Franks's probation in February 1994 for failure to report and pay fees. Franks was arrested three days later. But on February 18, 1994, Green, acting on the recommendation of the Wise County Adult Probation Department, asked the court to dismiss the motion to revoke. The request was granted and Franks was released from jail.

The judge modified Franks's probation to include sex offender counseling, and prohibited him from changing residence without the court's approval.

On July 17, 1995, Franks failed to attend a group counseling session, and the sex offender assessment-treatment program provider notified the Wise County probation office. Franks again failed to attend his scheduled sex-offender counseling in August 1995. Again the probation office was notified. The district attorney filed a second motion to revoke probation for failing to attend counseling. Franks was arrested and ordered to serve thirty days in the Wise County Jail.

Judge John Fostel modified the terms of Franks's probation in June 1996 to include no contact with any child younger than age seventeen. Two years later, he extended Franks's probation one year, to end April 2, 1999. The extension would allow Franks enough time to pay court-ordered fees and to complete the sex-offender-counseling program.

Six days following Opal Jennings's abduction, April 1, 1999, Franks appeared at the Wise County probation office with a fresh haircut and driving a vehicle that matched the description of the car driven by Opal's abductor. That was when Jesse Herrera, Franks's probation officer, called his friend Sergeant Harlon Wright, of the Wise County Sheriff's Office, and reported his suspicion of Franks's possible involvement in the Opal Jennings case. Wright, in turn, passed the tip on to the Fort Worth police that same day.

April 13, 1999, Judge Fostel discharged Franks from probation, stating, "The court is of the opinion that the ends of justice have been served."

Four months later, Mike Adair met with Sergeant Wright and Jesse Herrera for the first time since they'd provided the tip about Ricky Franks.

The news stories chronicling the series of events concerning Franks's legal problems led to a rash of tongue-wagging criticism.

"I know she disappeared March twenty-sixth, and he came in on April first," Wright said. "I know that agency had a lot of information coming in, and it had to be funneled through."

Indeed, more than twenty-five hundred tips had been generated. Franks's name was but one of many that had been passed on.

"Knowing the number of leads in a case of this magnitude, the Monday-morning quarterbacking will be humongous," Wise County sheriff Phil Ryan said of the lag time between the tip about Franks and his arrest. The sheriff added that if anything went right, it was that the Wise County community supervision department, the Wise County Sheriff's Office, and the Fort Worth police were talking to one another about the sex offenders under their watch.

As others scrutinized the effectiveness of the law enforcement community, Teresa Sanderford quietly wrote a short five-to-six-line letter to Ricky Franks at the Tarrant County Jail.

The letter asked Franks, if he took Opal, to please tell them where she was. The family cast no stones. Their interest was only focused on finding Opal. The family asked their pastor, Grady Brittian, if he would attempt to deliver the letter to Franks in jail.

On August 30, 1999, the Tarrant County grand jury met in one of the secured Grand Jury rooms of the Tarrant County Criminal Justice Center to consider the case against Richard Lee Franks. Metal detectors and armed security guards had protected the entrance ways of the building since a deadly shooting spree on July 1, 1992.

George Lott, disgruntled following a bitter divorce and child custody battle, had entered the fourth floor of the Second Court of Appeals in Tarrant County. Neatly dressed, Lott took a seat on one of the courtroom benches, placing his briefcase on his lap. Lott quietly opened the case and, with malice aforethought, gunned down Chris Marshall, a Tarrant County assistant district attorney. Lott also wounded three others, including two appellate judges, before reloading his nine-millimeter semiautomatic and chasing down thirty-three-year-old Dallas attorney John Edwards. Lott shot and killed Edwards in the stairwell of the courthouse. None of these men were responsible for Lott's divorce or custody decision, which had been handled in another state. Lott had simply lashed out at the judicial system itself.

Entering the Tarrant County Justice Center had taken the grand jurors several minutes as women's purses passed through the X-ray machine, and men had to empty their pockets of money, keys, and other items that would set off the metal detectors. They had stood by the bank of elevators in the center of the justice center and waited along with county employees to catch the next elevator going up. Each of the impaneled jurors anticipated a full day of testimony on the Richard Franks case.

The first day was tiring for Assistant District Attorney Robert Foran, the prosecutor Greg Miller had tagged to begin presenting the case. Foran, a man of medium height and brown hair, would be one of three assistant district attorneys to present evidence against Franks. Six members of the Franks family, including his wife, testified.

Judy Franks, her thin brown hair noticeably graying and the lines in her face deepened, testified under oath that her husband could not have kidnapped Opal Jennings because he had been with her at their South Fort Worth home the entire day.

No one who testified revealed anything new to the prosecution.

Presenting the evidence to the members of the jury was not the end of the intensive investigation. The search for Opal and evidence concerning her disappearance would continue throughout the grand jury process and on through the trial, if there was to be one.

"This is one of the most massive investigations I've ever seen in Tarrant County," Greg Miller commented after the first day of testimony. "We're going to lay it all out for the grand jury and see what happens. It's going to be a long and tedious process because we have a lot to bring to them."

The following morning, Richard Franks's mother, looking distressed and anxious, walked into the Tarrant County Criminal Justice Center on her way to testify before the grand jury on behalf of her son.

"I'm Richard's mother, and I'm proud to be his mother," Bessie Franks told reporters just before entering the grand jury chamber. "He's innocent. He is a good Christian boy, and the truth will come out."

In addition to Mrs. Franks, five other witnesses testified, including the man who sold Franks the black Cougar, and another who once got a ticket while driving the vehicle.

In all, more than twenty persons, for both the prosecution and defense, spoke before the grand jury. Proceedings were suspended until October 1999 while prosecutors waited for physical evidence to be returned from the FBI laboratory.

Meanwhile, the defense continued to hope there would be no indictment. Their client had persistently maintained his innocence, and his attorneys believed his diminished mental capacity led him to tell investigators what they wanted to hear.

"Under interrogation people will say things just to get the interrogators to leave them alone," Ed Jones stated. "This is especially true in Ricky's case, a person who has been diagnosed as mildly mentally retarded."

Jones's statement signified the course the defense would take if Franks was indicted and taken to trial.

Responding, Robert Foran insisted that prosecutors would not have presented the case if they thought the confession was false. Miller's prosecution team was certain they were building a case against the man who had kidnapped Opal Jennings. Only one remaining question was left to be answered: where was Opal?

CHAPTER 8

The grand jury had been read the sickening confession of Ricky Franks, describing the sexual advances of six-year-old Opal Jennings. They had listened to Franks deny the statement, contending he had been coerced into making the false confession. The panel had paid close attention to each witness. It was their duty to determine whether the facts and accusations presented by the prosecution warranted a trial of Richard Lee Franks for the kidnapping of Opal Jennings.

On September 21, 1999, state district judge Don Leonard extended the term of the grand jury hearing evidence in the Franks case. It was not an unusual move to lengthen the standard ninety-day term of service by another ninety days. It was no indication of the strength of the state's case. It merely allowed the panel to continue deliberations without interruption.

While the grand jury continued their discussions, parents across the North Texas metroplex continued taking extra precautions to protect their children.

About sixty parents and children met at W. R. Hatfield Intermediate School to learn how to prevent child abductions. The "Velcro method" was demonstrated with a five-year-old child. The child clung tightly to the instructor's arm while he walked around the room, sticking to him "like Velcro." Soon the room was filled with children clinging to a parent like a fabric sheet to freshly dried clothes.

Investigators from thirteen North Texas cities, as well as the county and state, continued to work the nearly three thousand leads concerning Opal's abduction. They hoped knowledge of the Jennings case would prevent such horror from ever happening again. Realistically, they knew that evil lurked near soccer and baseball fields, playgrounds, and other areas where children normally congregated. Their job was to continue to look for one little girl who had been a victim of such evil.

On October 20, 1999, a change in the weather prompted investigators to bring back search dogs to look again for signs of the missing six-year-old. The two highly trained dogs had last searched in the August heat. Investigators hoped the cooler temperatures would allow the animals to gain a better scent.

The canines sniffed around the lake near the intersection of Loop 820 and North Main Street, near Meacham Airport, and back to a quarry earlier identified by Franks as a place where Opal might be found. They turned up nothing.

More than a month after testifying before the grand jury, on November 4, 1999, and prior to the grand jury's decision on an indictment of her husband, Judy Franks was arrested on charges of providing her husband a false alibi for the day of Opal's kidnapping.

Judy, perhaps unknown to her husband, had a boyfriend. She frequently wrote Jerry Burrows at the prison where he was incarcerated, at the Texas Department of Criminal Justice. In one of her letters to

Burrows, Judy admitted she had given her husband an alibi for the day Opal Jennings was abducted.

Special Agent Andy Farrell learned of Judy Franks's relationship with Burrows when letters from Burrows to Judy were found during the search of her parents' house for evidence linking Ricky Franks to Opal. Shortly after the letters were given to Greg Miller, Farrell and Miller traveled to Huntsville to talk with Burrows.

A man in his forties, with receding brown hair, Burrows spoke openly with the prosecutor and FBI agent. He confirmed Judy's confession that she had given Ricky an alibi and even supplied Miller and Farrell with Judy's letter stating she had lied.

Miller was delighted with the hard evidence disputing Franks's alibi. He was uncertain if the grand jury had given any credence to Judy's testimony, but the obsessive prosecutor wasn't about to take any chances.

Along with Judy Franks's letter to her boyfriend, Miller had also obtained photographs from the FBI of a blue Mead notebook kept by Judy's mother. The notebook contained a daily diary of Mrs. Magby's medication and water consumption, as well as the goings and comings of Ricky and Judy. The notebook itself hadn't been seized, but an astute FBI agent had taken time to photograph the pages, unaware that they would play a big part in the prosecution's case.

On March 25, 1999, Mrs. Magby had written in the notebook that Judy and Ricky had stayed out all night. On March 26, the day of Opal's kidnapping, Mrs. Magby made a notation in her book that Judy and Ricky came in at 5:00 A.M., a statement in direct conflict with that given by Judy Franks during her grand jury testimony.

With Jerry Burrows's letter from Judy and Mrs. Magby's diary as evidence, Miller charged Judy Franks with the offense of perjury. In addition, she was also indicted for theft and forgery in connection with a 1996 stolen Internal Revenue Service tax refund check for $1,053.

The check was issued to a woman living with Judy Franks at the time of the theft. Judy had asked her aunt, a bank teller, to cash the check for her friend, who, Judy claimed, had lost her identification. The woman later complained she never received the IRS check and a short time later Judy Franks asked the woman to move out.

The forgery and theft charges were unrelated to the case against Ricky Franks.

After being indicted, Judy Franks was taken to the Tarrant County Jail, where Ricky Franks awaited word on the grand jury's findings. Her bond totaled $60,000. If convicted, Judy Franks could face up to ten years in prison for perjury and up to two years in prison for theft and forgery.

When Bessie Franks heard the news of her daughter-in-law's arrest, her heart sank. It was like a recurring nightmare. First Ricky arrested for kidnapping, then Judy for perjury, theft, and forgery. As Bessie had done with Ricky, she defended Judy, basing her advocacy on Judy's limited mental capabilities.

"Judy is a slow learner, too. She could have misunderstood some of the questions. I don't want to say anything bad about Judy, but I don't think she would be smart enough to lie on purpose," Bessie Franks told reporters.

Bessie wanted to help her daughter-in-law, but she was having a difficult time herself. Ricky was in jail, his half brother Harold had been in jail, and Bessie had tried to help both boys. Her limited financial resources had been stretched to the breaking point. The $800 she had used for gasoline and other expenses going to see her sons and their attorneys had just about tapped her out. She hoped Judy's parents would be able to help her.

That help didn't come for nearly a month. Once the Magbys obtained Brantley Pringle as counsel, Pringle posted the $60,000 bond and Judy Franks was released from jail.

Five days after his wife's arrest, Richard Franks learned that the grand jury had agreed to indict him for the kidnapping of Opal Jennings with the intent to harm or sexually abuse her. Assistant District Attorney Robert Foran announced that a second charge against Franks, of indecency with a child, would be dropped so that the prosecution could focus on the higher charge of aggravated kidnapping. Franks could be sentenced from five years to life in prison.

The Sanderford family was not surprised at the decision of the grand jury. Greg Miller had spent hours with the Sanderfords, keeping them informed of the investigative efforts, which continued to focus on finding Opal. He also counseled with them as to the prosecution's trial strategy, explaining that the case would be difficult, but pledging to do his best.

"We have such faith in the DA and the police," Teresa Sanderford, Opal's aunt, said. "We're just going to have to sit and wait to see what the judicial system has in store."

Teresa Sanderford didn't know Ricky Franks and had no idea if he was responsible for Opal's disappearance. She just knew the indictment of Franks gave the family little comfort. Even if Ricky Franks was eventually found guilty of taking Opal, she was still missing. More than a conviction of the person guilty of taking Opal, they wanted Opal back home.

* * *

The stage was set for trial. Richard Franks had been indicted for aggravated kidnapping by the grand jury. The next step was a trial based on the merits of the case. Greg Miller's prosecution team was ready to move forward. Ed Jones and Leon Haley were set to defend their client adamantly. A trial date of April 3, 2000, was set. Lawyers from the prosecution and defense would clash in one of the most anticipated trials in Tarrant County history.

Judy Franks visited her husband frequently at the Tarrant County Jail as he awaited his April trial. She stared at him through the Plexiglas window and spoke to him by telephone. Judy would have done anything for her spouse. Jailers at the downtown Fort Worth facility scrutinized Judy Franks closely each time she arrived to see the man accused of taking Opal Jennings.

Under that intense examination, early in January 2000, Judy Franks was again arrested while visiting her husband. Accused of attempting to smuggle a crack pipe into the jail for Franks, Judy spent one night in the county facility before her attorney posted a $1,000 bond and she was released. Judy was charged with possession of a controlled substance with the intent to deliver. Her troubles continued to mount.

Preparations were feverishly under way for the highly anticipated trial as searchers continued to look for Opal Jennings, and lawyers relentlessly reviewed all the evidence. Ed Jones, attorney for the defense, spent much of his time in the Cash America building in downtown Fort Worth poring over thirty-six bound volumes of FBI notes, exhibits, and evidence folders.

The six-story building housed the Fort Worth division of the Federal Bureau of Investigation. It was there that the evidence against Richard Franks was secured.

On March 26, 2000, exactly one year after Opal's abduction, almost to the moment, the Fort Worth skies turned a ghastly green, the air stilled. It was as though the heavens were mourning the loss of Opal Jennings.

At 6:15 P.M., the shrill sounds of emergency sirens blared throughout the city. The reverberation warned that a tornado had been spotted; everyone should take cover.

The early-season tornado started near Monticello and north of West Seventh Street, just west of the city's center. The damage in that area was a category F0, or light. As the path of the tornado traveled across the Clear Fork of the Trinity River, its damage increased to F2, significant. It remained at that level as it rampaged into the heart of the city.

Hail, the size of softballs, bombarded the area, traveling at an estimated speed of one hundred miles an hour. A nineteen-year-old man, unable to find shelter, was struck in the head, his skull fractured by the tremendous force. He was the first victim of the devastating storm that tore a two-mile-long swath. Only two other deaths by direct hail strikes had been reported in the twentieth century.

Hardest hit were buildings in the downtown area, including the Cash America building, where windows were sucked from their frames and shards of glass blew out at 150 miles an hour. Trees were toppled, buildings crumbled, and only steel beams remained on a cathedral's five-story tower. Pieces of glass, chunks of metal and building panels, continued to fall an hour after the storm had passed.

A second tornado destroyed more than one hundred

homes in neighboring Arlington and Grand Prairie and damaged more than one thousand others.

When the devastating winds had ceased, five people were dead and ninety-five injured. Of those who died, one man was crushed inside a collapsed industrial building, another was killed by flying debris, and another man drowned when his car was swept into the Trinity River. There was $500,000,000 in damage to commercial and public buildings. Downtown Fort Worth was in shambles.

Two days after the horrendous storm ripped through Fort Worth, FBI agents picked through paper strewn across the pavement near the Cash America building. They searched for any sensitive files that may have been blown out of the bureau's sixth-floor office. Wearing disposable gloves, twenty agents looked through even the smallest scraps of paper that had been scattered outdoors.

It was impossible to determine if any sensitive files had been lost. Paperwork had been left on agents' desktops when the storm hit, but sensitive files were believed to be safe in cabinets. The FBI planned to inventory its documents to determine whether any confidential papers were missing.

In his Arlington living room, Greg Miller sat stunned as he watched news footage of the Cash America building on TV. It was 7:00 P.M., just forty-five minutes after the tornado had struck downtown Fort Worth. Miller could see papers blowing out of the shattered windows and knew that anything left unsecured would be lost. His heart sank as he thought of the materials for the Franks case being held for safe-keeping at the FBI office.

Miller grabbed his phone and called Andy Farrell.

Farrell failed to call back, and by 10:00 P.M., Miller was growing frantic. He had to know the status of the case files.

The prosecutor's phone finally rang at a little after ten o'clock. It was Bruce Shinkle, another agent of the FBI.

"I have some good news and some bad news," Shinkle announced.

Miller drew in a deep breath. "Give it to me," he said, expecting the worst.

"Well, the good news is the notebooks were locked in the basement vault and we still have them," Shinkle said.

Miller let out a small sigh but knew the bad news was yet to come.

"However," Shinkle continued, "when the tornado hit, the fire alarms went off and activated the sprinkler system in the vault. The vault is flooded."

When Miller replaced the phone in its cradle, he leaned forward, resting his head in his hands. Months of work *literally* could be going down the drain.

The next morning, Farrell and Shinkle made arrangements for the notebooks to be specially treated. First they were placed in a vacuum chamber, the air removed, and the temperature dropped to some point well beyond freezing. The process extracted all of the water out of the notebooks. The pages, in essence, were "freeze-dried." After there was a stabilization period, the temperature was gradually raised back to room temperature. The notebooks had been saved, but each and every page contained in the thirty-six volumes had been stuck together.

The job of carefully pulling each of the hundreds of pages apart fell to Miller and Farrell. The task was tedious. The two men grew tired of the painstaking work, but it had to be done. Through it all, they knew they had been lucky. Most of the FBI files that were upstairs in the bureau's offices were never seen again.

In light of the extreme natural disaster, the recovery process of the evidence notebooks, and a request by the defense for more time in reviewing the thousands of pages of FBI files, Judge Robert Gill ordered a two-month postponement of Franks's kidnapping trial. Greg Miller was ready to go forward, but he admitted the delay could help with the effects of pretrial publicity. The trial originally had been set for one week after the one-year anniversary of Opal's disappearance. There had been substantial media coverage concerning Opal and the upcoming trial, which might have caused the defense to ask for a change of venue to another Texas city. Miller didn't want that to happen. He wanted the trial to take place in Tarrant County—the place where the crime had occurred and where he knew citizens wanted justice for Opal.

It would be June 2000 before Richard Lee Franks would finally be tried for the aggravated kidnapping of Opal Jennings.

CHAPTER 9

In April 2000, Judy Franks appeared before Tarrant County district judge Sharen Wilson on charges of aggravated perjury. The stout, forty-year-old wife of Ricky Franks lowered her head, the dark roots of her tinted hair showing. Judy stood before the bench and admitted she had provided a false alibi for her husband when she testified before the grand jury. In exchange for her guilty plea, two unrelated charges—one for forgery and the other for theft concerning an IRS check—were barred from prosecution. The charges weren't dismissed, but she couldn't be prosecuted for them in the future.

Judge Wilson, known for her stern demeanor and tough judgments, granted Judy Franks five years' deferred adjudication probation. The perjury conviction would appear on any criminal background check but would not be denoted as a felony conviction. Judy would retain her right to vote and maintain other privileges not allowed convicted felons.

Deputy District Attorney Greg Miller told reporters, "The plea agreement was basically what I offered from the beginning of the case." Miller had no interest in sending the mentally slow wife of accused kidnapper

Ricky Franks to prison. His focus remained on convicting her husband for the aggravated kidnapping of Opal Jennings.

Judy's false alibi was not seen as a deliberate criminal act by her attorney, or by the lawyers for Ricky Franks. They understood that Judy had made the bogus statements out of affection and concern for her husband. Ed Jones and Leon Haley claimed they had had no plans to call Judy to testify in the June trial, stating she didn't figure into the defense of her husband.

Jones and Haley were too busy working on pretrial maneuvers to worry about Judy Franks's grand jury testimony. Their strategy was to put their client in the best position possible prior to the beginning of trial.

The defense team filed a motion to have Judge Robert Gill removed from the case based on Gill's early involvement in the investigation. According to the motion, in the first sixteen hours after Franks's arrest, Gill had learned too much about the case to be an impartial jurist. After being supplied with enough information about the defendant to support the issuance of both warrants, Gill had signed each document.

The motion read, "Judge Gill, based on his involvement and participation in the investigation of the defendant, is biased and prejudiced against the defendant such that a fair trial cannot be had by the defendant."

In addition, the motion asked for Gill's removal as trial judge based on the fact that it was Gill who set Franks's bail at $1,000,000 and that the district judge had never appointed counsel to help Franks during the long hours he was in custody.

Patrick Davis, a third attorney to join the Franks defense team, claimed the motion didn't question Gill's competence or character, but it was filed to make certain the judge hadn't been a witness to any issues or material facts that could prevent their client from getting a fair trial. The motion would give the experienced judge the option of removing himself from the legal proceedings, or appointing another judge to decide the matter.

Two additional pretrial motions were also filed. One asked for a hearing on the admissibility of Franks's statement given to police soon after his arrest. It was important to the defense team that the prejudicial words of their client admitting he had picked Opal up at her residence not be heard by the jury. They certainly didn't want the twelve-person panel to hear that Franks claimed the six-year-old child made sexual advances toward him.

In the second motion the defense asked the court to throw out any other written or oral statements that might have been taken from their client shortly after his arrest and detention. Haley, Jones, and Davis knew that any statements Franks had made concerning Opal's whereabouts were potentially devastating to their defense.

Two months after the disastrous tornado had spun through Fort Worth, the city that Will Rogers declared was "where the West begins," some high-rises, including the Cash America building, were still closed. Plywood covered broken windows, making the building look as deserted as an Old West ghost town.

The building initially was thought to be so severely damaged that it would have to be demolished, but tenants eventually were informed that the building could be repaired and they would be back in their offices in about eighteen months. Many offices, like the FBI, had made arrangements to share space with others. Some worked from card tables set up in their living rooms, and one operated from his car on a cell phone. It was basically back to business for those who worked in the downtown area.

And it was back to court for Richard Franks. The two-month postponement, asked for and received by his attorneys, was over. It was time for the much anticipated trial of Richard Lee Franks for the aggravated kidnapping of Opal Jennings.

On June 26, 2000, the day before Franks's scheduled kidnapping trial, his three gritty lawyers appeared in the courtroom of Judge Robert Gill for a pretrial hearing on the motions that had been filed with the court. The men were as diverse in their appearance as they were in their approach to the law.

As lead attorney, Leon Haley, an attractive, well-dressed African American, controlled his emotions and presented his cases in a calm, confident manner. Edward Jones, a younger, less experienced but exuberant attorney, often showed unabashed emotion in the courtroom. The third lawyer on Franks's defense team was Patrick Davis. Davis, clean-shaven and wearing wire-rimmed glasses, generally sat silently watching court proceedings with an open law book in front of him. Davis was not heard from until he rose to object to a point of law. Davis, well versed in appellate law, was on the team to make certain the pretrial hearing and the trial were run according to the letter of the law. Davis would also file Franks's appeal to a higher court in the event he was convicted of the offense.

The stern-faced Judge Gill, brown hair slicked to one side, with a short mustache in a neat trim line beneath his nose, was set to hear arguments from the defense in support of their motion to suppress statements given by their client in the hours prior to his official arrest and arraignment. The state, represented by Greg Miller, Robert Foran, and Lisa Callahan, would present evidence in support of the defendant's voluntary statement. They were prepared to squelch any objection to the presentation of Richard Franks's confession.

Investigator Kathy Manning was the first to be called. Blond hair neatly coiffed, and dressed in a business-style suit, Manning testified before the court that she had verified the arrest warrant against Franks, had been one of six investigators to initiate the arrest, and had prepared the Miranda warning to be read to Franks. Manning also established that Franks had acknowledged he understood his rights and had placed his initials at the end of each statement.

In addition, Franks had been presented a consent-to-search form for his vehicle. The form had been read to him and he had signed it. Franks verbally had admitted he understood that the officers would be searching his car for evidence, and had expressed no objection or asked any questions.

The veteran investigator, who had moved to the District Attorney's Special Crimes Unit, from the Fort Worth Police Department, told Judge Gill that Eric Holden, an expert polygraph examiner, had spent hours with Richard Franks, ultimately ending the interview with a statement from the accused.

"He hadn't been forced, coerced, or threatened to make the statement," Manning testified, adding, tongue in cheek, that guns hadn't been drawn, he hadn't been tricked, and Franks hadn't been intoxicated at the time the statement was given.

At that point in the proceedings, Lisa Callahan, an assistant district attorney for nine years, who had worked two years in the Crimes Against Children Unit, presented Franks's written statement into evidence. If the confession drew any negative reaction from Judge Gill, he didn't show it. He remained stoic throughout the reading.

"We gathered the appropriate paperwork we needed to bring him across the street to be arraigned," Manning stated. "And an arrest warrant had also been prepared, so we waited until that was finished before coming across the street into this building."

Manning, confident in the unit's procedures and self-assured in her testimony, explained that Ricky Franks was put in the bailiff's office behind the courtroom to wait for Judge Robert Gill to take the bench. Franks had remained in the bailiff's office about forty-five minutes before he was taken before the judge for arraignment. At that time the judge went over the Miranda warning in great detail.

"At no time did Ricky Franks invoke any of his rights," Manning stated firmly.

"Did he at any point in the bailiff's office offer any voluntary statements?" ADA Callahan asked.

"Yes. He said that he didn't do it, that he didn't want to be in trouble. He was just trying to say something to keep himself out of jail," Manning responded.

"Did Danny McCormick make a response to that?" Callahan questioned.

"Danny asked him, 'Is what you said not the truth? All we want is the truth. You need to tell us what the truth is.' Franks said, 'No. I told you the truth. I just don't want to go to jail,'" Manning answered.

Patrick Davis rose from his seat and objected. Davis believed the court was going to hear the objection to the arrest, then the motion to suppress Franks's statements. However, Judge Gill announced he intended to consider all the defense motions at once. Davis sat down, obviously unhappy with the court's decision.

When Manning's testimony continued, she told the court that while she and Charlie Johnson waited in the car with Franks, and while McCormick was getting the arrest warrant prepared, Franks again began to talk freely.

"He again said that he didn't do it. I said, 'Well, everything that we've gone through tonight, did you make that up? Are you not telling us the truth?' He said, 'No. I'm telling you the truth. I just don't want to go to jail. I don't want to be in trouble. They are twisting my words around.' I said, 'How are they twisting your words around? What's wrong with what's been said?' And he said, 'I just don't want to go to jail.' I said, 'If you could tell us where the body was, then we could show the judge that what you put in that paper, everything in it is the truth.' He was concerned the judge wasn't going to believe that he had let Opal out of the car and she was still alive," Manning testified.

Edward Jones began his cross-examination of Manning by asking when she initially had received a copy of the seat belt warrant, a warrant that would allow investigators to pick up Ricky Franks and question him without formally charging him with any crime. Jones learned Manning first acquired a copy of the seat belt warrant on August 13, and again requested a copy, to make certain the warrant was still outstanding, on August 17, the day Franks was arrested.

"Are you in the normal practice of making arrests for ticket warrants?" Jones asked, expecting a negative response.

"Yes," Manning replied.

Jones stared at Manning questioningly. If he doubted the investigator's statement, he decided not to pursue the matter.

Jones next established that all of the officers present when Franks was arrested were with the Tarrant County District Attorney's Office. There had been no one from the Saginaw Police Department or from the FBI.

When questioned, Manning admitted that Franks had asked her how much money it would take to get him out of jail and that she hadn't checked to see if he had the necessary funds on his person to pay for the seat belt ticket. He also had asked where his car had been taken.

During Kathy Manning's testimony, Ricky Franks sat quietly at the table beside his attorneys. Dressed in a dark suit, white shirt, and multicolored dark brown tie, Franks appeared nothing like the scruffy, long-haired man described by the young witnesses of Opal's kidnapping. He showed no emotion and asked his attorneys no questions while Manning was on the stand.

In cross-examination Edward Jones repeated many of the questions asked earlier by Callahan. He then questioned Manning concerning Ricky Franks's mental abilities.

"At the time that Mr. Franks was arrested and questioned, did you have any personal knowledge regarding his IQ level or his mild mental retardation?" Jones inquired.

"No," Manning stated.

Jones continued his questioning, implying that Ricky Franks was unable to understand the Miranda warning, therefore he couldn't have waived his rights. He then asked about his client's condition during the long hours of interviewing.

"Did Mr. Franks get any sleep from the time that he was taken into custody, prior to his signing the statement, I believe, at eight A.M.?"

"No," Manning responded flatly.

"Are you familiar with the requirements regarding, upon arrest, taking someone before a magistrate without unnecessary delay?" Jones asked.

"Yes, sir."

"And in this case you don't believe that you, in not booking Mr. Franks in until after two o'clock the next day, hadn't taken him without unnecessary delay regarding the ticket warrant?" Jones pressed.

"That would be true. That was not an unnecessary delay," Manning answered with confidence. Manning was a seasoned officer who had testified in court numerous times. She knew well she was to answer the questions directly, giving no additional information not specifically requested by the defense.

Ed Jones knew he was not going to get any more than the basics from Manning. He moved on, questioning Manning and hoping to make points related to the defense motions.

"Did you inform the judge that Franks had recanted and said that he didn't do anything or know anything?" Jones asked.

"I didn't speak with the judge, no," Manning replied.

"Had the judge arraigned him?" Jones pushed on.

"At that point, no," Manning responded.

"But, yet, you didn't let the judge know that; is that correct," Jones said, his tone more statement than question, his voice raised slightly.

"That's correct," Manning said.

Jones passed the witness to the prosecution.

Lisa Callahan, a striking young woman with long dark hair and large bright eyes, which sparkled through fashionable glasses, approached Kathy Manning for redirect examination.

"Now, counsel asked you whether or not you knew anything concerning the defendant's IQ. In conversing with him, you talked about a number of issues, bond, his feelings about whether or not the judge would believe him, stuff to that effect. Did he appear to speak and respond in a normal fashion?" Callahan asked.

"Yes, he did."

"Were you able to understand him completely?" Callahan inquired.

"Absolutely."

"Was what he said consistent and logical with what the issue was at the time?" Callahan asked.

"Yes, it was."

"Was his vocabulary normal?" Callahan queried.

"Yes, it was."

"Did his mental ability seem up to the task of dealing with the situation at hand?" the prosecutor continued.

"Yes, it was," Manning answered.

Callahan's last questions were in response to the time it had taken to get Ricky Franks arraigned. Through Manning, the prosecutor established that the paperwork prepared in order to get Franks booked in jail was begun at 6:00 A.M., soon after Eric Holden's interview with Franks was concluded. Regular procedures had taken them until later in the day to have Franks actually arraigned and then booked into the Tarrant County Jail.

Kathy Manning was dismissed and Eric Holden, a licensed polygraph examiner, with two degrees in psychology, was called to testify.

Holden established that he had never heard of Ricky Franks until called by the Special Crimes Unit to interview him; that no investigator had spoken to Franks regarding Opal Jennings prior to Holden arriving in Fort Worth; and that it had taken about thirty to forty minutes to be briefed by investigators before he began his discussions with Franks.

"Why did you go talk to Ricky Franks more or less right away?" Miller asked.

"Well, because of the time of the evening. I wanted to determine that he wanted to take the polygraph examination. I needed to find out if he understood what the examination would be about and if he was a decent subject capable of being tested effectively. That would be based on his fatigue and his willingness to cooperate. I wanted to establish whether he was really going to take the test and if I would administer it to him based on his condition," Holden stated.

"How long did that initial conversation take?" Miller asked.

"About five to ten minutes," Holden replied.

"Based on your observation and comments and responses of Ricky Franks, what conclusion did you arrive [at]?" Miller asked.

Patrick Davis was on his feet. "Your Honor, I object to any conclusions. I don't think it's even relevant. At this time you're determining the motion to suppress a number of things. Mr. Holden's conclusions have no relevance or bearing on this hearing, as to my client's legal rights," Davis argued.

Without hesitation Judge Gill responded, "Overruled."

Davis took his seat and Miller continued his questioning.

"He was anxious to take the polygraph test. He wanted to take the polygraph test. He understood it was about the Opal Jennings case and he indicated that he felt rested and was in good shape. He said he had eaten and he was ready to take the test. So, based on that, I concluded that we would proceed," Holden answered.

Holden explained that he then set up the polygraph equipment in a room designated for conducting the examination. Holden then began the initial interview with a more in-depth evaluation of Franks's physical condition and his understanding of the issues they would cover. Holden then proceeded with the interview.

"During this process, did you obtain a consent from Ricky Franks?" Miller asked.

"I did."

Holden explained that whenever conducting an interview for law enforcement, he always issued the Miranda warning so that the person knew their rights. If, however, he was interviewing for a defense attorney, the interview was conducted under the attorney-client privilege, therefore the Miranda warning wasn't given.

"Who is involved in deciding what questions are going to be administered?" Miller asked, sitting at the prosecution table.

"I initially develop the issues that I want to test over. The development of the test questions is really a combination of efforts—in this case between Mr. Franks and myself. I would talk to him about questions, make sure he is clear on them, get his language for what he thinks the question is asking, design a test question that he says he's very clear and can explain to me what that question means. Then I tell him we've got a good test question here, find out how he's going to answer it, and make sure he's very clear about that. Each of the questions is designed in that way," Holden explained.

"Did Richard Franks have to approve the questions that you were going to ask him?" Miller asked.

"Absolutely."

Holden continued by explaining that if there was a problem with a question, anything that would cause Franks to say it wasn't a good question, it wasn't clear, or it couldn't be answered yes or no, then it would be back to square one. They would start all over.

At the defense table Edward Jones and Leon Haley

had their heads together whispering, perhaps discussing rebuttal questions for Holden. Holden's explanation of their client's participation in the questioning process for the polygraph didn't fit their profile of Franks as mentally incapable.

"Was Richard Franks comfortable with the questions that you and he designed for his test?" Miller questioned Holden.

"He indicated he was. Yes, sir," Holden responded.

"What happens after the questions are designed?" Miller questioned.

"At that point the questions are all entered into the computer. At that point I begin to explain the actual attachments that would be placed on him, what they do, how they work. How the computer gets the data based on physiological reactions from the examinee. I explain the actual test procedure to him at that point and go through the test procedures with him. I make sure he's clear how long each chart will take, how many charts will be run, and how long the whole procedure will occur. I explain to him that he will not feel anything from the attachments or the test receptors around the chest and belly. He will feel the pressure on the arm cuff; I make sure he's clear about that. And then we begin the test process after I give him the final instructions about sitting still, looking straight ahead, making sure he doesn't have to go to the bathroom, and he has plenty of water and feels good—" Holden explained.

"Object to the narrative," Davis interrupted.

"Overruled," Judge Gill responded.

After waiting for the judge's ruling, Holden continued. "Then we get the last commitment: are you sure you want to proceed with the test? If he says yes, we do. If he says no, we go home."

Still sitting at the prosecution table Miller asked, "What time was the first test run?"

"The first test, which was a practice test, was conducted at two-oh-one A.M.," Holden said.

"When you ultimately gave him the test for the subject matter, what time was that?" Miller asked.

"About two-oh-five, two-oh-six, somewhere in that area of the morning," Holden stated.

Holden explained that four tests were administered to Ricky Franks. He stated that up until the point he administered the tests, he had no idea Richard Lee Franks was involved in the abduction of Opal Jennings.

When the test was concluded, Holden had gathered up all the chart data, removed the attachments from Franks's body, asked him if he needed to go to the bathroom and if he was comfortable. Holden had informed Franks it would take about twenty minutes to evaluate the charts, grade them, and make an assessment.

"Initially, what did you do?" Miller asked.

"Initially I numerically scored them and numerically evaluated them. For reliability purposes I want to know how the computer graded it, if the computer saw it in the same way that I did. If there is a disagreement, it causes some concern. I had three computer evaluations. There are three computer algorithms in the computer; one from Johns Hopkins University and two other independent evaluations that are used by the Department of Defense, law enforcement agencies, and private examiners. They're algorithms that grade and evaluate polygraph charts. So, when I completed my evaluation, I went back in. Ricky was in the room with me when I did the computer assessments of each of the sets of polygraph charts," Holden explained.

"Did you inform Richard Franks of the results of the

polygraph?" Miller asked. "And is that something
that is required by Texas state law?"

"I did. It's required if the person appears deceptive.
The requirements—" Holden began before being
interrupted by Ed Jones.

"Judge," Jones said as he stood to address the
bench, "I object to any results being presented to this
court. They are inherently unreliable and inadmissi-
ble in court."

"Overruled," Judge Gill stated without hesitation.

Franks's eyes narrowed and his lips pursed as he showed
emotion for the first time during the proceedings.

As Jones sat down, Miller urged Holden to continue.

"The law states that if a person is deceptive, you
must advise the examinee of that deceptive opinion
and afford them an opportunity to discuss the issue
and to clarify it or tell you what may have caused the
problem," Holden finished.

Holden informed the court that he had informed
Franks of his test results about 3:00 or 3:15 A.M.

"At that time, did Mr. Franks begin to give you a different version than what he had previously given
you?" Miller questioned.

"He did."

Holden explained that he then asked Franks to clarify the incident for him, and as he did, Holden began
to take notes. The polygraph examiner told the court
that the conversation with Franks took between two
and 2½ hours. It occurred somewhere between 3:00
and 6:00 A.M.

"During this portion of your meeting with Richard
Franks, did he want to tell you what you put on this
paper?" Miller asked, holding the statement Franks
had made the morning after his arrest.

"He did. He had a story to tell and he told it,"
Holden responded. Holden elaborated by stating

that he had written Franks's statement word for word and that Ricky Franks had signed and initialed it.

Holden added that he had allowed Franks to smoke, drink soft drinks, and to use the bathroom. Holden said he also asked Franks to write how he was treated on the last page of his statement. Holden acknowledged he had been impressed with Franks's handwriting and that virtually all of the words had been spelled correctly.

"When you told him you were impressed, what response did Richard Franks make?" Miller asked.

"He looked at me, smiled a little bit, and winked," Holden said.

"He winked?" Miller said with surprise.

"Yes. He winked."

Holden stated he then gave his handwritten notes to Charlie Johnson to be typed. He smiled as he admitted he had to help Charlie Johnson in transposing the notes due to his own poor handwriting.

When Miller concluded his questioning, Leon Haley stood to begin the cross-examination. A man of medium stature, Haley still commanded a presence in the courtroom.

Referring to Eric Holden's two degrees in psychology, Haley asked, "So you have some understanding about the makeup of the mind of people and how you can mislead them into making false statements; is that correct?"

"I'm not sure I have that clear a picture of the makeup of the mind, but I'm familiar with some of the issues you are addressing," Holden answered.

Haley switched his focus to the size of the room his client had been kept in and to Franks's demeanor during the questioning.

"The room was kind of sterile, wasn't it? Just a little room—a table and a chair, correct?" Haley asked.

"Right."

"When you got in there, he was kind of like cowered over in a little corner, just sitting in a chair. Isn't that right?" Haley asked, painting a picture of his client as a frightened victim.

"You are asking me to account for his state of mind. He was happy to take a polygraph and that's what he wanted to do. That's what I was there for. I asked if he really wanted to do it, and he said yes. As for the arrest, I'm sure no one is glad to be arrested, period, for any reason," Holden stated.

Miller was pleased with Holden's testimony and his ability to withstand the defense attorney's probing. An expert witness, Holden had testified in hundreds of trials. The defense wasn't going to trick him into making a statement he wasn't prepared to back up with facts.

"Wouldn't it have made a difference to you what they had told him in terms of how you would have questioned him and prepared your discussions with him before you gave him the polygraph?" Haley asked in an effort to find out if Franks had indeed been questioned before Holden's arrival.

"It was important for me to know whether they had interviewed or interrogated him before I started," Holden responded. "Had they done that, I wouldn't have proceeded."

Holden stated that once Franks had agreed to take the polygraph, he then went to the investigators to learn more facts of the case. He needed the information at that point in order to formulate questions for the testing. He told Haley he still didn't know Franks was a suspect, only that he was to question him to determine if he was a likely suspect.

Determining that Holden could have spent as much as four hours with Franks prior to administering the polygraph, Haley asked Holden if he had had any concern that Franks needed rest before taking the test.

"Not at all. Based on what he indicated to me, how good he felt, how rested he felt, that he had eaten, I wasn't overly concerned about it," Holden stated.

Haley continued, wanting to know how far Holden had pushed his client.

"It's the policy of twenty-seven years, and my reputation pretty well substantiates this, if at any time he would have said, 'I'm tired,' which at one point he did, it was over," Holden responded.

"According to your evaluation, it appeared that he might have been deceptive. Is that fair?" Haley asked.

"Yes, sir."

"Now, let's talk about this word 'deceptive.' The fact that it appeared that he may have been deceptive didn't mean that he was actually lying, though. Isn't that fair to say?" Haley asked.

"Sure," Holden admitted.

Haley's serious look vanished momentarily and a slight curve of his lips was visible.

"Is there any reason why you didn't allow him to just take—to say, 'Let's try it again, maybe something's wrong, let's try it again'?" Haley questioned.

"There's no procedure that you just keep doing it over and over. I had conducted four exams at that time, three repeats of the same questions over and over and over. Because there was consistency every time I asked the questions on each of the three charts that pertained to the Opal Jennings matter, I had no reason to believe it would change on chart four or chart five or chart six. The law says two. I run a minimum of three," Holden elaborated.

"Did you discuss with him why he may or may not have passed?" Haley inquired.

"I asked him if there was anything going through his mind, what was going on with him. I asked him if he wanted to talk to me. He said he did. I asked him to explain to me, if he could, what was going on with him. Did he lie to me about anything that we had talked about? What might have caused the problem with him passing the test," Holden explained.

"You said you read him those warnings, did you actually read them to him or did you hand him the paperwork and tell him to read it?" Haley questioned.

"I went over them with him when I went over the consent form, as I was filling it out. I read portions of each of the paragraphs to him and specifically the Miranda warnings. I read those Miranda warnings to him," Holden stated. "In fact, if I might just put in one additional thing, we have people that are ordered to take the test—for example, police officers. We have totally different forms which our attorneys have devised that say, 'I understand I'm being ordered to take this test.' So we are very cautious about that. If a person tells me, 'I don't want to take this test,' whatever the reason is, I don't administer it. That's been my policy for twenty-seven years and it will remain my policy.

"I didn't see personally or hear anything from Mr. Franks that indicated he didn't understand what he was doing; he didn't understand where he was; he didn't understand what we were going to talk about; he didn't understand that he could stop at any time he wanted to; he didn't say, 'I don't want to talk to you' or 'Get me a lawyer.' It was whatever he wanted to do; it really made no difference to me at that point."

"Did you tell him if he took the test he'd be all right, they would leave him alone, anything like that?" Haley asked.

"I never told him that he could or couldn't do

anything. I didn't tell him he might go home, might not go home, or he could stay. I didn't get involved in that because I didn't really know what his status was, quite frankly," Holden admitted.

"If you didn't know what his status was, why would you focus on the Miranda warnings out of the statement he signed?" Haley asked.

"We've done that for the last ten years or so with everybody that we administer a police test to or a law enforcement test. It makes no difference who it is. They are all treated the same. Mr. Franks was just another test subject," Holden said.

"Are you telling this judge that after he takes the test and you tell him that he's deceptive, that he sits with you and goes, 'I tell you what, let me just tell you what happened,' and you just sit there and listen to him give his story, and when it's all over, he looks at you and says, 'I'm tired, I want to stop'? Is that what you are telling us?" Haley asked sharply.

Franks had listened to his attorney closely. When Haley began to dispute Holden's testimony, the defendant smirked slightly.

"No, that's not what I'm telling you," Holden said calmly. "I wanted to know what he could tell me to clear up the deceptive readings. I did what's called a directed interview on him. When I attempted to interrogate him, he stopped me and told me he didn't want to talk to me."

Switching gears, Haley asked, "So the state calls you and asks you to come over. So now you are an agent of the state. Is that fair to say?"

"That's a legal judgment. I don't know. I know I'm working for the state," Holden said coolly.

"And you were being paid by them," Haley declared.

"Yes."

"And when you got that statement, you got your money and you were out of there, correct? I mean, let's just be fair about it. Is that correct?" Haley said accusingly.

"I don't remember who paid me. I billed them. They paid me at some time later," Holden answered frankly.

Haley left the subject of Holden's payment and focused on Richard Franks's academic level.

Holden informed the court that Franks had told him he had graduated from high school in Justin, Texas. Franks said he had been in special education and described himself as a slow learner because he had difficulty reading and couldn't spell well.

Haley pressed, asking if Holden was able to discern if Franks had been functioning on a fifth-grade level, or what level he may have been on during their discussions.

Holden responded by stating that he felt Franks had communicated very well. He admitted he hadn't considered Franks's educational achievement level when talking with him, but that each person he tested was evaluated on an individual basis.

"What I'm getting at is that, if you knew my client had had some special disability problems, you would have operated a little differently in administering that exam. Is that fair to say?" Haley asked.

"In a sense," Holden responded. "But it wouldn't affect how I administer the interview or the test. It would affect how I design the test questions, or if he wasn't capable of understanding, I would have terminated the test," Holden said.

"If someone brought a person into your office, let's say they were ten or twelve years old, you would have some concerns about giving them a polygraph exam, wouldn't you?" Haley inquired.

"Absolutely, but you still have to evaluate it, individual by individual. There is really no blanket that will cover that issue," Holden responded.

Haley questioned when and how Holden had concluded the interview.

"I had been instructed by the district attorney investigators that the moment he said, 'I want to stop, I don't want to talk to you, I'm tired, or I want a lawyer,' I was to stop immediately. I was not to proceed further," Holden explained. "At the end of the interview, after the testing and evaluations were completed, I told him I thought there was more, that I thought he knew where Opal Jennings's body was, and that I thought he had caused her death. At that point he stood up and told me, 'I don't want to talk anymore. I'm tired.' I said, 'Then the interview is over.' I never began an interrogation on him."

The expert witness reiterated that he had asked Franks to write in his own words how he had been treated during the interview and to confirm that he had not been abused in any way.

On redirect Greg Miller had little to ask the polygraph examiner except, "Let me ask you, from a polygrapher's point of view, do you see a difference between giving a ten-, eleven-, twelve-year-old juvenile a polygraph as opposed to an adult who may have a below-average IQ?"

"Sure. There's a difference," Holden replied.

Miller nodded his head. Holden's statement had blocked any attempt by the defense to present their client as a childlike figure, rather than a grown man of low intelligence. Miller was pleased with Holden's testimony. He had presented to the court, not only Franks's ability to understand what was asked of him, but his deception regarding questioning concerning Opal Jennings's disappearance.

Eric Holden was excused from further questioning during the pretrial hearing. He surely would be called to testify during the trial, but at this point in time the defense was merely attempting to prove their client's statement should not be allowed into evidence when the trial began.

Danny McCormick was the next state's witness, called by ADA Robert Foran. McCormick walked to the stand stiffly, his shirt revealing a rigid back brace beneath. McCormick had experienced recent back surgery and apparently still suffered from the effects.

McCormick was asked many of the same questions his coinvestigator Kathy Manning had been asked. Foran concentrated on the arrest warrant, the Miranda warning, the statement Franks had signed, and the recanting of that statement.

Ed Jones cross-examined McCormick. He asked the investigator how many certified peace officers were present when Ricky Franks was arrested for the outstanding seat belt ticket.

"I believe there were seven," McCormick responded.

"Did you tell Mr. Franks that he was the focus of an investigation in the Opal Jennings disappearance?" Jones asked.

"I never told him he was the focus of the investigation," McCormick stated.

"He was just another person that you pulled off the side of the road for a ticket warrant with seven officers and [dragged] down to the Tarrant County District Attorney's Office and questioned; is that right?" Jones asked sarcastically.

"That's not correct," McCormick said.

Moving on to the Miranda warning, Jones asked,

"Were you aware Ricky was a slow learner or of his mental retardation at that point?"

"Not that I recall, no, sir," McCormick responded.

"So when you administered these warnings, you administered them to a person that you believed was not slow or mentally retarded; is that correct?" Jones inquired.

"That's correct."

"Are you aware of what you are required to do before questioning a juvenile? Before taking them before a magistrate and ensuring their rights are read to them?"

Robert Foran stood behind the prosecution table and voiced his objection to the defense questions based on irrelevancy. After all, Ricky Franks was a thirty-year-old man, not a juvenile. His objection was overruled by Judge Gill and McCormick was allowed to answer the question.

"We're required to take them before a magistrate," McCormick said.

"Isn't it true it's because a person of tender years or tender mind may be intimidated by someone and, therefore, needs to have the warnings given to them by a neutral and detached magistrate?" Jones asked, attempting to make a case based on Franks's mental capabilities.

"Yes, sir."

"Did you ever tell the judge that Ricky had recanted his statement a number of times?" Jones asked.

"No," McCormick acknowledged.

When ADA Foran began to question McCormick on redirect, he asked if the investigator had told the judge the number of times Franks had also reaffirmed his statement was true and correct.

McCormick admitted he hadn't told the judge that

Franks had recanted or reaffirmed his statement concerning Opal Jennings's disappearance.

"Let me ask you, at the conclusion of reading back his Miranda warnings and reading him back the statement in its entirety, did Ricky Franks want to sign that statement?" Foran asked.

"Yes, sir."

"Did he do so freely and voluntarily?"

"Yes, sir."

Foran passed the witness back to Ed Jones for further questioning.

"Would Mr. Franks have freely and voluntarily come by the Tarrant County District Attorney's Office and given those statements if it wasn't a direct result of the arrest and questioning regarding the disappearance of Opal Jennings?" Jones asked.

"I don't know," McCormick said, shaking his head. "Are you asking me if he would have voluntarily come up and told us about it? I don't think so. Probably not, no."

The state rested on the motion to suppress the statement given by Richard Franks to Eric Holden. It was the defense's turn to introduce witnesses in support of their motion. Their first two witnesses were called to shed doubt on the validity of the arrest warrant.

Janet Van Zandt reluctantly took the stand. Van Zandt was a clerk in the Municipal Court of the City of Fort Worth and didn't know until the morning of the hearing that she was going to be called to testify. She really didn't want to be involved in the case. She had been responsible for issuing the warrant for Richard Franks's failure to pay his seat belt ticket.

Van Zandt explained that when a ticket was issued, the person was given thirty days to go into the municipal court and pay the citation off. If the person failed to do so, Van Zandt would take the information provided by the officer who issued the ticket and write up a complaint. Franks had been issued the ticket for failure to wear a seat belt on April 8, 1999. On May 8, 1999, if he hadn't paid the traffic ticket or hadn't contested it in some legal fashion, then the arrest warrant would have been prepared. In Franks's case, that's just what was done. On May 8, 1999, a valid open warrant for Richard Franks had been issued.

Lisa Guerra, the second defense witness, confirmed that her coworker, Ms. Van Zandt, had prepared the arrest warrant in question. She admitted, as had Van Zandt, that the warrant hadn't been signed in her presence. But under-cross examination she swore that knowing Van Zandt well, she would never have signed a false arrest warrant.

The final defense witness was Daniel S. Lowrance. Lowrance, who held a Ph.D. in psychology, had been hired to conduct an IQ test on Richard Franks to help prove he was mentally deficient. Having performed more than ten thousand such tests, Lowrance was considered an expert in the field.

Lowrance had met with Richard Franks on March 19, 2000, and administered the Wechsler Adult Intelligence Scale (WAIS), the widely accepted test to measure intelligence.

"Could you briefly tell the court your findings regarding Mr. Franks in the IQ test that you have given him?" Ed Jones asked.

"His verbal IQ is sixty-five, his performance IQ is sixty-nine, and the full-scale IQ is sixty-four," Lowrance reported.

"So you classified, on the basis of this test, Mr.

Franks in the mentally deficient range. Is that correct?" Jones asked.

"Mild mental deficiency, yes," Lowrance responded.

"At what age would his mental IQ level leave him equal to the functioning of his mind?" Jones asked.

"I think you are asking me his mental age. His mental age would be similar to, or on the average of that, a fourth-grade child, somewhere around ten. Maybe as high as eleven," Lowrance said.

Greg Miller rose to cross-examine the psychologist directly. He crossed the courtroom and asked if he could see Dr. Lowrance's file. Looking through his metal-framed glasses, Miller leafed through the doctor's notes. Miller was silent as he flipped the pages. He didn't buy into the doctor's theory that Ricky Franks was comparable to a ten- or eleven-year-old. Miller believed Franks knew what he was doing when he snatched Opal Jennings from her yard and was fully aware of what he was saying when he gave his statement to Eric Holden. Miller looked up and addressed the witness.

"I noticed in going through your file here, I don't see a copy of the statement which is the subject matter of this hearing," Miller said slyly.

"I object, Your Honor," Jones said loudly. "That goes outside the scope of this witness's knowledge. He was called simply to—"

"Overruled," Judge Gill said.

Jones, cut off by the judge before completing his objection, sat down.

"I'm going to show you what has been admitted as State's Exhibit six. Have you ever seen that document before?" Miller asked, handing the witness Ricky Franks's signed statement.

"No."

"I noticed there are not any police reports or prior

offenses or statements or anything like that," Miller said, still flipping through the doctor's folder to make his point.

"I have no knowledge of any of that," Lowrance stated.

"You said his verbal IQ was sixty-five, correct?" Miller asked.

"If I could see my file, I'll be sure. Sounds right," Lowrance responded.

"Sure. Okay," Miller said, handing the folder back to the witness. "I'm not trying to trick you."

"I thought maybe it was a memory test," Lowrance said with a slight smile. "Here they are. Verbal IQ is sixty-five, performance is sixty-nine, and full scale is sixty-four."

"Are you familiar with the phrase 'adaptive behavior'?" Miller asked.

"'Adaptive behavior' is the person's mental capacity to adapt to the demands of their environment, social, functional daily skills, daily-life skills, things like that," Lowrance explained.

"How did you determine the mental age?" Miller inquired.

"IQ scores and the standard scores on the achievement testing," Lowrance said.

"Did you give him any tests to measure his adaptive behavior skills?" Miller asked.

"No, sir."

"Would you agree with me that the real-world experiences of a thirty-year-old male normally would be different, significantly different, than a ten- or eleven-year-old?" Miller pressed.

"Absolutely, yes."

After establishing that Dr. Lowrance had spent 5½ hours with Franks during his testing, and that Franks had been quite talkative, Miller passed the witness, assured that he had made his point. Ricky Franks's

IQ may have been tested at 65, but his adaptive behavior skills far surpassed his mental competence.

Leon Haley stood and announced that the defense rested. Miller offered no other evidence for the prosecution.

After taking the motion to suppress and the motion to withdraw from hearing the case, Judge Robert Gill announced his decision. Both motions were denied. The criminal defense attorneys would have to find a way to disarm the effect of having Judge Gill preside over the trial and the impact their client's statements would have on the jury.

They wouldn't have long to find out. The trial would begin the next morning at nine o'clock.

CHAPTER 10

On June 27, 2000, the Fort Worth courthouse was abuzz with activity. It was a typical hot Texas day. Men had their suit coats thrown over their shoulders and women dabbed their moist brows with tissues. Dozens of people had parked their cars at Fort Worth's only subway station and taken the short ride to the downtown outlet mall, crossed Houston Street, and made their way to the Tarrant County Justice Center.

A wave of citizens joined family members of Richard Franks and Opal Jennings to garner seats for one of the most publicized trials of the new century. News media, which had heralded reports of the kidnapping of Opal Jennings for fifteen months, selected their places on the courthouse steps to gain interviews from principal figures in the trial.

As Audrey and Robert Sanderford walked out of their front door on their way to the Tarrant County Justice Center, their eyes moved upward. A sign that had been affixed to the front of their home on March 26, marking the one-year anniversary of Opal's disappearance, hung overhead. The sign read OPAL'S PLACE, and featured a photo of Opal that had been seen on flyers, posters, and TV screens across the county. What Audrey called "hope chimes" had been attached to the sign. As they walked to their car, purple petunias Opal planted the year before had sprouted and served as a reminder of the cheer Opal had brought into their lives. Sorrow and dread filled Audrey's heart. She missed Opal terribly and now she would have to sit through the trial of the man accused of taking her away. It would be difficult for Audrey, who had been hospitalized for emotional breakdowns more than once during the past year. She was uncertain how seeing the man accused of taking Opal and hearing his excuses and denials would affect her.

Audrey and the rest of the Sanderford family stood in the security line, dropping cell phones, keys, and sunglasses into the small bowls provided outside the walk-through metal detectors just steps into the front doors of the courthouse. Women placed their handbags, men their briefcases, on the conveyor belt that traveled through an X-ray machine to guarantee the safety of those that entered.

Prior to the July 1, 1992, shooting spree of George Lott in the older historical Tarrant County Courthouse, just blocks from where Franks would be tried, security had been minimal. But with the deaths of Chris Marshall, head of the Tarrant County District Attorney's Appellate Division, as well as Dallas lawyer John Edwards, and the wounding of three others, including two judges, security in each of the county's courthouses had been intensified dramatically.

The Sanderfords entered Judge Gill's courtroom and sat on the right side reserved for them. Impartial spectators, along with area reporters, scattered themselves along the length of the benches in the center. The Franks family had reserved seats on the left side of the courtroom, closest to Ricky Franks. The first row of each of the three sections remained empty for security purposes. No one other than law enforcement personnel would be allowed to occupy those prime viewing areas.

Greg Miller, Robert Foran, and Lisa Callahan entered the doors of the 213th District Court from the front of the courtroom, armed with investigative reports and enlarged maps. Their private offices were housed on another floor of the Tarrant County Justice Center, a maze of small spaces secured behind a locked door only accessible by attorneys, staff, and those brought into the inner sanctum for interviews.

Leon Haley, Ed Jones, and Patrick Davis walked into the courtroom from the rear, toting binders filled with notes and witness lists, confident of their defensive strategy.

Everyone was present in the courtroom—everyone but Opal Jennings. The six-year-old had been gone for over a year. No one knew her whereabouts—no one, according to Greg Miller, but Richard Franks.

Miller, Foran, and Callahan were prepared to prove that Franks killed the child, although he was only being tried for aggravated kidnapping. Without a body, Miller knew it would be difficult, if not impossible, to convict the sex offender of murder. Thirty years earlier, the case would never have been prosecuted for murder without the victim's body, even if someone had confessed to the crime. But under the Texas Penal Code rewritten in 1974, the victim's body was not needed for prosecution. Circumstantial evidence was all that was considered necessary to take a case to trial for murder.

But even without a murder conviction, Franks

faced life behind bars if jurors found him guilty of aggravated kidnapping. Because Opal was under the age of fourteen, prosecutors needed only to show that Franks took her somewhere, not that she was forced or restrained. By Texas law, children younger than fourteen cannot give their consent; therefore, any seizure of a child would be deemed a kidnapping.

Following the earlier pretrial hearing standoff between the prosecution and defense, speculation ran high that Miller would rely heavily on Franks's confession to secure a conviction. Leon Haley and Ed Jones, who had lost the motion to suppress Franks's statement the previous day, were set to counter the potentially negative impact Franks's confession might make. It appeared they would present a defense that would concentrate on Ricky Franks's mental retardation and charge that the confession had been coerced.

Sitting on a raised bench above the courtroom and flanked by both the Texas and American flags, Judge Gill asked both the state and the defense if they were ready to proceed. As each side responded in the affirmative, nausea gripped the stomach of Leola Sanderford.

Greg Miller, the lead prosecutor for the state, walked the short distance from the prosecutor's table to the jury box. Miller, whose gravelly voice resonated throughout the courtroom, was a seasoned prosecutor. He delivered his remarks with passion and conviction. What he may have lacked in substantial evidence, he made up for in his firm conviction that Ricky Franks was guilty.

Miller told the jury the state would prove through eyewitness testimony that Richard Lee Franks abducted Opal Jennings. Miller stated that investigators had tracked down numerous leads and had tried to eliminate Franks as the possible assailant.

"Couldn't do it," Miller said. "You know why? He took her."

Miller declared that the crime was solved when Ricky Franks was arrested.

"We will call two inmates who heard Franks confess to the crime," Miller told the twelve-person panel. "One will tell jurors that Franks said, 'If they find her body, they will find the evidence to link me to this crime.'" Miller paused to let the statement sink into the minds of each juror.

Then Miller mentioned that there was Franks's statement, which Judge Gill had ruled admissible the previous day, in which Franks said he gave Opal a ride to a convenience store, but he dropped her off safely after rejecting her repeated sexual advances.

Miller planned to build his case around Franks's own words and persuade the jury to find him guilty of aggravated kidnapping.

The defense was just as determined to do all it could to help the jury find their client innocent of the horrendous crime that had gripped Tarrant County for more than a year.

"None of the state's witnesses will testify about physical evidence linking Ricky Franks to the case," Edward Jones stated in his opening remarks. "This isn't a case of circumstantial evidence, but of absolutely no evidence whatsoever. The person responsible for the disappearance of Opal Jennings is *not* in this courtroom," Jones said, putting emphasis on "not" as his voice grew louder.

Jones set the stage for their defense when he told the jury that Ricky Franks had below-average intelligence and was coerced into making a statement, which he later recanted.

"This case is about the Tarrant County District Attorney's Office overreacting in an attempt to solve this terrible, terrible disappearance."

Then looking at each juror individually, Jones challenged them by saying, "You, as Tarrant County citizens, deserve better and Opal deserves better. At the close of all the evidence, you tell the Tarrant County District Attorney's Office, you tell the Saginaw police, you tell the FBI, to go get Opal's abductor."

Opal's mother, Leola, squeezed Teresa's hand and took a deep breath. The trial of the man charged with kidnapping her daughter was about to begin. She sat quietly, remembering Opal.

Everyone in the courtroom took in a breath as the defense concluded their opening statement and the prosecution waited to call their first witness. Tension was high on both sides of the aisle.

Teresa Sanderford glanced at her husband, Clay, as she heard Robert Foran call her name as the state's first witness. She pushed the low swinging dark wooden door that separated the inner courtroom from the gallery. She walked slowly to the stand. Her long brown hair brushed the shoulders of her dark clothing. Teresa's hand shook slightly as she raised it in order to swear to tell the truth.

The court reporter, sitting just in front of the witness-box, poised her hands over the keys of her machine, ready to take down every word of the Franks trial.

Teresa was nervous as she sat before Judge Gill, the filled gallery, the jury, and the accused, Ricky Franks. While other witnesses waited in an adjoining room for their turn to take the stand, Teresa kept her eyes on Robert Foran. She deliberately avoided the intense stare of the defendant.

Teresa explained that at the time of Opal's abduction, she was living with Audrey and Robert Sanderford, her grandson Austin, and other relatives on North Hampshire in Saginaw, Texas.

"How old was Austin?" Foran asked.

"He was twenty-two months old," Teresa replied.

Opal, Teresa's great-niece by marriage, was described by Teresa as a six-year-old kindergartner who loved school, did well, and was very bright. Teresa's shoulders relaxed and she smiled as she spoke of Opal.

Foran produced an enlarged photo of Opal, her eyes sparkling and her smile radiant. Teresa's voice broke slightly as she identified the endearing girl in the photo as Opal Jennings and confirmed that it was how she had looked at the time of her disappearance.

Using additional photos that had been blown up for easier identification, Foran had his witness point out various streets and houses in her small Saginaw neighborhood.

"Now I want to direct your attention back to March 26, 1999. Were you at home that afternoon?" Foran asked.

"Yes. I was waiting for my husband to come home because we were all going to go out to dinner," Teresa answered.

"Were other people at home?" Foran questioned.

"Yes. Opal was there. My grandson Austin, my mother, Audrey Sanderford, and her husband, Robert Sanderford," Teresa said.

She then explained that she had been in the family kitchen while Robert was in the living room watching the news with Audrey.

"At any time that afternoon, did they leave?" Foran asked.

"Robert had gone outside because the kids were getting a little bit far away. You could hear their voices. The windows were open and everything. He told them to come back up closer in the yard," Teresa said.

"Did you see them there in the front yard?" Foran asked.

"I saw them most of the time, but they could step out of my view," Teresa responded.

Teresa explained that she could hear Opal, Austin, and their friend Spencer running and yelling, being kids. Then she heard Austin crying.

"Would you describe for the jury what drew your attention?" Foran prodded.

Teresa took a deep breath. She would never forget the sound of her grandson's cry that day. She heard it in her dreams, on occasion even in her waking hours. It made the hair on the back of her neck stand.

"He was crying like I had never heard Austin cry before. He was just totally brokenhearted and devastated. I had never heard him cry like that," Teresa said, her voice a bit lower than before.

Ricky Franks sat expressionless between his attorneys. His head was held high, but his eyes avoided Teresa Sanderford as she continued to tell the jury about her grandson's cries.

"What did you do when you heard that?" Foran asked.

"I went immediately outside. He was sitting right outside the front door in a chair, a little settee my mother had set out there. He was just crying," Teresa explained.

"What did Austin say to you?"

"He told me that Opal was gone," Teresa said. "I asked him, 'Gone where?' And he said, 'Gone bye-bye.'"

Spectators in the gallery shuddered as they heard the unsettling words of Opal Jennings's aunt. They could only imagine the terror the child's words had sent through her.

Leola Sanderford and her baby, Opal Jo'Dace Jennings, born
November 24, 1991. *(Photo by Teresa Sanderford,
courtesy of Leola Sanderford)*

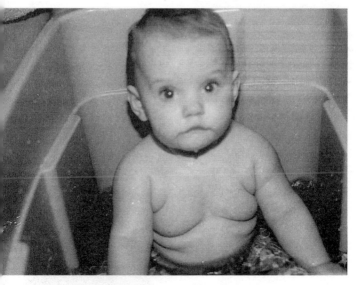

Opal had big blue eyes and light brown hair.
(Photo by Teresa Sanderford, courtesy of Leola Sanderford)

Opal and her new baby sister, Courtney. *(Photo by Teresa Sanderford, courtesy of Leola Sanderford)*

Opal was six years old at the time of her abduction. *(Photo by Teresa Sanderford, courtesy of Leola Sanderford)*

Opal lived with her grandparents in their home in Saginaw, Texas for six months prior to her abduction.
(Photo courtesy of the Tarrant County District Attorney's Office)

Austin Sanderford, Opal's two-year-old cousin, was playing with Opal when she was abducted. *(Photo by Teresa Sanderford)*

An aerial view of the neighborhood—the arrow points to the location where Opal was taken. *(Photo courtesy of the Tarrant County District Attorney's Office)*

A closer look at the quiet street and the tree where Opal sat with her playmates when she was approached by Ricky Franks. *(Photo courtesy of the Tarrant County District Attorney's Office)*

More than 100,000 flyers were distributed across Texas and the U.S., some even reaching foreign countries. *(Photo by Teresa Sanderford)*

MISSING

OPAL JO JENNING KIDNAPPED ABOUT 5:30 ON FRIDAY MARCH 26 1999 IN SAGINAW,TX LAST SEEN BEING FORCED INTO DARK PURPLE ALMOST BLACK CAR MAY HAVE TAN OR BROWN TOP BY LATE MODLE BELIVED TO BE A MERCURY SEDAN A TALL WHITE MALE WITH BROWN HAIR IN A PONYTAIL WITH FACIAL HAIR
AGE: 6 HAIR: BROWN EYES:BLUE ABOUT 4 FEET TALL WEIGHT:60LB
IF YOU'VE SEEN OR HAVE ANY INFORMATION ABOUT OPAL PLEASE CALL SAGINAW POLICE AT 817-232-0311

More than 100,000 flyers were distributed across Texas and the remaining United States, some even reaching foreign

Opal's family displayed some of the tributes left at the site of her abduction in their home, with Opal's photo. Here many prayers were said for her safe return. *(Photo by Teresa Sanderford)*

Hundreds of citizens from around Texas converged on Saginaw and the northern area of the state in search of Opal Jennings. *(Photo courtesy of Texas EquuSearch)*

Members of Texas EquuSearch, a volunteer organization, joined the search for Opal. *(Photo courtesy of Texas EquuSearch)*

Spencer Williams, the three-year-old witness to Opal's kidnapping, described the abductor's car as dark, with a star on the back. The star he referenced appeared on the Texas license plate. *(Photos courtesy of the Tarrant County District Attorney's Office)*

The trunk of Ricky Franks's car revealed a stop sign used by school crossing guards. As a registered sex offender, he was forbidden to go within 1,000 yards of a school.
(Photo courtesy of the Tarrant County District Attorney's Office)

The FBI carefully dismantled the car in search of forensic evidence linking him to Opal Jennings's disappearance. No clues were found. *(Photo courtesy of the Tarrant County District Attorney's Office)*

Richard Franks was arrested August 18, 1999, for the kidnapping of Opal Jennings. *(Photo courtesy of the Tarrant County Sheriff's Office)*

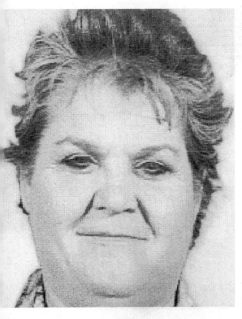

Judy Magby Franks's mug shot at the time of her arrest for perjury. *(Photo courtesy of the Tarrant County District Attorney's Office)*

Ricky Franks's defense team:
Top, Leon Haley;
Right, Edward Jones;
Bottom, L. Patrick Davis.
(Author photos)

Lead prosecutor, Deputy Chief District Attorney Greg Miller.
(Author photo)

Assistant District Attorney Lisa Callahan. *(Author photo)*

Danny McCormick of the District Attorney's Special Crimes Unit. *(Photo by Kathy Manning)*

Mike Adair *(front)* of the Special Crimes Unit watches the Franks trial unfold with Danny McCormick. *(Author photo)*

Kathy Manning, investigator for the District Attorney's office and James Neal of the Saginaw Police Department await their turn to testify. *(Author photo)*

Forensic psychologist Dr. Randy Price explains a point to defense attorneys during a trial recess. *(Author photo)*

Ricky Franks stares at the courtroom gallery during a brief recess. *(Author photo)*

Leola Sanderford talks with relatives and Deputy Chief DA Greg Miller on the final day of Ricky Franks's trial. *(Author photo)*

Robert Sanderford, Opal's grandfather, sat quietly as the evidence against Ricky Franks was presented. *(Author photo)*

Teachers from Opal's school wept as they said good-bye to her following a memorial service on January 24, 2004. *(Author photo)*

Audrey Sanderford finally found closure with the discovery of Opal's remains five years after her abduction. She met with well wishers following the moving memorial. *(Author photo)*

A white cross bearing the name of Opal Jennings rests with seventy-five others in a special place known as Our Garden of Angels. Each cross represents a child taken too soon by violent means. *(Author photos)*

Teresa explained that Austin was able to indicate a direction in which he had seen Opal leave. He had pointed toward her sister's house, where Austin's cousin lived.

Foran asked Teresa to step down from the witness stand and move to one of the enlarged photos of her neighborhood that had been placed on an easel. She turned her back toward Franks as she pointed out her mother's house and the lot where the children had been playing at the time of Opal's kidnapping. She identified the house across the street from Audrey and Robert's as the one where she, her husband, and Austin were currently residing. With a trembling hand, Teresa then pointed to the house two doors down from her own, where Spencer Williams lived, and her sister's house on the corner of North Hampshire and Worthy.

She explained that after talking with Austin, she hurried toward her sister's house, stopping momentarily to ask a dozen kids who were playing in the area if they had seen Opal. She then returned to the Sanderford house.

"When we arrived back there, my mother called nine-one-one and she asked me to go to Spencer's house to see if Opal might have gone over there," Teresa explained.

"How much time had gone by since the first time you heard Austin crying and the time you went across to Spencer's house?" Foran inquired.

"Maybe five minutes, seven."

The state's witness explained that she first had asked Spencer's great-grandmother if she had seen Opal, then went to the door and spoke with Charlene, Spencer's grandmother. "I asked Charlene if I could talk to Spencer."

"Would you describe for the jury Spencer's demeanor at the time?" Foran asked.

"He was very excited. He wanted to tell me about Opal and what happened to Opal when I asked him. He was just really excited, superexcited," Teresa reported, her voice growing stronger as her testimony continued.

"When you say 'excited,' was he happy or was he upset?" Foran asked to clarify.

"He was very upset."

"What did he say?"

"He told me Opal had been kidnapped," Teresa answered.

There was a gloomy stillness over the courtroom as Teresa described the child's words. The image cut deep into the hearts of the Sanderford family. The Frankses sat silent.

Teresa described how she had asked Spencer's grandmother if she could take him to her house. As they walked across the street, Spencer told Teresa a man had grabbed Opal and put her in a car. Spencer described the car as "purpledy black" and the man as having long hair and a baseball cap. The four-year-old had been keyed up and had talked rapidly as he described for Teresa the events surrounding Opal's kidnapping.

"Now," Foran began, "I want to direct your attention back to a time period before March twenty-sixth. Did you observe any vehicles in the neighborhood behaving in a suspicious manner?"

Teresa took in a deep breath. "Yes," she responded, "I observed a car, a black car with tinted windows that went extremely slow up our street. It was probably no more than five miles an hour."

Handing Teresa a photo of Ricky Franks's Mercury

Cougar, he asked, "Does this bear a resemblance or similarity to the vehicle that you saw?"

Teresa studied the photograph before responding. "Very, very similar, yes."

"Do you remember approximately what time all of this occurred?" Foran asked, taking the photograph from her.

"Between five-thirty and a quarter to six," Teresa replied.

"Approximately how many times did you see the vehicle behaving strangely and driving slowly prior to March twenty-sixth?" Foran inquired

"Two or three different times," Teresa said.

Teresa told the twelve-person jury that it appeared to be a man driving the vehicle, but she couldn't give a definitive description of him.

Foran returned to the prosecution table and sat beside Miller and Callahan as Leon Haley rose to address Teresa.

Although Teresa had begun to relax during Robert Foran's questioning, her anxiety level rose as the defense attorney walked toward the witness stand.

Haley attempted to put Teresa at ease, and after a brief introduction, Haley clarified that the location of where the children had been playing on the day of Opal's disappearance was a vacant lot adjoining the Sanderford property.

"Did y'all have a dog at the time?" Haley asked.

"Yes."

"Did you hear the dog at all barking or making any type of noises that would give you some concern that maybe the children could have been in trouble?" Haley inquired.

"No."

"When Austin told you Opal had gone bye-bye,

and you proceeded to walk in the direction he pointed, he said, 'No, car,' correct?" Haley asked.

"Yes."

"He was letting you know walking is not going to do us any good because she went in a car, right?" Haley questioned.

"Not necessarily, because we're talking about a two-year-old," Teresa replied. "To a two-year-old 'bye-bye' can be next door or back inside the house."

"You saw several children playing and you talked to some of the children. Did they tell you they had seen a car circling the area?" Haley asked.

"Yes, they did."

"Did they tell you that they saw Opal in the car?" Haley asked.

"No."

"Did the children tell you that the car was a purplish car that they saw circle?" Haley questioned.

"No. They said it was a dark car," Teresa answered.

"They told you it was a dark car, no specific color. Is that fair to say?" Haley asked.

"I don't remember," Teresa said, her brow wrinkled.

"You would have told authorities back then whatever you recalled because it would have been fresh on your mind. Is that fair to say?" Haley asked.

"No, not necessarily," Teresa said, shaking her head. "The reason being is because the first night you talk to them, you are so upset that some things that you remember don't come back for a little bit later. But most everything that was of great importance I told that night."

"Spencer told you Opal was kidnapped. What do you think he meant?" Haley inquired.

Teresa looked at Haley questioningly. With a small shrug, she replied, "That Opal was kidnapped. That someone had taken Opal."

Haley returned to the subject of the car the abductor drove on March 26, 1999, specifically the color. Teresa admitted that she had written a note that Spencer had told her the car was a purply pink and had passed that information along to the Saginaw police. She denied, however, that she hadn't told authorities on the night of the abduction that the car was dark in color.

Holding a photo of Ricky Franks's black Mercury Cougar, Haley asked if Teresa was claiming it was the actual car seen on North Hampshire on the day Opal disappeared.

"No, I'm saying it's a car very much like that one," Teresa testified.

Smiles crossed the faces of the Franks family and whispers were exchanged. They believed it hadn't been Ricky's car the children had seen; they believed he was not the one seen driving around the Saginaw neighborhood; they believed in Ricky's innocence. They felt Haley was making that clear to the jury.

"When you say to us that you saw a car in the area, was it actually a black car or was it actually a dark car?" Haley asked.

"It was a black car," Teresa said with confidence.

"Do you know whether the person you saw in the car was a black male, white male, or a Mexican male?" Haley prodded.

"No, I don't," Teresa answered.

Leon Haley was pleased with Teresa Sanderford's testimony. She couldn't identify Ricky Franks's car as the one seen driving in the neighborhood and she couldn't put his client in the car.

At the end of questioning, Teresa walked to the bench where her husband sat in the courtroom. She took her seat beside Clay. He put his arm around her and gave her a hug. Clay knew how difficult it had been for Teresa to relive the events of March 26. She had answered all the questions with direct, straight-forward answers. She had done well and was greatly relieved. But there were still hard times ahead. Other witnesses would be testifying about the day Opal was taken and, with each telling, the Sanderford family would be forced to relive the most horrifying day of their lives.

In response to the calling of her name, Charlene Williams slowly shuffled toward the witness stand. Walking with the aid of a cane, she pushed down heavily on the instrument with some difficulty as she stepped up and settled into the witness-box. Spencer's grandmother was in ill health and her gait reflected the multiple problems she suffered. Charlene watched as Lisa Callahan approached.

"May I approach the witness, Your Honor?" Callahan asked.

"I'm sorry, hon. I didn't hear that," Charlene remarked.

"I was addressing the judge," Callahan stated.

Gallery spectators smiled.

For thirty-four years Charlene Williams had lived on North Hampshire Street in Saginaw, Texas. She had watched children of all ages play in the vacant lot across from her house. Never had she experienced the fear, the horror, she had on March 26, 1999. Now, sitting in the Tarrant County Justice Center, she would be asked to relive the events of that day.

As Robert Foran had done with Teresa Sanderford, but without asking her to step down from the witness-box, Callahan asked Charlene to identify a photo depicting her Saginaw neighborhood. Then Callahan turned to the day Opal was taken.

"Opal and Spencer and Austin were playing across the street, what were you doing?" Callahan asked.

"I was in the house playing Free Cell, a game on the computer," Charlene answered.

Callahan asked Charlene to describe what happened when Spencer ran into her house.

"He said, 'Grandma, Grandma.' I said, 'What?' And he said, 'Somebody took Opal.' And I just looked at him and I said, 'Spencer, you are watching too much television. What happened?' And he just told me that somebody took Opal. I still didn't believe him and I said, 'Oh, honey, just go out and play.' He said, 'I don't want to go in front.' I said, 'Then go in the backyard,' because I thought it pertained to what had been going on in Dallas, with the newscast of something that had happened there," Charlene explained.

"What happened next?" Callahan encouraged.

"It wasn't two or three minutes later that Teresa came and knocked on the door and said, 'I've got to see Spencer.' And I said, 'He's in the backyard.' She said, 'Opal is gone. I have to talk to him.' Then I went and got him," Charlene added.

"Did you talk to him about what had happened?" Callahan asked.

"He said that they were playing on the lot and a car pulled up on the east side of the street, heading south, and a man got out of the car, picked her up, knocked her in the car, and took off," Charlene said.

"Did he say anything about what Opal did when the man picked her up?" Callahan inquired.

"She was crying."

Charlene explained that Spencer told her the man said, "Hi" before he grabbed Opal, then knocked her in the car by striking her in the chest with his hand. Spencer had also said that the man had driven to Opal's aunt Pat's house, pulled into the driveway, made a U-turn, and headed back up Hampshire.

"Did he say anything concerning the man's appearance?" Callahan asked.

"Just that he was slender, tall, and that was it," Charlene answered.

"Did Spencer describe the car to you?" Callahan questioned.

"He said it was a dark car. I asked, 'What did it look like?' He said, 'Looked a little bit like Mommy's.' His mother has a sports car," Charlene responded.

Callahan asked what color Spencer's mother's car was and was told by Charlene that her daughter's car was black.

Callahan smiled at Charlene Williams to let her know she had done well; then Callahan turned her witness over to the defense.

The defense's cross-examination of Charlene Williams fell to Edward Jones. His brunet hair, dark brown mustache, and goatee accented his handsome face. He approached Charlene with the respect he would have given his own mother.

Jones reiterated many of the questions asked by Callahan for clarification. He then asked Charlene, "Did you notice anything strange in the moments preceding Spencer coming in and telling you about Opal? Anything that would take your attention outside?"

"No. Just that he came through the door like a rocket," Charlene explained.

"Did you notice anything weird in the neighborhood in the weeks before?" Jones asked.

"Not really. We had a lot of construction going on, a lot of building on the different houses in the block. Repair work. But nothing out of the usual, outside of normal every week happenings," Charlene replied.

As Callahan had, Jones asked Charlene to point out

the positions of each of the houses on her street from a photo presented to the jury.

Charlene described how she had driven around the neighborhood, to the nearby convenience store, and to the Dairy Queen, looking for a dark car with a child inside. She admitted she had seen none.

The elderly grandmother was excused and as she slowly made her way to the rear of the courtroom, Patricia Barrett, Teresa Sanderford's sister's, walked to the witness stand. Pat's hair was a shade darker and a few inches shorter than that of her sister's. The women were not only sisters, but close friends.

In Greg Miller's recognizable style, he strolled to where Patricia Barrett had taken her seat to the left of Judge Gill.

Pat testified that she had no firsthand knowledge of Opal's kidnapping. Like Teresa, she hadn't seen the abduction, had only heard about it from family. But like Teresa, Pat had seen a car cruising the neighborhood in the weeks leading up to Opal's disappearance.

"And why did the car catch your attention?" Greg Miller asked.

"It was going slower than normal, or a little bit more cautious is a better way of putting it," Pat answered.

Pat described the vehicle as black with tinted windows.

Miller handed his witness a photo of Ricky Franks's car and asked, "Is that car similar or dissimilar to the vehicle that you saw in your neighborhood in the days preceding Opal's abduction?"

"Similar," Pat responded.

"The back portion of the car, would you describe it as sort of being boxlike, or boxy?" Miller asked.

"Boxy, yes," Pat agreed.

"Now, admittedly, you aren't saying that this is the car that you saw," Miller stated.

"No. I said it looked like the car," Pat responded.

Leon Haley had few questions for Patricia Barrett. He got right to the point.

"All this similar and similar-like, the bottom line is that the car that you see in this photo, you aren't saying that is the car that you saw in the neighborhood; is that correct?" Haley asked.

"No, I can't say that," Pat said honestly.

"Do you know what model of vehicle you saw riding through the neighborhood?" Haley inquired.

"Black Cougar, kind of like that one," Pat said, motioning toward the photo of Franks' car in Haley's hand.

"Now you are saying a black Cougar?" Haley asked with a trace of surprise.

"Or one like that," Pat said. "It just looked like a black car with tinted windows."

"You don't know if it was a Cougar or not, do you?" Haley asked.

"No, not really," Pat answered truthfully.

"You are not saying that you saw Ricky Franks riding in the neighborhood in a car like that, are you?" Haley pressed.

"No. I'm not."

Once again the defense had emphasized the point that the car seen in the Sanderford neighborhood before Opal's abduction, and the day she was taken, could not be identified as belonging to their client.

Pat Barrett's short time on the stand was over. The case was moving along quickly when James "Trey" Barnes was announced as the state's next witness.

Known as Trey to friends and family, he was one of the

boys playing ball in the street the day Opal disappeared. Robert Foran asked the tall, slim fourteen-year-old if he had noticed anything unusual on March 26, 1999.

"A car kept passing by us," Trey stated.

He explained that he and his friends had stopped tossing the ball when the car passed by so that they wouldn't hit the vehicle. He added that the car had driven past five or six times and had come from the direction of Opal's house.

"Do you remember the color?" Foran asked.

"It was a purplish color," Trey responded.

Trey was unable to tell what make or model it was, but, like Teresa and Pat, Trey remembered the windows were tinted.

As had been done with Teresa and Pat, Trey was shown a picture of Ricky Franks's black Cougar and asked if he was able to say if that was the car he had seen on March 26. And like the sisters, he was unable to identify Franks's car as the one he had seen the day Opal disappeared.

Edward Jones walked toward Trey with a reassuring smile. Jones planned to continue the defense's attack on the identification of the car seen in the Saginaw area. He believed they were creating significant doubt in the minds of jurors that the car seen by witnesses on March 26 wasn't the same car owned by their client.

"When you talked to the police regarding this incident, do you remember telling them that the vehicle had very, very shiny wheels?" Jones asked.

"Yes, sir."

"By very, very shiny wheels, do you mean chrome wheels?" Jones pursued.

"Yes, sir."

"And that's something that you were sure about when you told the police about that, isn't it?" Jones asked.

"Pretty sure."

"Okay. Isn't it also true that you told the police that the vehicle sat either higher in the front or higher in the back, that it wasn't level?" Jones questioned.

"Yes, sir. It was higher in the front," Trey said.

"And you told them it was a dark purplish color; is that correct?" Jones asked.

"Yes, sir."

"And that it had dark-tinted windows so that you couldn't see the driver inside," Jones stated.

"Yes, sir."

"And you got a good look at this car, didn't you?" Jones asked.

"Not really."

Trey's response seemed to surprise the defense attorney.

"You didn't really get a good look at the car?" Jones asked.

"No."

"Were you throwing the ball across the street?" Jones inquired.

"Yes, sir."

"Okay. And every time that you threw the ball across the street, you had to wait for the vehicle to go by, right?" Jones questioned.

"Yes, sir."

"So you would wait for it to go by, you looked at it enough that you knew that it had very, very shiny chrome wheels, right?" Jones asked.

"Yes."

Trey reported to the jury that one of the boys he had been playing ball with was Mike Logan. Although Mike had told police that the car that had driven by them on March 26 had antennas on the back, Trey didn't recall seeing them.

Jones handed Trey the photo of his client's car,

which the state had introduced into evidence, and asked if the wheels were shiny or not. Trey answered they were not. He also confirmed that there were no antennas attached to the back of the automobile and noted that there was one antenna on the front, with a Jack in the Box ball attached. He agreed that the vehicle in the photo was not higher in the front than it was in the back.

Ed Jones walked back to sit with Ricky Franks and Leon Haley. He gave Franks a slight smile, obviously pleased with the way questioning was going.

The teen was excused and Spencer Williams was called. The two crossed in the aisle, Spencer nearly half the size of the tall teenager.

Smiles crossed the faces of jurors and spectators alike as the small boy walked briskly to the front of the courtroom. His blond hair was neatly parted and his clothes freshly pressed. Because of Lisa Callahan's experience in the Crimes Against Children Unit of the DA's office, she had been selected to question five-year-old Spencer.

Not much more than the top of the boy's head could be seen as he sat in the witness chair, trying to peer over the stand in front of him. Spencer leaned toward the microphone to answer each question asked by Callahan.

Spencer told the court that he was five years old and that he was in school. Callahan ran through a series of questions to show that Spencer knew his colors, the alphabet, and the names of his pets. He told Callahan the types of games he and Opal played, along with his little friend Austin.

When Callahan began questioning Spencer about the events of March 26, the boy suddenly began responding, "I forgot." The boy could no longer respond as he had when he first spoke with authorities.

"When y'all were looking at the ant piles, what happened?" Callahan asked.

"I forgot," Spencer said, glancing toward Franks, then quickly looking away.

Realizing that Spencer frequently looked at the stern-faced defendant before responding to her questions, Callahan walked to the witness stand and positioned herself between the boy and Franks, successfully blocking the direct line of sight.

"Did you see a person come up?" Callahan rephrased her question.

"Yes. A man," Spencer replied.

"Did you see what he looked like?" Callahan continued.

"Yes."

"What did his hair look like?" Callahan asked.

"I forgot," Spencer said, looking to the rear of the courtroom where his mother stood.

Leon Haley rose to address the court.

"Your Honor, at this time, I would move that the witness is incompetent to continue testifying based upon his age and tender years. I know that the state is doing this in good faith; they can get out anything they want from him, but he's incompetent to testify. I would ask that the court reject his testimony at this time. I'm not arguing about what he's said so far, but I'm saying that he not continue anymore," Haley argued.

Judge Gill responded immediately. "I find that he has sufficient intellect to accurately relate transaction. Just because he doesn't remember one or two things doesn't mean he's not a competent witness."

Haley sat down, his face void of any expression

that would indicate if he was frustrated by the court's decision.

Callahan smiled as she redirected her attention to the boy. With much prodding, and a smile from his mother, Spencer told the attentive jurors that the man wore a red hat, his hair was long, and he wore it in a ponytail. The man said hi; then he took Opal and put her in his car. The five-year-old was relating the events of the day much easier than earlier in his testimony. He told of the man hitting Opal in the chest and hearing her scream before the man drove away.

Spencer's mother's stomach knotted as Lisa Callahan passed her son on to the defense for questioning. Callahan had been patient with Spencer, but his mother feared the defense would be far more aggressive.

Deciding there would be no positive result from questioning Spencer, Leon Haley declined to cross-examine the boy.

Spencer's mother breathed a sigh of relief as she smiled at her young son walking toward her.

CHAPTER 11

The state's case against Richard Franks was proceeding as Greg Miller had expected. Each of their witnesses had provided the information they intended for the jury to hear concerning the day Opal was taken. It was now time to call investigators to introduce Ricky Franks and connect him to the crime.

Mike Adair, assistant chief investigator for the district attorney's office, was first to be called. Adair had been assistant chief for five years and with the DA's office for twenty years. Prior to joining the DA's investigative unit, Adair had served ten years with the Arlington Police Department (APD).

Adair took his seat in the witness chair, adjusted the lapel of his dark suit, and pulled the thin microphone toward him. Adair explained to the jury how he had assisted the task force by taking some of the possible leads in the Opal Jennings case to check out. One of those leads had been Richard Lee Franks. He was not asked, however, to explain that the lead had come from Jesse Herrera, Franks's probation officer, prior to contacting Franks. It was from that conversation, however, that Adair knew that Franks drove a black Cougar and had cut his long hair, shortly after Opal Jennings's disappearance.

Adair spoke matter-of-factly about driving to Franks's residence for the original interview. He told of seeing two vehicles parked in Franks's driveway, a black Mercury Cougar and a white Chevrolet, which appeared to be a Chevrolet Lumina.

"As a result of your initial conversation with Ricky Franks, were you left with the impression that he didn't know the Saginaw area?" Foran asked.

"Yes. I came away with the impression that he wasn't that familiar with Saginaw," Adair stated.

When Foran asked Adair if he knew whether Franks had ever worn his hair in a ponytail, the investigator testified that Franks said he had worn his hair long enough to have a ponytail and had, at times, pulled his hair back. Adair later stated that at the time of his interview with Franks, on August 4, 1999, the defendant was wearing his hair short.

Adair explained that he had met with his team of investigators, decided to begin a surveillance of Franks, and, finally finding him alone, took him into custody for an outstanding seat belt warrant. He told the jury that Franks was taken to the Special Crimes office on West Belknap and informed that he was under arrest for the traffic ticket. He also was informed they were investigating another matter.

Mike Adair was an excellent witness. His voice was strong, yet not overwhelming, as he explained the procedures he and his unit had followed in apprehending Franks.

Under cross-examination by Leon Haley, Adair acknowledged that when he first attempted to make contact with Franks, he hadn't been at home. Adair had left a business card with Franks's wife and it had been Franks himself who had called to make an appointment with Adair the next day.

Haley turned his attention to his client's arrest.

"Y'all didn't arrest him for your safety; you wanted to be able to get access to him. It was pretty much like a pretext arrest so that you could talk to him about this. Is that fair to say?" Haley asked.

"There was no pretext," Adair said. "We had a reason for talking to him and we knew there was a warrant for him."

"And y'all surrounded his vehicle, you tell him politely that he has a warrant for his arrest, and y'all are taking him into custody. Is that fair?" Haley said mockingly.

"Yes," Adair answered simply.

Adair acknowledged that there were no uniformed officers present at Franks's arrest. He also admitted that the investigators had blocked Franks's ability to leave and that he offered no resistance when he was told he was under arrest.

"All he had to rely on was that y'all were telling him the truth as to who y'all were. Am I correct?" Haley questioned.

"Yes," Adair replied.

"I mean, you could have been some terrorist organization pulling over and snatching him off the street, for all he knew. Is that fair?" Haley asked.

Suppressed snickers spread through the gallery.

"Well, we identified ourselves as police officers," Adair explained.

"Was anybody there to help him to go get assistance from his family, anybody else, to say, 'Oh, by the way, he's been arrested; he's with that group over there,' nobody, like that?" Haley asked.

"There was a clerk at the grocery store that knew Ricky and said he was going to call Judy and tell her that he'd been arrested and was being taken downtown," Adair explained.

Before the court Haley described the room at the Special Crimes Unit office as "little bitty," but Adair called it small.

The supervisor of the special investigative force acknowledged that Franks had been arrested at about 8:30 P.M. and had been left in the room at his office for about two hours without being interviewed. He confirmed their offices were downtown across the street from a magistrate and the county jail, where Franks could have been booked in.

"Did you allow him to make a phone call?" Haley asked.

"No, we didn't," Adair answered honestly.

Continuing his questioning, Haley asked about Eric Holden and when he had arrived in Fort Worth to talk with Franks. Adair testified that Holden arrived about 10:30 P.M., that he had talked with Danny McCormick, and then began his interview of Franks. That interview ended with Franks giving a statement about 8:00 A.M. By that time Franks had been in custody almost twelve hours.

"He didn't get any sleep. You're aware of that, right?" Haley inquired.

"Yes."

"Would you say he smoked about, what, three packs of cigarettes?" Haley asked.

"A lot."

"How many Dr Peppers did he drink?" Haley asked.

"I don't know."

"Did you give him any candy bars?" Haley asked.

"They may have. I don't know," Adair said.

When asked if they provided a sandwich or meal for Franks while in their custody, Adair stated they asked

if he wanted a hamburger or something, but he said
he was satisfied with the Dr Peppers and cigarettes.

Moving on to the black Mercury Cougar owned by
Franks, Adair admitted it was Judy who most often
drove the vehicle.

Adair acknowledged that at no time while Franks
was in custody did they allow him to attempt to make
the $125 bond.

Haley believed he had made his point with the jury.
DA investigators had taken his client off the street, kept
him in seclusion for more than seventeen hours, from
the time of his arrest until his release, and denied him
the opportunity to make bond. He passed the witness
back to Robert Foran for follow-up questions.

Foran stood, not only to cross-examine Adair but
also to defend the actions of the supervisor and his
investigators at the time of Franks's arrest.

Through questioning, Foran established that
Franks, having talked to Adair earlier, was aware he
was a DA investigator at the time of the arrest. In addition, other investigators at the scene identified
themselves before placing Franks in handcuffs. Lastly
Adair restated that Franks had agreed to talk with Eric
Holden and to wait until he drove from Dallas to Fort
Worth, accounting for the time delay in taking the defendant before a magistrate.

Leon Haley adamantly disagreed.

"Your Honor, I object," Haley said loudly as he
stood before the court. "The delay had nothing to do
with waiting for Mr. Holden. The delay had to do with
him not being taken to a magistrate or a judge. I
object, that's an improper manner in which he's misleading the jury."

Ricky Franks watched his attorney intently. He may
not have understood the argument Haley was making,

but he appeared pleased with the way in which he delivered it.

Judge Robert Gill looked down from his elevated bench and announced, "Overruled."

Foran continued with fervor, asking rapid-fire questions.

"Did you see if he needed to go to the bathroom?"

"Yes, sir."

"Just sitting in a room smoking cigarettes and drinking Dr Peppers?"

"Basically, yes."

"Anybody yelling at him?"

"No, sir."

"Threatening him?"

"No."

"Telling him what to say?"

"No."

"Telling him what to do?"

"No."

"Did y'all attempt to get a statement first?" Foran asked.

"No, we didn't."

"When you originally spoke to Richard Franks on August fourth, he wasn't in custody, was he?" Foran pressed.

"No, he wasn't."

After making his points to the jury, Foran asked to approach the bench. Judge Gill nodded. Foran, Haley, and Jones moved to stand by the wooden ledge at the front of the judge's bench.

"Judge, I have an issue of law to take up outside the presence of the jury," Foran announced.

Once the jury was secured in the jury room adjacent to the courtroom, Foran continued. "I believe the defense has implied to this jury that there was undue delay in booking Franks in, when, in fact, this defendant voluntarily took them around, pointing out possible locations for the body—" Foran stated.

"That's after the fact, Judge," Haley interrupted.

Jones argued that their client's statement had not been introduced to the jury and should not have been brought up by the prosecutor during his questioning.

"And I don't see the relevance of where he went, to prove that he was not booked in on time," Haley argued, pointing out that the prosecutor had mentioned Franks taking the investigators to possible sites where Opal could be found.

"When did the event supposedly occur?" Judge Gill asked.

"Right after the arraignment, when they were taking him back. Judge, the reason I approached is because Franks took them to various locations where Opal might possibly be. And they have talked about Franks not being booked in immediately, it was some hours later. They have misled this jury as to why," Foran explained.

"But was there an undue delay before the giving of the statement?" Judge Gill asked.

"I think what they have implied is a general misconduct on the part of the police, a pattern of misconduct that they want to argue was part of the statement-taking process and continued afterward. It's unfair and misleading," Foran argued vigorously.

"I don't think the witness answered in a misleading fashion," Judge Gill remarked, terminating any further discussion on the issue.

Neither Haley nor Foran had any additional questions for Mike Adair.

After a brief recess for the jury to smoke if they wished, enjoy a drink, or take a bathroom break, court reconvened with the state calling Eric Holden.

Richard Franks's narrow eyes followed Holden as he approached the witness stand. Franks pressed his lips tightly together, giving an aura of anger.

Just as he had done in the pretrial hearing the previous day, Holden testified that he had been called to the Special Crimes Unit on the evening of August 17, 1999, to interview someone. Holden was a skilled witness, often looking directly to members of the jury as he spoke.

Greg Miller led Holden through the questions he'd prepared in an effort for the jury to understand the procedures the polygraph examiner followed before, during, and after he spoke to Richard Franks. When Miller asked Holden to tell the jury his conclusions regarding Franks, Holden looked toward the jury and said, "My conclusion was that he was relatively bright. He was conversing very normally. There was virtually nothing that I talked with him about that he didn't communicate back to me in a very conversant way. Talked to me smartly, if you will. He didn't appear to me to be disadvantaged in the sense of his ability to communicate, to understand, and to deal with me on virtually any issue that we talked about. I was relatively impressed with him."

Franks's posture relaxed and he smiled at Holden's depiction of him. He had spent years with people telling him he was stupid, he appeared to like Holden's positive description of him.

Holden informed the jury that Franks not only told him he was familiar with Saginaw but, for a portion of his life, had grown up there. When Holden had asked him if he was accustomed to wearing a hat or cap, Franks said he wore one regularly, most often a red ball cap with a red dog on it.

Leon Haley's white teeth shone bright against his ebony skin as he approached Eric Holden. The shrewd defense attorney and the expert witness had been down the question-and-answer path the day before. Holden knew that Haley would try to poke holes in his testimony by playing up the significant amount of time he had spent with Franks, the late hour of the interview, and his client's lack of food and sleep—Holden was right. Haley then zeroed in on Holden's fee for conducting the interview.

"How much did you get paid for your services?" Haley asked.

"I'm going to guess, Counselor. I think eighteen hundred dollars," Holden answered.

If Haley expected to get a reaction from any member of the jury after hearing the large amount of money paid to Holden for a mere twelve hours of work, he was disappointed. The twelve jurors remained expressionless, but a low whistle could be heard from the rear of the courtroom.

"So eighteen hundred dollars and we got us a statement, right?" Haley asked, inferring that the amount of Holden's fee was payment for obtaining the defendant's statement.

"That was the time that I committed. The time that I spent," Holden said, unshaken.

"Did you put this red hat in your notes?" Haley questioned.

"I did not," Holden stated.

"So that's the first time I'm hearing about this red hat, right?" Haley asked.

"As far as I know."

"Is there anything wrong with him having a red cap?" Haley asked.

"No, sir."

"Did you ask him if he had any black tennis shoes, or blue clothes, or black clothes?" Haley pressed on.

"No, sir."

Haley continued by establishing that Holden's interview with Franks had not been videotaped or recorded on audiotape. The only accounts of the proceedings were Holden's nearly illegible handwritten notes and the typed copy. Holden also admitted that Franks had become agitated at the end of the interview, had stated he was tired and wanted to stop. At that request Holden immediately had ceased to question the suspect.

As he had done in the pretrial hearing before Judge Gill, Haley asked about Franks's mental capacity and if Holden would have interviewed a ten- or eleven-year-old child in the same manner. The crafty attorney continued to build his client's diminished-capacity defense.

"Sometimes children can be manipulated. Would you agree with me on that?" Haley asked.

"Sure."

"And mentally retarded people can be manipulated. Is that fair?" Haley pushed on.

"They can be, sure," Holden admitted without hesitation.

His point made, Haley turned the witness over to the prosecution.

During redirect, Miller asked Holden why Franks had become agitated during the interview.

"He became agitated at the very end of the interview, shortly before I terminated it," Holden explained. "Based on everything that I had been told by him and what he had said to me, I told him that I believed firmly that he had caused the death of Opal Jennings and knew where her body was."

Loud murmurs could be heard from the Franks family. They were obviously unhappy with Holden's testimony and, in particular, Holden's accusations concerning Ricky's knowledge of the crime.

Miller completed his questions by asking Holden—as he had the previous day—if he had told Ricky Franks he was impressed with both his handwriting and his spelling. When Holden answered yes, Miller set Holden up for the response he wanted the jurors to hear.

"What response did Ricky Franks give you?" Miller asked.

"He looked up at me and smiled and winked."

After Miller left, in the minds of the jurors, the image of Ricky Franks coyly winking at Eric Holden, he passed the witness.

Haley attempted to counter the picture Miller had painted of his client as a sly, competent adult by asking Holden if Franks actually winked, or if he could have been so sleepy at that point that his eyes were blinking. But Holden stood firm, he stated to him it appeared to be a wink.

The defense counsel asked Holden why, if he had been so impressed with Franks's handwriting, hadn't he simply asked him to write a statement, rather than writing it himself. Holden denied he had written a statement, saying that he simply had taken notes based on what Franks had told him while they talked.

With Holden still in the witness-box, Haley asked permission to approach the bench. Speaking softly and leaning uncomfortably over the bar to speak, Mr. Haley addressed the judge: "Your Honor, I'm only doing this for cautionary purposes because I don't want to open the door to anything. I would like to be able to ask Mr. Holden: isn't it true that when Mr. Franks got agitated at him, Mr. Franks was telling him, 'I didn't kill her.' I just want to ask that one question, but if the court tells me that I'll be opening the door to a whole bunch of words, I'm not going to ask that question."

"I'm not going to tell you anything," Judge Gill stated with a stern face. "If you ask the question and if the prosecution wants to go into something, I'll rule at that time. I'm not going to advise you how I'm going to rule on something that may or may not happen."

Haley thought for a moment before announcing he had no further questions for Eric Holden.

The last witness of the day was Kathy Manning. Investigator Manning explained to the jury that she was the person responsible for learning about the outstanding traffic warrant for Richard Franks and for securing a warrant for his arrest. Manning, as Holden had done before her, repeated much of her pretrial testimony during the kidnapping trial itself.

Most important, Manning was the vehicle used by the prosecution to introduce Richard Franks's statement into evidence.

Approaching the witness, the dark-haired Lisa Callahan handed a piece of paper to the blond-coiffed Manning.

"Is this the statement that was taken from Richard Franks on August 18, 1999?" Callahan asked.

Manning responded affirmatively, adding that she had witnessed Franks sign the statement, as had Danny McCormick.

"At this time, Your Honor, the state would offer State's Exhibit twelve for identification, subject to tendering it to defense counsel for their inspection," Callahan said.

"Judge, if you would note our prior objection to the statement for legal reasons," Edward Jones stated.

"Those objections are noted and overruled," Judge Gill responded.

"Ms. Manning, let me present you with State's Exhibit twelve. If you would go ahead and read that out loud to the jury, and if you could please read it slowly," Callahan instructed.

As Callahan handed Manning the paper, Ed Jones again objected, this time to the reading of the statement to the jury. He contended that if they wanted to read it, they could do so themselves. He asserted that Manning reading the statement would be improper.

Judge Gill promptly overruled the objection.

The prosecution was pleased with the ruling. They wanted the confession heard aloud. They wanted the jury to listen to the damning language, for the Frankses to hear Ricky's own words, and the news media to capture every remark. They wanted Ricky Franks exposed for the convicted child molester, and kidnapper, they knew him to be.

Manning cleared her throat and began by reading the Miranda warning that Franks had initialed; then she began reading Franks's statement.

The courtroom was perfectly quiet. Only the voice of Manning broke through the eerie silence. Jurors leaned forward slightly to be certain to hear each word of the defendant's much anticipated statement. Franks sat back, seemingly undisturbed by what was about to be read in court:

"'My name is Richard Lee Franks. My date of birth is August 3, 1969. I live at [address blacked out] Sheridan in Fort Worth, Texas. I have completed twelve years of school and I can read and write the English language.

"'On March 26, 1999, I went to Saginaw, Texas, to see my brother Danny—'" (That was a correction. The typed copy said "Donny" and he changed it to "Danny," placing his initials above that name.)

"Excuse me," Leon Haley interrupted. "Your Honor, may I approach the bench for a second?"

"You may," Judge Gill said.

Manning sat back as Haley argued that the defense had a prior motion before the court about getting into Mr. Franks's criminal record and that record, including his probation, appeared in the statement that was about to be read.

Greg Miller, who had followed Leon Haley to the bench, attempted to set the record straight.

"There is nothing in the statement about a prior record," Miller informed the judge.

Judge Gill instructed Kathy Manning to proceed with the reading of the statement as Miller and Haley both returned to their seats.

"'When I saw Opal Jennings and two other kids, a boy and a girl playing in a field beside a house, this was about four P.M. in the afternoon or a little later. I was driving a Ford Cougar and was by myself. I went by Danny's house, saw the girls and a boy playing outside, outside playing in the field. I stopped to talk to them and Opal said, "Where are you going?" I was in the car and Opal was talking to me through the fence. She asked where I was going and I told her that I was going to see if my brother was home so I could go visit with him.

"'I told Opal, if he's not there, I'm going home. She said they might be at work. And I then asked her how she was doing and she said she was doing good in school. She said that she was getting good grades. She came up to the car on the driver's side. The driver's door was open. She came up to the door, gave me a hug and shook my hand. I asked her if she was passing and she said, "I hope so." I then told her that if she was doing good in school, then she would. I said, "I hope you pass." The other kids wanted her to hurry up so she could play with them. I said, "You need to get back and finish playing what y'all are playing." They were playing some kind of ball.

"'She reached in the car. I thought she was going to grab me. I didn't know what she was going to try to do, so I pushed her hand and said, "What are you trying to do? I'm not the one to be doing it with." I didn't want to do nothing that would get me in trouble. She was just a kid. I don't see myself doing nothing like that. I was afraid she was going to make a pass at me or get me to take her somewhere. She was wanting me to take her to the store. She went around to the front of the car to get in the passenger side. I was afraid she wanted me to take her to have sex with her or something.'"

Shocked spectators sucked in a breath that was audible throughout the courtroom. Jurors, attempting to keep their faces void of expression, wrinkled their brows as if not understanding the words Manning read.

"'I took her to the store. She got in the passenger side. The other two kids were outside playing. I told her I was going to bring her back so she could finish playing with the other two kids. I took her to the convenience store a block from the house. I sat in the car and she got something to drink.

"'She bought a Coke and then she came back to the car. She said, "Thank you for bringing me up here." But I said, "I won't do it again." Opal tried to move over toward me. I didn't know what she tried to do. She tried to grab me between my legs. She grabbed my dick. She wanted me to fuck her. I told her no. She said, "Fuck me." She tried to take her pants off. I told her no. She asked me why and I said because I don't do that. She asked me why and I said, "Because you are too young and I could get in trouble for it."

"'She unzipped my pants, took my dick out. She had

it in her hand. She went down like she was going to go down on it. I pushed her back. I put my dick back in my pants. She was sitting beside me. When she went to bend over, I pushed her back. I said, "I'm not going to have sex with someone younger than I am."'"

Spectators twisted uneasily in their seats. The faces of the Sanderford family didn't reveal any of the anger or sadness they felt in their hearts. Miller had prepared them for what would be revealed in court. If jurors were adversely affected by the words of the defendant, they held their emotions close. The Frankses, on the other hand, whispered their disbelief that Ricky could have made the disgusting accusations. His mother merely put her face in her hands as Manning's voice reverberated throughout the courtroom. Ricky Franks stared at the table in front of him, while his attorneys watched each member of the jury closely to interpret any consequence that might surface later.

"'I told her that she needed to get out of the car,'" Manning continued. "'This happened on the way back from the store. I took her to her house and left her off the same place where I talked to her at. I don't know if she went in the house or not. I just wanted to get away from her. When I dropped her off, she gave me a hug and I left. The other two kids were in the field playing.

"'Everything in this statement is true and correct and I said it in my own words. I stopped the interview at my request when I got tired. I was treated good tonight and everything I said is in my own words.'

"And again, the initials, 'RLF.' Underneath that is typed Richard Lee Franks and then Richard Franks's own signature. The date, August 18, 1999. The time, eight A.M. Witnessed by Danny McCormick."

The words of the defendant hung in the courtroom

like an unnatural fog. When Leon Haley began to question Manning, he wanted not only to detract from the possible impact of his client's words, but to refocus the testimony on the arrest, detention, and questioning of Ricky Franks.

After having Manning restate the procedures followed the day of Franks's arrest, Haley asked, "You're familiar that no evidence obtained by an officer or person in violation of any provision of the [Texas] Constitution or the laws of the state of Texas, or the [U.S.] Constitution or the laws of the United States of America, shall be admitted into evidence against an accused on trial in any criminal case. You're aware of that, correct?"

"That's true," Manning agreed.

"And you're further aware that any case where the legal evidence raises an issue the jury shall be instructed that, if it believes or has a reasonable doubt that the evidence was obtained in violation of the provision of this article, the jury shall disregard any such evidence so obtained. You're aware of that, correct?" Haley continued.

"That's true," Manning responded.

It was unclear if members of the jury understood the defense counsel's technical reference to the law as it pertained to the acquisition of his client's statement, but Haley felt he had made his point. He passed the witness.

ADA Callahan countered Haley's insinuations of misconduct by having Manning once again tell the jury that Franks's statement was taken properly in accordance with the law and that he had stated he understood his rights before they proceeded.

The bantering, back and forth, on the issue of Franks's ability to comprehend the procedures continued for several minutes. When both prosecutor and defense counsel announced they had no more questions for Manning, Judge Gill recessed court for the day.

The damning statement of Richard Lee Franks had not been forgotten during the rapid-fire redirect and recross-examination by the two attorneys. The words of Ricky Franks would ring in the ears of those who had been present in the court for some time.

As Judge Gill dismissed court for the day, the statement of Ricky Franks was on the minds and lips of everyone who had been present to hear Kathy Manning read the declaration. It wouldn't be until the jury returned with their verdict that the impact of the offensive words "She asked me to fuck her" would be known.

CHAPTER 12

Day one of the Richard Franks kidnapping trial had ended with the shocking written statement of Franks accusing Opal Jennings of attempting to seduce him. Heads were still reeling over the language and insinuations made by the defendant.

The previous day's testimony concluded with a member of the Special Crimes Unit; the second day began with another. Danny McCormick, tall, lean, his shaven head shining under the courtroom's fluorescent lighting, ambled to the front of the courtroom to be sworn in. He moved stiffly, as he had during the pretrial hearing, hampered by a tight back brace, the result of recent back surgery.

Like Mike Adair and Kathy Manning, McCormick also had served as a police officer. Ten years on the Denton, Texas, force had prepared McCormick for his position as a Narcotics Field supervisor, prior to being tabbed as a member of the elite Special Crimes Unit.

Unlike Mike Adair, who had dressed in a conservative dark business suit, McCormick's attire had more of a Western flavor, from his handlebar mustache down to his cowboy boots.

The veteran lawman had been assigned to the Opal Jennings case immediately after word of her abduction, long before the tip concerning Ricky Franks had reached the Special Crimes office. In fact, it had been McCormick who had passed the Franks lead on to Mike Adair.

McCormick reiterated that Manning had discovered a traffic warrant for Franks and the warrant was served by their personnel on August 17, 1999. The black Mercury Cougar driven by Franks had been secured and preserved for trace evidence.

"We have heard the use of words like 'pretext' and stuff like that in this trial," Robert Foran stated. "When you arrest someone on a valid traffic warrant, are you allowed to inquire into the traffic warrant if you want to?"

"Yes, sir," McCormick replied.

Ricky Franks sat silently beside his attorneys, watching McCormick with his head held high and a bit of a smirk on his pimpled face.

"Are you allowed to inquire into other criminal matters?" Foran asked, attempting to counter the defense's accusations concerning Franks's arrest.

"Yes, sir."

Even if investigators had used the traffic warrant as an alleged reason to detain Richard Franks and question him about the Opal Jennings kidnapping, McCormick made it clear that they had been within their legal rights.

After McCormick stated he had read Franks the Miranda warning, the assistant district attorney went through each section of the warning, with McCormick verifying Franks's initials on each paragraph.

Investigator McCormick explained to the jury and spectators how Eric Holden was called to the office to interview Franks. They were provided a larger room in which to meet, and no law enforcement personnel were present during their discussions. McCormick verified that Franks had been given frequent bathroom breaks, provided beverages, and was allowed to smoke. He made it clear that once Eric Holden's interview with Franks had concluded, he had taken the interviewer's notes and had Investigator Charlie Johnson type them up on one of their investigative forms. McCormick added that in order for the statement to be valid, it had to have the Miranda warning on the front face of the statement. Franks then signed the statement, never indicating he didn't understand what was going on.

Ricky Franks eyed McCormick carefully as the investigator spoke of his interview with Holden. His blank expression failed to give away his inner thoughts.

Leon Haley walked to the middle of the courtroom and addressed McCormick. "On August 17, 1999, y'all made a decision, after following him and his wife around that particular day and waiting until he was alone, y'all made a calculated decision that what y'all were going to do is mess with Ricky. Isn't that fair to say?" Haley said accusingly.

From his seat at the prosecutors' table, Robert Foran announced, "Objection, argumentative."

"Sustained," Judge Gill ruled, agreeing with the assistant prosecutor.

Haley amended his questioning to indicate that the task force had been in possession of the arrest warrant for four days before seven plainclothes investigators in unmarked cars made the arrest.

The ardent defense attorney also presented, through McCormick's testimony, that they had the option of leaving Franks's car at the convenience store and having his wife pick it up, or having it towed to the downtown police pound. McCormick had to admit that the team had opted for one of the investigators to drive the Cougar to the county garage.

"But as y'all drove it off, assuming that Ricky had actually been involved in this matter, you could have been contaminating evidence; isn't that true?" Haley asked, setting into motion possible questions that any evidence that may have been found later in his client's vehicle was possibly tainted.

Following inquiries about the interview room in which Franks was held, and whether Franks had been left alone for long periods of time, Haley concentrated on his client's family.

"During all that period of time, he's at a place he's never been before and you are telling me he didn't ask to go home?" Haley declared.

Haley looked surprised, even bewildered, when McCormick responded by telling him that the defendant had not asked to go home or asked to speak to any of his family. In fact, McCormick insisted that Ricky Franks had sat in the interview room drinking Dr Pepper and waiting for the arrival of Eric Holden, seemingly unconcerned about his detainment. As hard as Leon Haley tried to get McCormick to acknowledge that he, other investigators, or Eric Holden had *interrogated* Mr. Franks, rather than *interviewed* him as they insisted, McCormick held fast to his denial.

Then the questioning turned biting as Haley drilled the investigator about evidence that authorities obviously had expected to be found in the defendant's car.

"You told him that there was blood in that car; isn't that correct?" Haley said sharply.

"He was told there was some blood in the car," McCormick replied matter-of-factly.

"And you were lying to him, weren't you?" Haley said, his voice rising.

"No, sir. I was told there was."

"You know now that there was no blood in that car that leads my client to Opal Jennings. Isn't that fair?" Haley adamantly pursued his questioning.

"That's correct," McCormick acknowledged.

Judy Franks smiled as Haley's cross-examination took on a combative edge.

"Somebody told him there were hair fibers in that car. Are you aware of that?" Haley questioned.

"Yes, sir."

"And y'all were lying to him about that, too, weren't you?" Haley accused.

"I was not, no, sir."

"You know to this day that after all of the tests were done, that there are no hair matches to my client in that car dealing with Opal Jennings. Is that fair?" Haley asked pointedly.

"That's correct, yes, sir," McCormick conceded.

Repeating that absolutely no blood was found in Franks's vehicle, making certain the jury was fully aware that his client's car couldn't be linked to Opal Jennings by forensic evidence, Haley charged Mc-Cormick with lying to his client through interrogation tactics, not interview techniques. McCormick responded to Haley in the same unruffled, controlled manner he had maintained throughout the questioning, denying the allegations.

Haley's voice softened, but his intensity remained. "Y'all were just in there nicely, politely accusing him and lying to him. Is that fair to say?"

"No, sir," McCormick responded calmly.

But McCormick had to agree with Haley that Franks had changed his story a number of times and that at some point he had told the investigators, "I'm being confused." McCormick also admitted that they had not informed the judge who arraigned Franks that he had recanted his story. Then the investigator disclosed that at some point Franks insisted he didn't kill Opal Jennings, maintaining that the officers were twisting his words.

Haley's face remained stoic, but his dark eyes reflected pleasure with McCormick's acknowledgments. He hoped reasonable doubt was looming larger in the minds of the twelve jurors. The skilled attorney knew not to lie back, but to continue pressing forward, to keep the focus on the investigation itself and off his client.

"The bottom line is, y'all are talking to this man," Haley said as he pointed toward Ricky Franks, "and you ask him, 'Can you tell us where you might put a body?' Isn't that right? Y'all had him running all around town trying to find a body, correct?" Haley asked this in an effort to prove his client had no real knowledge of where Opal Jennings might be.

"We went to two places, yes, sir," McCormick admitted.

"And found absolutely nothing; isn't that right?"

"That's right."

"And all of y'all are standing out there looking real silly with a mentally retarded person. Y'all were looking real silly out there finding absolutely nothing. Isn't that true?" Haley said mockingly.

"We didn't find anything, no, sir," McCormick replied, ignoring the attorney's snide remarks.

Franks's two half brothers sneered at the witness as they listened to Haley chip away at the investigative tactics used on their younger brother.

Haley had managed not only to have one of the principal investigators acknowledge that they had found no body and no physical evidence linking his client to Opal Jennings, but had once again managed to instill in the minds of the jury Ricky Franks's diminished capacity.

Haley summed up his cross-examination of Mc-Cormick by questioning him as to why Franks's statement had not been recorded on either audiotape or videotape when the technology was available. He asked why they had decided to obtain a written statement signed by Franks, in lieu of any sound-recorded or video-recorded transcript.

"When something is as serious as this, so important in trying to find out the true person that abducted Opal, we don't have anything other than that statement from my client; is that fair?" Haley asked, again allowing his annoyance to show through to the jury.

"We have the statement, yes, sir," McCormick responded flatly.

Haley had no more questions for Danny Mc-Cormick. As Haley walked back to sit beside his client, Robert Foran rose to ask additional questions in an effort to clear up what could be some misunderstandings in the minds of jurors.

Foran reiterated that Franks had given a consent to search his vehicle, that the tests they had discussed with the defendant had been presumptive tests, not confirming tests, and that those tests had indeed indicated the possible presence of blood—that was exactly the information they had given Franks on the night of his arrest.

"So there wasn't a lie. That's the information you had as a result of the tests that Max Courtney provided to you," Foran declared, referring to the owner of a Dallas forensic laboratory.

Turning his attention to the interview room Haley had characterized as small and daunting, Foran used his own gift of cynicism to make his point.

"Are there bars on the windows?" Foran asked.

"No, sir," McCormick replied.

"We don't have a rack in there to put them on, do we?"

"No, sir."

"We're not torturing him in there?"

"No, sir."

"We didn't deprive him of basic necessities, did we?"

"No, sir."

"And you gave him Dr Pepper. Is that some sort of truth serum?" Foran asked amid the muffled snickers of several in the court's gallery.

"Not that I know of," McCormick stated, maintaining the stoic expression he had throughout the battery of questions fired at him by the prosecutor.

In response to Foran's questions, McCormick described Franks as being indecisive, saying that he had taken Opal, then recanting more than once during the time he was being taken to and from the magistrate. The defendant had also given a number of explanations why blood would be in his car. He said Opal fell and scratched her leg, then said that she ran and fell, hitting her head on a rock, bleeding in the car when she got back in.

Foran lastly questioned McCormick about a fictitious scenario told to Franks by Special Agent Lori Keefer. She had told Franks about another abduction in Keller, Texas. The ploy had been used as a "checks and balances" because of Franks's recantations. The fake story would have given Franks an opportunity to admit to something that was absolutely untrue, an indication that he was of the mind to confess to any crime just to please the investigators.

"How did he respond to the false scenario?" Foran asked.

"He got angry about it," McCormick replied. "He said no way he did that. He said, 'I knew if I told you about Opal, I would get blamed for everything else.' He never admitted to the false scenario."

Franks never so much as flinched as McCormick explained the anger he had displayed during their discussions while driving around Fort Worth in search of the body of Opal Jennings. He remained silent, staring blankly as McCormick talked about him as though he weren't in the courtroom.

His testimony complete, Danny McCormick stiffly rose from the witness chair and walked back to his seat in the courtroom gallery. It had been a long, sometimes grueling session. He had told the truth and hoped the members of the jury understood the Special Crimes Unit's investigative procedures, as well as their respect for Ricky Franks's rights.

As McCormick pushed open the wooden gate dividing the gallery from the court, Ricky Franks's half brothers stared at him with obvious despisement, their eyes following him from the witness chair to his seat beside Kathy Manning. They didn't believe the declarations of the lawman. They agreed with Leon Haley, their brother had been manipulated into making statements the investigators wanted. Their resentment grew.

The state's next witness was as sharp a contrast to the career lawman as the dark of night is to the light of day. Andrew Bouyer was a three-time convicted felon: burglary of a vehicle, burglary of a habitation, and theft from a person were among his multiple arrests, along with at least one term in the Texas Department of Corrections Institutional Division. At the time of Franks's trial, Bouyer was on probation for assault causing bodily injury.

Bouyer wasn't exactly the type of witness prosecutors

relished using. His criminal record could be exploited to discredit his testimony, but Greg Miller had decided to take the chance, betting that what Bouyer had to tell the jury would far override the negative impact of his own deviant behavior.

"Let me just get this out," Miller began with a shrug, "because I don't know if it's going to be a big deal or not. You were up here yesterday, right?"

"Yes, sir."

Bouyer had been ready to testify, but the length of the prior testimonies had put his appearance off for a day.

"Did you have any lunch money (yesterday)?" Miller asked.

"Yes, sir."

Miller's head snapped toward Bouyer, surprise shone on his face. "You did?" Miller asked, his voice rising. "Who gave you the money?" Miller questioned.

"You," Bouyer replied honestly.

"Okay, all right. I was going to ask for my money back," Miller said, to chuckles from the audience. Miller had lightheartedly defused any questions that may have come during cross-examination as to whether Bouyer had been paid for his testimony.

Settled down in the witness chair, Bouyer told the jury that he first had met Ricky Franks when they were both put in the small cells on the fifth floor of the Tarrant County Jail. According to Bouyer, there were few prisoners being held in that section. He and Ricky Franks had become friends, more as a matter of convenience than common interests.

"When I first went over there to his room, I asked him for a cigarette, because I didn't have none at the time. He gave me one and I went and talked to one of the other guys who I knew in the pool. They told me, 'That's Ricky Franks over there. That's the guy on the Opal thing,'" Bouyer informed the court.

"Did Ricky Franks tell you anything about Opal Jennings?" Miller asked.

"When I first knowed him," Bouyer began in broken English, "he told me that he picked her up, took her out to eat. She offered to have sex with him and he dropped her off somewhere. He said he dropped her off back at her home."

Members of the Franks family shook their heads in obvious disagreement, while Ricky Franks sat expressionless.

"Did he tell you anything else about Opal Jennings?" Miller nudged.

"No, sir. But, later on, he tried saying that they forced him to say that. But they didn't force him to say it to me whenever I first heard it, so that's why it was confusing to me," Bouyer rambled on.

The response obviously angered Rodney Franks, whose jaw tightened as the veins in his neck expanded, reflecting the disdain he felt for the state's witness.

Miller asked Bouyer if he had been trying to interrogate Franks, play some kind of psychological games with him, or trick Franks into telling him something. Bouyer emphatically denied the allegation.

"Later on, did Ricky ever express some concerns to you about the authorities finding Opal's body?" Miller continued.

"He told me if they find a body, then they're liable to link something to him," Bouyer stated.

Whispers buzzed around the courtroom. Franks was on trial for kidnapping, not murder, and although Opal had not been seen in more than a year, this was the first time during the trial that speculation of her death seemed to be confirmed.

"Did he tell you anything about the car he was in when he picked up Opal?" Miller inquired.

"Not really. He just said it was his car and told me it was black," Bouyer stated.

In only a few short minutes, Miller had made the points he had planned and was ready to pass the witness to the defense. The assistant district attorney could only hope the jury gave at least some credence to the former convict's testimony.

Edward Jones walked toward the witness, determined to discredit the former con. Jones induced Bouyer to admit he had gone by the alias "Chris Freeman" and that his term in the Texas penitentiary had been for four years. Concentrating on Bouyer's criminal record, Jones hoped the jury would see the convicted felon as an unreliable witness, not to be believed. Then, as Miller had predicted, Jones attacked Bouyer's motivation for agreeing to testify in court against his client.

Citing two pending counts of aggravated assault of a public servant against the state's witness, Jones asked, "Now for your testimony here today in front of this jury you received a deal, didn't you?"

"Yes, sir," Bouyer admitted.

"They thought your testimony was so important here today that they offered you something when you were looking at four to forty years in prison; is that right?" Jones asked.

"Yes, sir."

"And, stop me if I'm wrong, your testimony was so important that they offered to reduce your cases. You could have gotten four to forty years, but they're reduced to one-year misdemeanor probation; is that right?" Jones questioned.

"I'm going two years' probation, yes," Bouyer responded truthfully.

Murmurs spread across the courtroom. Most in the audience were unaware that such agreements were regularly entered into in order to obtain needed testimony. Only time would tell if the jury would believe Bouyer.

As Jones continued his cross-examination, Bouyer admitted that while in county jail he had occasionally read the newspaper to Ricky Franks, not because Franks couldn't read, but because he often didn't understand what was written. Through Bouyer, Franks had kept up with his case. Many of the things written about Franks in the paper had upset him and, according to Bouyer, Franks was a nervous wreck at times.

Through the defense's questioning, Bouyer restated his prior testimony that in talking with Franks he appeared worried that if a body was found, he would then be charged with a more serious offense. Then, in order to counter the accusations made by Bouyer, Jones returned to the witness's criminal record and the deal he had made with prosecutors.

Miller had expected Jones to attack his witness, but he had to do something to try to redeem him. Miller asked Bouyer to explain that the two counts of aggravated assault occurred in the Tarrant County Jail. Bouyer had been extremely upset when taken to jail, venting his frustrations on the two deputies. He had bitten both, but neither had required medical attention.

Then Miller addressed an issue he thought obvious: jail inmates seldom confide in jailers or deputies; it's to other inmates they turn for conversation, for purging their souls.

As Bouyer was excused, Assistant DA Miller believed the prosecution wouldn't have the same challenges to their next witness. James Blackburn, although a former jail inmate, was not facing new charges and wouldn't benefit in any way from testifying. In fact, it had been Blackburn who had contacted them from his home in Grapevine, Texas, after seeing a news report on Channel 4 Fox News.

Blackburn had violated his misdemeanor probation and was serving a six-month county jail sentence when he met Ricky Franks. As a jail trustee (inmates who work for the sheriff's department cleaning cells, serving meals, and delivering commissary), Blackburn was forbidden to speak to other inmates. It had been Ricky Franks who chose to speak to him.

"At first he told me that him and his wife just drove past Opal Jennings's house to see how close it was to their house," Blackburn told Lisa Callahan, who had been chosen to question Blackburn. "Then later, he said that he did pick her up, but after fifteen or twenty minutes, she was gone."

"Did he say anything about seeing her before that date?" Callahan asked, backtracking a bit.

"Yes. He said he'd seen her in her neighborhood for about a year. Out in the front yard, playing in the front of the house," Blackburn explained.

Two spectators quickly glanced at one another, Blackburn's words ringing in their ears. "He'd seen her in her neighborhood for about a year." Had Franks been stalking Opal, waiting for an opportune moment in which to grab her?

"Did he say why he had gone there to begin with?" Callahan asked.

"He said to get satisfaction," Blackburn stated.

Although faces of the jurors remained expressionless, a few of them widened their eyes at the witness's statement. Members of the audience could only imagine how the convicted child sex offender planned to gain the pleasure he claimed he desired. The Franks family, continuing to believe in Ricky's innocence, could be seen shaking their heads. They didn't believe Ricky had made such a statement to the man on the stand, a man they believed was obviously lying.

Leon Haley was also unhappy with Blackburn's statements. On cross-examination he questioned Blackburn's motives for coming forward.

"You say you were sitting at home and you saw the news and you decided you would just come on down here," Haley said smartly.

"Yes, sir," Blackburn responded.

"All right, are you happy?" Haley quipped.

"I suppose, sir," Blackburn replied, unaffected. He was excused.

Audrey Sanderford watched as Blackburn walked from the courtroom. She wasn't pleased with the way the trial was going. She and Greg Miller had disagreed on a number of issues before the start of the trial, and as it proceeded, she had more questions than answers. Audrey wanted a definitive conviction, one in which there was no doubt left as to who took Opal. She feared the circumstantial evidence being presented against Ricky Franks would not be enough to convince her, or the jury, of his guilt. And Audrey wanted more—more than a conviction, Audrey wanted Opal to come home. Her attention returned to the courtroom as another state's witness was called to the stand.

CHAPTER 13

Greg Miller and Andrew (Andy) Farrell had been friends for several years. The chief deputy prosecutor and the fifteen-year veteran of the FBI had worked many cases together. Each respected the other. Farrell, a member of the FBI's Special Crimes Unit based in Fort Worth, had been assigned to head up the Opal Jennings investigation from the onset. Miller felt confident Farrell's testimony would help him persuade the jury of Ricky Franks's guilt.

After the noon break, Andy Farrell, an attractive middle-aged man of medium build and dark hair, took the stand. Explaining the multijurisdictional task force that had joined in an effort to find Opal Jennings, Farrell told jurors that within the command post there were different tasks.

"One of the first things we established was a tip line, both an 'eight hundred' number and a local number. We also established a post office box," Farrell explained. "One desk at the police department would get those leads. If they came in telephonically, they would complete a lead sheet. The lead sheet would then be routed to what was called an intelligence desk. They would look at it and try to assign initial priority to it based on the investigative plans that were going on at that time. And then the lead would be forwarded to case agents or supervisors, who would review that lead, verify the precedence that was put on it, and then decide what should be done about the tip.

"Daily, agents would come into that command post. They would receive leads from the lead box. There would be a morning briefing, where we discussed leads that were going on, different things that were occurring. And then there would be an evening briefing, where we'd do the same thing."

Through Farrell, Miller wanted the jury to understand the exact procedures taken with each lead that had been received by the task force. If they understood the care and precision that was taken with each lead, they would understand how the information concerning Ricky Franks had been handled.

Farrell continued by stating that lead sheets were three-part carbonless papers, assigned a priority of A, B, C, or D, with A being the highest priority. Leads were then put in various notebooks, based on a system developed for maintaining them. Farrell told the court that there had been some three thousand leads in the Opal Jennings case.

Answering questions concerning the car driven by the abductor, Farrell explained that the bureau utilized all witness descriptions of the kidnapper's vehicle used in the abduction to come up with a general description of the car.

"The vehicle description that we released was a dark-colored car, two-door or four-door, possibly a Chrysler product. I think there was also a description of possible rust spots on the vehicle," Farrell said. The FBI agent's coolness and authoritative delivery left no doubt he was a no-nonsense professional.

"Was there any discussion or information early on

in the investigation that perhaps a Cougar may have been involved?" Miller asked.

As the FBI special agent testified, Ricky Franks sat quietly between his two attorneys. He showed little emotion, making observers wonder if he understood Farrell's testimony. It was clear to others that Greg Miller was attempting to put Ricky Franks's Mercury Cougar at the scene of the crime. Did Ricky Franks understand?

Farrell responded by stating that the boys playing ball in the street at the time of the kidnapping had mentioned seeing a dark Cougar in the neighborhood. He also confirmed that Spencer Williams had mentioned seeing a medallion-type figure on the car that had taken Opal away. Through Miller's questioning, Farrell was able to tell the jury that Franks's black Cougar had a medallion on the landau portion of the roof.

In reference to procedures the FBI utilized in processing Franks's vehicle for blood, hair, and fibers, Farrell stated that a spot near the right hip of the driver's seat was tested with luminol, as well as a subsequent field test, and the substance tested positive for the presence of blood. They had sent a swatch and the swabs from the tests not only to the FBI lab, but an independent lab as well. Along with the specimens from the driver's side, floor mats that had tested positive for the presence of blood were also sent to the two labs.

Farrell informed the jury that both the FBI lab and Lab Corp were concerned with the specimens due to the length of time between when Opal Jennings had been abducted and when Ricky Franks's car was processed. Five months in the hot Texas heat would surely have deteriorated any evidence that had been found. Likewise, in the five-month period in which Franks would have been driving the vehicle, fingerprints could have been wiped away and any hair or fibers vacuumed up. It wasn't a surprise to anyone in the gallery that not one shred of DNA linking Ricky Franks to Opal Jennings could be found in his black Cougar.

"When did you become aware of a lead pertaining to Richard Franks?" Miller asked.

"The lead was received early on at the command post, reviewed, and assigned a B priority, then put in the lead pool. When I really focused on it was at the time the Tarrant County District Attorney's Office contacted me," Farrell responded.

The FBI veteran stated that investigators had focused on A priority leads until July, when the FBI realized that there were leads that hadn't been addressed. Area agencies cooperated in addressing the leads in July and August 1999. Ricky Franks's name appeared on one of those lead sheets. It was discovered he had lived in the Saginaw area for about ten years, and that familiarity with the region increased interest in him as a person to be considered a suspect.

"Let's just sort of jump off into this area," Miller said, shifting the attention away from Ricky Franks momentarily. "Prior to the arrest of Richard Franks on August 17, 1999, had there been a couple of other people that you had looked at fairly heavy on this case?"

"Yes, there were," Farrell answered.

"Was one of those individuals a man by the name of Jackie Lee Richardson?" Miller asked.

Spectators whispered to one another in hushed tones. Who was Jackie Lee Richardson? And how did he fit into the Opal Jennings case?

"Yes."

During Miller's direct examination of Farrell, the jury learned that, after receiving a call concerning Richardson, Farrell himself had interviewed Richardson concerning Opal's abduction. Richardson had been cooperative and had provided hair samples for testing.

Farrell explained that at the time of the investigation, Richardson was driving a Buick Regal two-door, brown in color, with a torn-off landau roof. Farrell had first seen the vehicle off State Highway 121 and Haltom Road. The car had been pushed up into the trees, generally undetectable from the road.

"The battery was gone from the vehicle. The cap over the master cylinder and the engine were gone. The interior was torn apart. It had a small doughnut tire on the driver's side, rear of the vehicle," Farrell explained.

"Did it appear to you that the vehicle was operable?" Miller asked.

Muffled snickers could be heard from the rear of the courtroom. Two men covered their mouths as they suppressed laughter at the obvious answer to Miller's question.

"No, sir," Farrell said.

Farrell established that when he had found Richardson's vehicle, he didn't believe it had been involved in Opal's abduction. In addition, Richardson was fully cooperative, had a corroborated alibi, and his only form of transportation on the day of Opal Jennings's kidnapping was a bicycle.

Farrell stated that Jackie Lee Richardson had been excluded as a possible suspect in the case, both by alibi and lack of physical evidence. The FBI agent named other men who had been investigated as the kidnapper, but they, too, had been excluded from any further suspicion.

"Did you try to eliminate Richard Franks as a suspect?" Miller asked.

"Yes, sir."

"Were you able to do that?" Miller questioned.

"We were not," Farrell stated.

Andy Farrell's testimony was tedious but important. Miller needed for the jury to understand how Ricky Franks had come to the attention of the task force and why he instantly became a person of interest. Farrell told the filled courtroom that two of the methods used to eliminate persons from suspicion were a substantiated alibi and lack of physical evidence linking them to Opal. He emphasized that, in reference to Ricky Franks, an alibi could not be established. Only Opal Jennings could verify if Ricky Franks was telling the truth about their encounter as he described it.

Miller lastly asked Farrell if he had learned that Franks had a number of jobs, had a valid Texas driver's license, and was married, demonstrating to the jury that Richard Franks, although often described as slow, was perfectly capable of sustaining a normal life.

Judge Gill could see that the jury was ready for a break. Eyes were heavy, bodies slumped. Just after Miller passed his witness to the defense for cross-examination, Judge Gill announced it was time to recess for lunch. As the families and friends of both Ricky Franks and Opal Jennings scurried to find a nearby place to eat, Franks was taken to a holding cell at the rear of the courtroom, where he would be given a meal tray and told he could rest before court was called back to order.

Greg Miller took the crowded elevator to his sixth-floor office, where he would eat lunch, if time permitted. The anxious prosecutor always returned to his office during the noon hour when in trial. He would go over notes, talk with witnesses, plan strategy. Only when he was satisfied with his preparation would Miller take a Lean Cuisine from his small office refrigerator, pop it in his microwave, and sit down for a few minutes of rest. But more often than not, Miller would settle for drinking a diet Coke and skip eating altogether.

Following the noon recess, Edward Jones was slated to cross-examine Special Agent Farrell. It was expected to be a lengthy cross, considering Farrell had been in charge of the huge investigation.

After a few initial queries, Ed Jones focused his questioning on Spencer Williams and his description of the vehicle driven by Opal's abductor.

"Spencer was taken to CarMax and asked to point to a vehicle that was the same body style as the one involved in [the] abduction; isn't that true?" Jones asked.

"Yes," Farrell answered.

"He pointed to a Chrysler New Yorker as the body style of the car; isn't that true?" Jones inquired.

"Yes," Farrell said, "I think it was also based on the emblem."

"That's true. Based on the emblem," Jones repeated, energized that the FBI agent was leading him down the road of questioning he had intended to travel. "Isn't it true that Spencer said it had a star on the trunk?"

"Yes."

"You know that Dodge and Chrysler both have the star on the back of the trunk above the keyhole," Jones stated.

"That's correct."

Jones went through Spencer's full description of the car, including the shiny wheels and the back half of the roof being brown.

"And so, isn't it true that Spencer's identification of the vehicle doesn't match with the vehicles that have been shown to the jury? Isn't that true?" Jones pressed.

"Yes."

Jones felt he had made a significant point and raised more than enough reasonable doubt in the minds of the jury. Jones moved on to the suspect's description.

Farrell acknowledged that Spencer Williams had told authorities the man was not white, not black, but a dark male. Other persons, too, had told investigators it was a dark-complexioned man, some even stated it was an older male with a wrinkled face.

After casting uncertainty as to the description of the perpetrator, Jones moved on to the number of suspects that could possibly be considered in the case, citing that a large NASCAR race being held at Texas Motor Speedway, mere minutes from Saginaw, had an estimated two hundred to three hundred thousand additional people in the area at the time Opal was taken. Then there was a teenage jogger who had spoken to a Hispanic male with a loose ponytail who had stopped to ask for directions. The man had caused the girl to become fearful. The time had been about 5:15 P.M. and the location was about a quarter of a mile from where Opal was taken, approximately fifteen minutes later.

Jones introduced additional sightings of similar automobiles, other Hispanic males seen in the neighborhood, and varying accounts of what the vehicle first identified as the getaway car looked like. The defense attorney talked about other attempted abductions in the area and other suspects investigated by the task force. Farrell's cross-examination was intended to present doubt in the minds of jurors, and to have them ask key questions. Was Ricky Franks, a non-Hispanic man, the real kidnapper? Exactly what was the accurate description of the car the abductor was driving? Only time would tell if Jones had developed skepticism in the jurors' minds, but at least some Sanderford family members themselves were beginning to question Franks's guilt.

In closing, Jones asked Agent Farrell, "Would you agree with me that there is a lack of physical evidence against Ricky?"

"That's a true statement, yes," Farrell admitted.

After Ed Jones passed Andy Farrell back to Greg Miller, and before he had made it back to his seat, Miller was on his feet ready to correct any misnomers that may have been instilled in the jurors' minds.

"Please tell the jury who saw the abduction of Opal Jennings," Miller stressed in an effort to have jurors disregard the other persons who had seen one or more Hispanic males in the area at the time of the kidnapping.

"Spencer Williams and Opal's two-year-old cousin," Farrell replied.

"Prior to the defendant's arrest you got approximately twenty-three hundred leads. After Richard Franks was arrested, tell the jury how many leads came in concerning Richard Franks and his background," Miller continued, with a renewed fire in his belly.

"The majority of the additional seven hundred leads that we received related to Mr. Franks and/or information about him," Farrell responded.

Miller recapped Spencer Williams's varying descriptions of the car that was used to whisk his friend Opal away. "Has Spencer been relatively consistent on his description of the man that took Opal Jennings?" Miller asked.

"On the man, he has been, yes," Farrell acknowledged.

After having Farrell go over, point by point, Spencer Williams's rendition of the events of March 26, 1999, Miller asked one final question.

"Do you think Spencer Williams was mixed-up when he said Opal was kidnapped?"

"No, sir," Farrell answered.

Farrell was excused and jurors took a long, deep breath as the prosecution prepared to call another witness.

"Call Jesse Herrera," Miller announced.

From the back of the courtroom, a small, dark-skinned Hispanic man walked toward the witness chair. No one seemed to know who he was, but Jesse Herrera was a name known to the Franks family. As a convicted sex offender, Franks had met with Herrera twice a month for two years in Herrera's office at the Wise County Courthouse. The two men had gotten along reasonably well, although Franks was unwilling to follow many of Herrera's directives.

As Herrera took the stand, Franks pressed his lips tightly together, creases formed around his eyes. Franks and his family believed if not for Jesse Herrera, Ricky Franks wouldn't be on trial for the kidnapping of Opal Jennings.

Greg Miller took care while questioning the Wise County probation officer. He had been cautioned not to mention Herrera's occupation or make any reference to his professional association with the defendant. Any such reference would be considered prejudicial.

According to Texas law, Franks's previous probation for indecency with a child would be withheld from the twelve men and women who would determine his guilt or innocence.

"When is the last time you saw Richard Franks?" Miller asked.

"April 1, 1999," Herrera said, his voice breaking slightly. The young Hispanic probation officer nervously adjusted his dark-rimmed glasses. Herrera had experienced some personal difficulty since the arrest of Franks for the crime that had gripped North Texas for months. Not unlike sex offender probation officers everywhere, Herrera felt tremendous remorse that one of his charges might have reoffended.

Continuing his questioning, Miller asked when, before April 1, had Herrera seen Richard Franks.

"March tenth," Herrera stated.

Miller checked his notes, pushed his glasses up the bridge of his nose, and asked, "During the times that you would see Richard Franks, did you have an opportunity to determine or view his physical appearance?"

"Yes, sir."

"Let's talk about from 1997 to March 10, 1999. Was Mr. Franks's appearance during that span of time consistent with the way he looks in the courtroom here today?" Miller asked.

All eyes in the courtroom shifted from Herrera to Ricky Franks seated at the defense table clothed in a dark blue jacket, white shirt, and dark tie. Herrera's attention had also moved to the defendant, then returned to Miller.

"No, sir, it wasn't," Herrera answered.

"Would you tell the jury what the difference was," Miller encouraged.

Herrera took a long breath and, without looking

at Franks again, replied, "He had long hair, usually scruffy-looking, didn't shave very often. He normally wore a T-shirt. Every now and then, he'd wear a cap and he'd wear blue jeans."

Jurors studied the defendant. Herrera's description of Ricky Franks was a far cry from the clean-cut man they saw sitting quietly in the courtroom.

Herrera testified that he didn't recall the color of the cap most often worn by Franks, but stated he had seen Franks's hair worn long in a ponytail.

"When he appeared on April 1, 1999, did anything catch your attention?" Miller questioned.

"He had a fresh haircut. Really short, a clean cut," Herrera responded.

"When he came to the meeting, how did he get there?" Miller continued.

"He came up there with his wife, Judy. They appeared to be in a black Mercury Cougar," Herrera said, avoiding the cold stares of Franks and his family.

"When you saw Richard Franks in the Cougar, what did you think?" Miller asked.

"Initially I had this weird feeling in my stomach," Herrera responded, touching his midriff with his right hand. "The description matched a flyer that I had on my filing cabinet at the time."

Herrera then explained that after seeing Franks and making note of the changes he had made in his appearance, and noticing the car he was driving, he'd contacted the Wise County Sheriff's Office and given the information to a deputy.

Miller pressed on with his questioning, connecting the dots that he felt would reveal Richard Franks as Opal Jennings's kidnapper. Miller persisted by asking Herrera about a conversation he'd had with Danny Doyle, Franks's half brother. The conversation hadn't been a pleasant one. Doyle had wanted to know if

Herrera had ordered his brother to cut his hair. When Herrera told Doyle he hadn't, and refused to discuss it with him, Doyle became very angry.

Greg Miller slowly walked from the witness stand, where he had stood to question Herrera, back to his seat at the prosecution table. He was pleased that through Herrera's testimony he had presented evidence that Richard Franks intentionally had altered his appearance after the disappearance of Opal Jennings. He hoped the jury found Franks's actions as deliberate as he had.

As Miller settled in his chair, Leon Haley stood to question Herrera.

"There's nothing wrong with having your hair in a ponytail, is there?" Haley asked.

"No, sir."

"The times you have seen him, sometimes he didn't have his hair in a ponytail, did he?" Haley questioned.

"That's correct."

Herrera agreed with the defense attorney that on occasion Franks would wear his hair straight down, at shoulder length, or occasionally have it shorter. But Herrera emphasized that he had never seen Franks with his hair shorter than just above the collar until after March 26, 1999.

Then Haley did something Herrera hadn't expected. Haley asked the witness to step down from the stand and for Ricky Franks to walk over to where Herrera stood.

The audience, along with jurors, watched intensely as Richard Franks stood and walked toward his adversary. Franks stared sternly at his former probation officer, while Herrera avoided eye contact.

Herrera's stomach churned and his jaw tensed as Franks approached. Following his attorney's instructions, Franks turned his back toward Herrera.

Gesturing as Haley requested, Herrera showed the jury where Franks's hair had lain at its longest.

With relief, Herrera took his seat as Franks returned to sit beside Ed Jones.

"Did you ever see Ricky Franks with a red cap on?" Haley asked.

"Not that I recall," Herrera stated.

"Living around here with the Texas Rangers, a lot of people have red caps, wouldn't you say?" Haley asked.

"I'm sure there are," Herrera replied. He was doing as he had been taught in probation training—when testifying, keep your answers short, don't expound or give personal opinions.

Haley established that many times when Franks had appeared in Herrera's office, he had been accompanied by his wife, Judy. Herrera couldn't disagree with Haley's portrayal of Judy as a wife who tried to run her husband's business, often wanting to stay in with Ricky as he met with Herrera. He explained that occasionally Franks would ask his wife to leave and "get out of my business," but that she would soon return wanting to know about their discussions.

Judy Franks smiled as she listened to herself described as a meddling wife.

"She was kind of running the show, wasn't she?" Haley asked.

"She did a lot, yes, sir," Herrera admitted.

Haley seized the opportunity again to portray his client as somewhat slow, living with his in-laws, seldom holding down a job, and blaming Franks's situation on his mental capacity.

Greg Miller wasn't going to let Leon Haley's implications slide. On redirect he quickly addressed Franks's ability to communicate.

"On all these times you saw Richard Franks, were

you able to carry on conversations with him?" Miller asked.

"Yes, sir, I was."

"Did you talk to him?" Miller continued.

"Yes, sir.

"Did you ever have any trouble communicating with him?" Miller wound down.

"No, sir."

"Thank you." Miller was finished, but Haley had two final questions.

"The bottom line is the one thing you knew is that he had some mental retardation. That's what you knew, isn't it?" Haley asked vigorously.

"I would say he's a slow learner," Herrera said firmly, finally having lost his initial nervousness.

"And with him being a slow learner, every once in a while, when you would have conversations with him, he wouldn't understand things and you would have to explain it to him. Isn't that fair?" Haley pressured Herrera.

"I probably had to explain some things to him," Herrera agreed.

Finally Herrera was excused. He drew in a deep breath and exhaled slowly. His testimony over, he was anxious to get back to Wise County.

The state's final witness was Lawrin Dean, a counselor at Psychotherapy Services. In 1999, Dean had conducted group therapy with about fourteen men, including Ricky Franks. She was cautious not to mention that the counseling sessions were for convicted sex offenders. Dean told the jury that Franks had last attended the group meeting on March 25, 1999, from 10:00 to 11:30 A.M., the day prior to Opal's abduction.

Miller, as well as many of the investigators on the

case, believed some unknown factor had been the catalyst for Franks's violent behavior. Something had made him lose control, seek out a victim, and ultimately select Opal Jennings as the object of his wrath. Miller suspected that unknown factor may have been something said in Franks's last treatment session.

During the session Franks had become angry, so irate, in fact, that he had stormed out in the middle of the group session. It was the next afternoon that Opal Jennings was abducted.

During her testimony Lawrin Dean told the court that throughout the six months Franks was in counseling, he consistently had long, stringy hair, was skanky-looking, and unkempt. Although she remembered Franks's long, brownish blond hair under a cap, the counselor couldn't recall the color of the hat.

When Leon Haley began his questioning, he went straight to the main issue of their defense. "Ricky was a little bit slow, wasn't he?" Haley asked.

"He functioned fine," Dean replied.

Although Haley continued to pound the question of Franks's mental retardation, none of the witnesses for the state would concur that the accused kidnapper was anything more than slow.

Greg Miller and his prosecution team had other witnesses to call—in particular, experts who would refute the defense's allegations that Richard Lee Franks's retardation limited his mental capacity to that of a child. However, the prosecutors decided to hold them in reserve as rebuttal witnesses. They'd be called after anticipated defense testimony in support of Franks's alleged retardation. Therefore, Greg Miller rose and addressed the court.

"Your Honor, the state rests."

CHAPTER 14

During what Judge Gill called a "stretch break," members of the gallery mulled around the hall outside the courtroom. Many waited with much anticipation for the calling of the first defense witness, while others voiced their disappointment. The latter had been waiting with eager expectancy for some new revelation connecting Richard Lee Franks to the Opal Jennings case, some "smoking gun" to prove without a doubt that Franks had not only taken the girl . . . but killed her.

Following the break, everyone took their seats as the defense called their first witness.

Judith Strine, an older, fair-skinned woman, walked to the witness stand to testify on behalf of Richard Franks. Strine nervously fidgeted as she awaited questions from Edward Jones. Jones planned to make her testimony quick and concise.

Jones asked the telephone assembler if she could tell the jury what she was doing on March 23, 1999, three days before Opal Jennings's disappearance.

"Me and my husband went to Saginaw, where I had had my wedding rings in pawn, and we had stopped between the Cash America and the Harvest

Grocery Store. We were parked . . ." Mrs. Strine
began to ramble.

"Slow down and let me help you through this,"
Jones instructed. He wanted to ask specific questions
and wanted Mrs. Strine to respond in such a way
that the jury would be able to understand her entire
testimony.

As instructed by Jones, Mrs. Strine stepped down
from the witness-box and walked to a map displayed
at the front of the courtroom. Before returning to her
seat, she indicated with a large X where the grocery
and Cash America pawnshop were located.

"What were you doing?" Jones asked.

"We were sitting in the car. I was trying to hurry him
up because I wanted my wedding rings," Mrs. Strine
said, referring to her husband. She explained they
had pawned her jewelry for $150 needed cash. They
had returned to the strip mall shop to reclaim the jewelry when she noticed a woman and a child coming
out of the IGA (Independent Grocer's Asso.) store.

"There was a gentleman that was following very
closely to them," Mrs. Strine testified.

"Who noticed the man and the little girl and the
older lady?" Jones asked.

"My husband. He noticed how pretty Opal's eyes
were. He said, 'That little girl has the prettiest blue
eyes,'" Mrs. Strine remarked.

"What was the little girl doing?" Jones questioned.

"She was holding her grandmother's hand as they
were coming out of the store," Mrs. Strine explained.

The witness stated she thought the little girl was
about five or six years old.

"What brought your husband's attention to that
person?" Jones asked, concerning the man who was
seen walking closely behind the child.

"Because the gentleman was following so close to

them, it was like he was just looking the little girl up and down, like any man would look a woman up and down," Mrs. Strine replied.

"How close was he standing to the little girl?" Jones asked.

"Not even that far apart," Mrs. Strine stated, raising her hands and holding them less than two feet apart.

"Give the jury a description of exactly what that man looked like," Jones instructed.

"He was five foot seven, brownish hair pulled back in a ponytail. His face looked like he had been working out in the sun. He had a dark complexion, wearing a red baseball hat. Apparently he'd been working out in the sun wearing sunglasses," Mrs. Strine said.

"Would you describe him as having a wrinkled face?" Jones asked.

"Yes, like somebody that had been out in the sun too long."

When Jones asked if the man appeared to be stalking the girl, Mrs. Strine concurred, stating that when the child and woman would stop, so would the man. When they continued on, he would follow. The witness implied that the stop-and-go behavior had occurred for several minutes before the man noticed her and her husband watching him from their car.

"How far away was he from you?" Jones questioned.

"From here to this lady here," Mrs. Strine said, pointing to the court reporter seated some five or six feet in front of her.

The witness reported that after hearing of Opal's disappearance, she had made a call to the FBI regarding what she had seen in front of the grocery store and pawnshop. She claimed the child had been Opal and the woman with her, Audrey Sanderford. She also stated that the man she saw following Opal matched the description released by police of her abductor.

Judith Strine commented that neither police nor the FBI had contacted her concerning her sighting. She did admit that the defense's investigator had met with her and her husband.

"You agreed to come forward and see if Ricky was the same person you saw that day outside the Cash America Pawn, three days before the disappearance; is that right?" Jones asked.

"Right."

Judith Strine had gone to the downtown Tarrant County Jail, accompanied by Clifford Ginn, the defense's investigator. As her husband waited downstairs to make his own identification, the witness saw Ricky Franks, standing about five to six feet away from her.

"You looked at Ricky, and is that the person that you saw outside the IGA and the Cash America Pawn three days before Opal's disappearance?" Jones asked.

"No, sir."

Jones passed the witness to the prosecution.

"I just have a few questions because I know you don't want to be here. Okay?" Miller said. "Let me point someone out to you."

Miller turned his back to the witness and raised the palm of his right hand.

"Audrey, would you stand up, please?" Miller instructed Audrey Sanderford.

Opal's grandmother slowly rose to her feet. Her face was drawn, her eyes revealed the strain of the last two days.

"Was this the woman who was with the girl?" Miller asked.

"Yes, sir."

"You described [the man] as five feet seven one hundred and seventy-five pounds?" Miller continued.

"Yes, sir."

"Your husband described him as six foot, two hundred forty pounds," Miller stated.

"Yes, sir."

"That's a pretty big difference, isn't it?"

"Right."

"And you are both adults."

"Yes."

"You are calm, you have your wits about you," Miller said.

"Yes, sir."

"Okay. Do you think we ought to give a four-year-old a little slack on his identification?" Miller retorted.

As soon as the words left Greg Miller's mouth, Edward Jones was on his feet. "Objection. Calls for speculation and irrelevant," Jones said loudly.

"Sustained," Judge Gill replied.

"That's all, thank you," Miller concluded, inwardly suppressing a sly smile.

Mrs. Strine was excused. Her testimony offered little in the way of condemnation *or* vindication for Franks.

On her way out of the courtroom, Mrs. Strine passed her husband on his way in. He was the next defense witness.

Billy Carl Strine and his wife had lived in Saginaw for about two years. Like he'd done with the wife, Jones asked Mr. Strine to identify for the jury the IGA food store and Cash America Pawn on an enlarged map.

At that point the direct examination was turned over to Leon Haley. Mr. Strine told the jury he believed the little girl to be about five years old and the woman with her in her fifties. Just as his wife had described minutes earlier, Mr. Strine testified that when the girl and woman would stop, or go, the man would follow suit.

"What was going through your mind at that time?" Leon Haley asked.

"Well, when the little girl and her granny came out, I told my wife, I said, 'Look at that pretty little girl. She has pretty eyes.' And my wife said yes. So they came out and he was like looking at this little girl and I said, 'Look at that son of a bitch looking at that baby that way.'"

Members of the audience smiled at Mr. Strine's frankness.

Mr. Strine explained that the man he saw was wearing blue jean overalls with stripes, sunglasses, and a baseball cap. His hair was in a ponytail. Mr. Strine stated the man wasn't black or Hispanic, but was a white man with a tan, sort of like he was dirty. As his wife had said earlier, Mr. Strine believed the man weighed about 240 pounds. "He had a pudgy belly," Mr. Strine explained.

With Haley continuing to question his witness, Mr. Strine stated he had notified a friend on the Saginaw police force about the incident on the Monday following Opal Jennings's kidnapping. He affirmed no one ever contacted him about the event, until the investigator for the defense, Clifford Ginn, did.

"When you went up to the jail, what did you say when you saw this young man?" Haley asked as he placed his hands on the shoulders of Ricky Franks. "Is he the person that you saw on March 23, 1999?"

"No, he is not the person that I saw," Mr. Strine replied.

Mr. Strine expanded his description of the man he saw with Opal Jennings and Audrey Sanderford, as about forty years old, with a mustache, and a face that was kind of crinkled. He said he would be able to identify the man if he ever saw him again.

"All right. But that person you saw stalking her was not my client," Haley reiterated.

"No, sir."

"Pass the witness, Your Honor," Haley announced.

Lisa Callahan would question Mr. Strine for the prosecution. After a few preliminary questions, Callahan struck on the discrepancies between Mr. Strine's description of the woman and that of his wife.

"You described the woman you saw with the girl as having orange or reddish hair; is that right?" Callahan asked.

"Yes."

"And your wife described her as a woman with blondish or grayish hair; is that right?"

"I don't know what my wife said."

"Would it be fair to say that you and your wife didn't really agree on the description of the woman?" Callahan said in a nonthreatening tone.

"I don't know what my wife said," Mr. Strine insisted.

Mr. Strine denied that his wife had ever told the FBI that his recollection of the event had come back to him after a period of time, that he initially had forgotten about it.

Callahan's cross-examination took but a few minutes. She ended by asking, "You didn't see the child taken; is that right?"

"Yes."

"You think in your mind that you know the man that took her, even though you weren't there and never saw it," Callahan accused.

"I didn't see the man take her, but I saw a man stalking her out of a grocery store, watching her walk with her granny that day that looked suspicious to me. Like he was going to grab her until he noticed I was watching him and he backed off of them, yeah," Mr. Strine said.

"Okay. So you knew what was in his mind?" Callahan asked.

"Oh yeah. I know what he looks like," Mr. Strine responded.

"Pass the witness," Callahan stated.

With no additional questions from the defense, everyone in the courtroom anticipated Leon Haley's announcement of his next witness.

Mouths dropped open, eyes grew larger with surprise, and heads turned to stare at Leon Haley as he declared, "The defense rests."

Taken by surprise, Miller's head snapped quickly to his left. He stared at Haley questioningly. He had anticipated the defense to call a number of witnesses to support their claim that Richard Lee Franks suffered from a low IQ. The prosecution's rebuttal witnesses were waiting in a nearby office, ready to give their own professional opinions on the defendant's alleged diminished mental capacity. The defense was also expected to produce witnesses that would support their allegations that Franks had been manipulated easily when investigators detained him more than twelve hours and gave him a polygraph test, which he had failed.

Outwardly Miller remained calm, but inside his heartbeat quickened. With the defense abandoning their predicted strategy, the assistant district attorney was prohibited from calling witnesses he had saved in reserve for rebutting their allegations. Miller feared the jury had been left with the impression that Ricky Franks was a mistreated retarded man who had been manipulated into making a false confession. He could only hope the jury would examine all the evidence and conclude, as he and the law enforcement community had, that Richard Lee Franks was guilty.

Leon Haley, on the other hand, believed the state hadn't proved its case. Prosecutors had presented no evidence linking his client directly to the crime; therefore, he felt it would have been overkill to present a lengthy line of defense witnesses.

As Miller, Foran, and Callahan digested the defense's unpredicted tactic, Judge Robert Gill recessed court for the day. Closing arguments would be heard the following morning at eight-thirty. The case would then be turned over to the jury. Only time would tell if the prosecution had been outmaneuvered by the defense.

The following morning the courtroom was filled to capacity. It was expected that closing arguments would be heard, the judge would charge the jury with the task of finding Ricky Franks guilty or not guilty of kidnapping, and they would retire to deliberate. It was anticipated that a verdict would be returned by late afternoon.

Greg Miller walked to stand in front of the jury box. As he looked into the faces of the twelve men and women, he saw nothing that would indicate if they were leaning toward guilty or not guilty.

Miller spoke in a strong, confident voice as he addressed the panel. "I believe that every one of you knows what happened to Opal. As much as everyone wants to see Opal walk through the courtroom doors, it's not going to happen. It's not going to happen."

Audrey Sanderford dropped her head, each inhalation coming quickly. She knew what Greg Miller said was the truth, but neither she, nor anyone close to Opal, wanted to believe it. Audrey wanted Opal to come home, and as long as the little girl's body hadn't been found, she held a glimmer of hope that her granddaughter was still alive.

Miller recapped the case, again explaining the manner in which Franks had appeared before and after Opal's abduction, the car he was driving, his familiarity with the area, and the statement he had given to investigators.

As expected, the defense disagreed with the prosecution. Ed Jones told jurors that the state hadn't presented any evidence linking his client to Opal. He focused on the car and the varying descriptions, and reminded them that several people reported seeing a Hispanic man with a ponytail in the neighborhood.

"The abductor is not in this room," Jones declared. "He never was."

When Leon Haley stood to complete the defense's closing statements, he picked up where Jones had left off, insisting that it was not Ricky Franks who had abducted Opal Jennings. Haley maintained that when Franks talked with the two inmates at the Tarrant County Jail, he simply had been repeating what he already had told investigators.

Haley emphasized Franks's IQ of about 65, the twelve-hour delay at the Special Crimes office, and his client's sleep deprivation during the ordeal. The defense attorney told jurors that the twelve-hour interrogation had left his mentally retarded client fatigued and willing to confess to something he didn't do.

"Investigators were messing with a weak person's mind," Haley stated. "His statement had more to do with authorities manipulating him. Ricky just told detectives what they wanted to hear, thinking that if he did, he could go home."

Then Haley made a charge to the jury. "That is how you get people on trial for something they haven't done. When the state begins to overreach, you (the jury) can prevent these things from happening."

Then, asking the jury to ignore Franks's statement, Haley explained: "He said it, but it isn't even true. There's no evidence to support it. It's not right to convict somebody because we're outraged about Opal's disappearance."

Haley accused investigators of being overzealous in pursuing the case against Franks because they were in a bind to solve the case.

In closing, Haley walked over to his client and, standing behind him, placed his hands on Franks's shoulders.

"He's just trying to go along, to get along with people, so he can go home. So I'm gonna ask you, can Ricky go home?"

Greg Miller buttoned his suit jacket as he rose to address the jury for the final time.

"Mr. Franks's statement is an incomplete confession, and that's enough to bring charges against him," Miller said. "He admits he talked to Opal. Opal tells him she makes good grades. There's only one way Ricky Franks could know that.

"He admits Opal got into his Cougar. He admits he took her to the store. That's enough. You can convict him."

Miller asked the jury to consider more than the defendant's statement, but to also take into account that he told the two jail inmates he had taken her. The lead prosecutor also denied defense contentions that investigators were pressured to make an arrest in the high-profile case.

Miller walked to the prosecution table, picked up a photo, and, holding it against his chest, walked back to the front of the jury box.

"I ask you to send a verdict that says crimes against children will not be tolerated," Miller said.

Then, turning the photo around, Miller softly said, "I want you to look at this little girl."

The jury gazed into the smiling face of Opal Jennings. No tears were shed, but silence fell across the entire courtroom. Only the low voice of Greg Miller could be heard.

"Look at the twinkle in her eyes, her precious smile. Don't reward Richard Franks because he was able to dispose of Opal. He got his satisfaction with Opal. He took her from us. Opal belongs to every one of us. Say a little prayer for Opal."

The courtroom remained quiet as Miller took his seat and waited for Judge Gill to address the jury. Greg Miller, Robert Foran, and Lisa Callahan had done their jobs to the best of their abilities. As in every trial, the verdict now rested with the jury. The verdict would be their report card. If the prosecution had performed well and made their case, Ricky Franks would go to prison for life. If not, then Franks could go free. Free to abduct, assault, and kill another North Texas child.

CHAPTER 15

Once the prosecution and the defense had completed their closing arguments, the jury was charged with the weighty task of determining the guilt or innocence of Richard Franks. Even though Greg Miller had indicated his belief that Opal was dead, jurors would only discuss evidence concerning the six-year-old's kidnapping.

To convict Franks of aggravated kidnapping, jurors had to find that he abducted Opal with the intent to terrorize her, inflict bodily injury, or violate or abuse her sexually.

To prove Franks abducted her, jurors would have to find that he held her in a place where she was not likely to be found. Because Opal was younger than fourteen, prosecutors only had to prove that Franks took her somewhere, not that she was forced or restrained.

If Franks was convicted of aggravated kidnapping, Judge Gill, not the jury, would assess his punishment. Because Richard Franks had a prior conviction for child sexual assault, he faced an automatic life sentence.

Spectators and members of both the Franks and Sanderford families nervously paced the courtroom and adjacent hall, anxiously looking toward the door that led to the jury room at the rear of the jury box. They also listened for the brash buzzer the jury foreman would press to indicate the twelve men and women had reached a decision.

One hour led to two, and there was still no word from the jury. Tensions mounted. When the buzzer finally sounded, indicating the jury was summoning the bailiff, all eyes darted toward the door to the jury room. But the jury hadn't reached a decision. Instead, they sent a note to Judge Gill indicating they were in disagreement over the testimony of five-year-old Spencer Williams.

The twelve-member panel filed back into the courtroom, taking their seats, where they had listened to testimony during the four-day trial.

State district judge Robert Gill held the court reporter's transcribed notes and read Spencer Williams's testimony. Young Spencer had testified that a man abducted his friend Opal from outside her grandmother's Saginaw home. He had explained that Opal screamed as she was being placed inside a man's car on March 26, 1999, while playing with him and her two-year-old cousin, Austin. Spencer had told the jury that the car taking Opal away was dark in color with a star on the back.

Jurors, having heard the testimony they requested, returned to the jury room to deliberate further. As the day dragged on with no verdict, the strain of waiting caused friction between members of the Franks family and some of the witnesses who had testified during the trial. Shouting erupted and television cameras moved in to catch the confrontation on tape.

Feeling television cameras had invaded the family's privacy, Harold Hemphill, Franks's half brother, raised his right hand toward the spying cameras, his middle finger extended as his remaining fingers

clenched into a defiant fist. Cameras recorded the ob-
scene gesture, further antagonizing Hemphill.
Rodney Franks later denied the allegation that he, too,
had "shot the bird" at the press, arguing that someone had misconstrued his actions when he innocently had scratched his head.

Even if Rodney Franks's explanation was true,
Leon Haley asked Rodney Franks and Harold
Hemphill to leave the courthouse.

Outside, on the steps of the Tarrant County Justice
Center, Hemphill and Rodney Franks continued to
expound on the injustice of their brother's arrest
and trial. Inside, the mood, although tense, was more
composed as the families of Ricky Franks and Opal
Jennings waited. The Franks family hoped to take
Ricky home; the Sanderford family knew that whatever the verdict, they might never see Opal again.

After they'd deliberated almost seven hours, Judge
Gill excused the jury panel for the night, asking
them to return at eight-thirty the following morning
to continue discussions. The jury hadn't indicated
they were hopelessly deadlocked, giving rise to the
hope that they would be able to agree on a verdict
eventually.

The defense saw the delay as a positive indication
that their client would be exonerated. "I think it's a
pretty good sign that they haven't come to a decision yet," Ed Jones told the crowd of reporters waiting for the long-expected verdict. "The longer they
take, it means they are really looking carefully at the
evidence."

Prosecutors declined to comment on the amount
of time being spent by the jury on deciding Franks's
guilt or innocence, but Greg Miller was leery. He
knew that, historically, the longer a jury took to reach
a verdict, the less likely a conviction. Perhaps the

best he could hope for was a hung jury. Miller didn't sleep much that night, and he rose early to drive from his home in neighboring Arlington to downtown Fort Worth and, once again, sit and wait for the jury's decision.

Perhaps it was the lack of sleep, perhaps the frustration at no longer having control over his case, but Miller looked fatigued. His normally clear green eyes were veiled with concern. When the buzzer sounded and a bailiff called Miller at his office to inform him that the jury was coming in, Miller simply straightened his tie and headed to Judge Gill's courtroom. The outcome of the trial was no longer in his hands. Miller, like the others who waited to hear the jury's decision, would have to accept their verdict.

As the twelve men and women filed into the jury box, their faces reflected the twelve long hours they had spent over two days in deliberations. There was no hint what their final decision would be.

In a strong, authoritative voice, Judge Gill spoke into the mike affixed to his bench. "The jury reports they are deadlocked on the guilt or innocence of Richard Lee Franks. I'm declaring a mistrial and will set a new trial date."

Leon Haley, Ed Jones, and Patrick Davis suppressed smiles at hearing the news. Ricky Franks turned to his family, his face expressing more confusion than relief. Even if Franks didn't realize what Judge Gill meant by mistrial, his attorneys knew it was a victory. They were encouraged that the jury had considered all the evidence and hadn't been swayed by the emotions surrounding six-year-old Opal Jennings's disappearance. But above all, they were pleased that Ricky Franks hadn't been found guilty.

Across the aisle Greg Miller, Robert Foran, and Lisa Callahan stood expressionless. Anyone that knew the three determined prosecutors knew that the mistrial was taken as a defeat. They had prepared well, and although there was no physical evidence to present to the jury, Miller remained resolute that he pursued the case against the right man.

"Ricky Franks took Opal Jennings. We'll try to do a better job the next time," Miller vowed.

Ricky Franks's mother clinched her hands and closed her eyes when she heard Judge Gill's words. Franks's wife, Judy, beamed.

Audrey Sanderford's tight lips, furrowed brow, and rigid posture gave away the anger she felt inside. She wasn't surprised the trial ended in a hung jury. She wouldn't have been amazed if Franks had even been found not guilty of the charges. Audrey had never accused Richard Franks of kidnapping her granddaughter.

"This has always been the state's case," Audrey later told reporters. "This was never my case. *My* opinion has no consequence in this."

Audrey's harsh words reflected the animosity she had developed for Greg Miller over the course of trial preparation. Audrey believed the focus of everyone connected with the case should be on finding Opal, not on convicting someone for her kidnapping.

"We need to get out there and work for Opal. We need to get back to the business of finding my child," Audrey stated.

As spectators exchanged opinions on the jury's inability to produce a verdict, and lawyers for both sides gathered their books and briefcases, Ricky Franks looked toward his family with an expression of dazed uncertainty.

Did Franks think he would be going home, as Ed Jones had asked the jury to let him do? Did he realize he would be confined to the Tarrant County Jail for an as-yet-undetermined amount of time awaiting a new trial?

His attorneys made no request to reduce the $1,000,000 bail set when Franks was first arrested.

When the bailiffs approached Franks, each taking an arm to lead him back through the underground passageway that led from the courthouse to the jail, he had a momentary flash of anger before he displayed what appeared to be a sense of understanding and acceptance.

Ricky Franks finally understood he wouldn't be going home that day.

The Richard Franks jury panel waited patiently inside the jury room. Greg Miller wanted to speak to them personally, as he did with every case—win, lose, or draw. He began by thanking them for their service and their efforts in trying diligently to come to a verdict. He then discovered the jury had twice been deadlocked, with six voting guilt and six favoring acquittal. The jury's final vote was split seven to five in favor of conviction.

"I'd like to ask you about my case. What didn't I do to persuade you Ricky Franks kidnapped Opal Jennings? What more could I have done?" Miller asked.

A middle-aged woman spoke up. "Look at the picture," she said, picking up a photo of Franks's car.

"What?" Miller asked, glancing down at the photo.

"Look at it the way a four-year-old would look at it," the juror stated.

Miller stared at the 8-by-10-inch glossy color photo of Richard Franks's Mercury Cougar. His forehead wrinkled as he attempted to understand what the woman was saying.

"The boy said there was a star on the back. You-all kept talking about the emblem on the trunk deck, look at the photo as if you were only about three feet tall. Do you know what you see?"

Miller continued to stare at the picture in which the rear of the Cougar was depicted.

"There's a star on the license plate. A four-year-old would see the star on the plate and remember it," she said.

The identification of the car had been a problem for the jurors. It was no wonder Spencer hadn't recognized any of the Dodge automobiles at CarMax, he hadn't been talking about an emblem at all, but the star that appears on the license plates of most Texas vehicles.

Miller swore he wouldn't let the identification of the car stonewall the next trial. He would cover it thoroughly, leaving no doubt in the next jury's mind.

September 18, 2000, was the date Judge Robert Gill set for the retrial of Richard Lee Franks, 2½ months after Franks's mistrial. Greg Miller vowed to present a stronger case.

"It will be a different trial," Miller announced with confidence. "We'll put on all of the witnesses that we would have used for rebuttal last time. We'll do a few things differently this time. Hindsight's a wonderful thing when you're a trial lawyer."

It was somewhat of a surprise that Leon Haley, Ed Jones, and Patrick Davis remained on the case to try it a second time. Most veteran court watchers thought the hung jury to be a victory for the defense and wondered why would the three lawyers risk taking on a case they could possibly lose.

On September 18, 2000, sixty-five prospective jurors sat in Judge Gill's courtroom ready to be questioned by both the defense and prosecution. From the sixty-five, twelve would try, as had their predecessors, to determine Richard Lee Franks's guilt or innocence.

The defense planned to focus on the police interrogation in which Franks had admitted he had had contact with Opal Jennings. They intended to concentrate on their client's mental state at the time of the interrogation and his diminished mental capacity. Haley felt that if the jury kept an open mind and gave Franks a fair trial, they would find him not guilty.

Greg Miller and his team were anxious to get on with the second trial. It had been an exhausting 2½ months preparing for their second courtroom faceoff. Miller had endured the constant questioning of Audrey Sanderford, the persistent scrutiny of the press, and harassment from one of Franks's relatives. He wanted the Ricky Franks case disposed of and a conviction secured.

Miller also had been living with the image of Opal Jennings in his head for more than a year—her luminous eyes, the way her mouth turned up at the corners when she smiled, the innocence reflected in her young face. Miller believed without reservation that Ricky Franks had kidnapped Opal, and he felt certain that Franks had killed her. It would be a no-holds-barred prosecution, even if it became the battle of the psychologists, one where the defendant's IQ would be evaluated by professionals brought in by both the defense and the prosecution. Miller pledged that every witness would be ready, every witness would be called. He knew that in the end Franks's mental capacity would be determined by the twelve-member jury.

Miller threw himself into the second trial with even more dedication than the first, promising himself that if the trial again ended in a hung jury, he would not be the one to lead the prosecution on a third attempt to convict Richard Lee Franks.

CHAPTER 16

Audrey Sanderford made her way into Judge Gill's Tarrant County courtroom, where she would once again hear testimony concerning Opal's disappearance. She looked frail. Her face was drawn, her posture slumped. A pink corsage was attached to the left side of her black-and-white jacket, a gift from friends who wanted to bolster her spirits for the difficult time ahead. Audrey's hair held a fresh rinse of dark brown color, but her efforts at looking her best had done little to mask the stress she was under.

Robert Sanderford followed shortly behind Audrey. It was obvious as they took their places on the wooden pewlike benches reserved for the family that they were no longer together. Audrey sat a couple of rows behind the front railing, while Robert took a place near the back of the room. They didn't speak.

Leola Sanderford, her dark bangs curled and her long hair reaching below her shoulders, took a seat next to Teresa. Leola's aunt had been her rock through the ordeal of her daughter's abduction, Franks's arrest, and the first kidnapping trial. She stayed close to Teresa, absorbing her strength.

For thirteen months Richard Franks had been in

custody in the Tarrant County Jail. With his bond set at $1,000.000, Franks's family had no way of securing his release, and even if they had, following his mistrial three months earlier, Franks's defense team hadn't asked for a bond reduction. Their client was protected in his present location, tucked away from the prosecution, the press, and even his own family. It had not been determined from whom the harassment received by Assistant District Attorney Greg Miller had originated, but speculation was high that members of Franks's family had initiated them. It was better if Franks's contact was limited.

As Ricky Franks traveled the now-familiar underground passageways to all of Tarrant County criminal courts, he ultimately entered the courtroom of Judge Robert Gill. His clean-shaven face revealed the sunless pallor of someone incarcerated for an extended amount of time. His hair was neatly trimmed, and he was dressed in a dark suit, white shirt, and tie, just as he had been only months earlier. Franks said nothing, but a broad smile crossed his face as he spotted his family sitting to the left of the defense table. His eyes then narrowed and his mouth formed into a tight line as Greg Miller and Lisa Callahan came into the courtroom and sat at the wooden table to the right of where Franks was sitting with his lawyers.

"Are both sides ready for the jury?" Judge Gill asked. Gill's demeanor expressed the command of the courtroom for which he was best known. Like the attorneys for both the state and the defense, it was believed Gill wanted this to be the last time he would preside over the kidnapping trial of Richard Franks.

"The state's ready," Miller replied. Lisa Callahan stood beside Miller. Absent was Robert Foran, who had been assigned another trial in another Tarrant County courtroom.

"Defense is ready, Your Honor," Haley stated.

"Good morning, ladies and gentlemen," Gill said as he addressed the jury. "We're ready to start the trial. I have to place you all under oath as jurors. Please raise your right hands."

Four women and eight men had been chosen from a jury pool of sixty-five to hear the second trial of Richard Lee Franks. The jurors raised their right hands and accepted the oath of service. Judge Gill explained the order in which the state and defense would present their cases, just as he had three months earlier to another jury, which had failed to reach a verdict for or against Franks.

"The state may read the indictment," Judge Gill said when he completed his comments to the jury.

Greg Miller rose from the prosecution table and moved across the courtroom to stand before Ricky Franks. Franks, likewise, rose and stood with his attorneys, facing Miller.

Commanding in a dark suit, white shirt, and patterned tie, Miller captured the attention of the jury, which listened intently to the formal charge of aggravated kidnapping. Although Miller looked at the defendant as he read the charge, Franks's eyes avoided the prosecutor's cold gaze.

At the end of the reading, Judge Gill asked, "Mr. Franks, to this indictment, you may plead guilty or not guilty."

Like he had during the first trial, Ricky Franks spoke in a soft but distinct voice. "Not guilty."

The formalities were over. It was time for the state to begin again with the prosecution of Richard Lee Franks. Lisa Callahan walked from where she had been sitting beside Miller and stood before the jury.

Casting a striking figure in her black suit, her long

dark hair shining under the bright lights of the court-room, Lisa Callahan began by asking a question.

"Ladies and gentlemen of the jury, I ask you, what are the odds? What are the odds that this defendant, Richard Lee Franks, is one and the same person who kidnapped Opal Jennings March 26, 1999?" Callahan pointed at the defendant as she spoke. "What are the odds?

"Now, we will be presenting to you evidence in this case, evidence of the defendant's actions and evidence of the defendant's deeds, in the months after this offense occurred. And we'll be asking you to consider at each step, what are the odds that a person could say the things this defendant did, and do the things that he did, and not be the guilty person?"

Callahan began to lay out for the jury the prosecution's case—how she and Miller would present their evidence—and named some of the witnesses they would call to prove Franks's guilt.

"We will present you evidence from people who were there right before the offense, when it occurred, and immediately afterward. The next group of witnesses will be individuals that knew this defendant, Richard Franks, for various periods of time. That the description given by Spencer Williams of a slender white male, with long hair and a ponytail, and wearing a red ball cap, fits this defendant. That the midsized dark car with dark tinted windows is a car that he was known to drive," Callahan explained.

The attractive ADA informed jurors that their witnesses would tell how immediately after Opal's abduction Franks had changed his appearance dramatically and that he had knowledge of the area where Opal was taken.

"What are the odds?" Callahan asked again. "Ask yourself, what are the odds that the same individual who would commit this crime would do these things, these attempts to change and avoid apprehension?"

Callahan touched on the upcoming testimony of investigators involved in the case and the statement Franks gave stating that he took Opal.

"Now, that is what the state's evidence will show you in this case. And I ask you, listen to every bit of evidence, absorb every detail, focus on every drop that we can bring you. Because at the conclusion of this case, we will ask you to find that the odds are not only beyond a reasonable doubt, but beyond any doubt that this defendant is one and the same person that kidnapped Opal Jennings on March 26, 1999, that he is guilty, and we will ask you to find him guilty."

As Callahan took her seat beside Greg Miller, Audrey Sanderford took a long, deep breath. She had not been well in the weeks leading to the second trial. The loss of Opal, the media demands, the stress of the first trial and the inconclusive outcome, as well as the strain the last eighteen months had taken on her marriage, had once again sent her to the hospital for a stress-related condition.

It was time to move on, but Audrey knew that would never be possible until Opal's kidnapper was brought to justice. But she wasn't sure that Ricky Franks was responsible. Greg Miller had gone over all the evidence and it was apparent he was convinced they were prosecuting the right man. The only thing Audrey was certain of was that she felt sympathy for Ricky Franks's mother and she wanted the whole thing to be over for both of them.

Leon Haley stood beside his client; then he walked to the jury box. His ebony face was serious before a small smile turned up at the corners of his full lips as he addressed the jury.

"What are the odds?" Haley began, repeating

Callahan's words. "That's good. What are the odds
that what they have told you is going to be totally different? There are always two sides to a story. So what
are the odds?"

Haley paced in front of the jury box, capturing the
attention of each juror.

"I anticipate the odds are going to show this. It's
going to show that a little bitty girl named Opal Jennings was playing in her yard, like any little child
would play. And the odds of somebody coming and
snatching a little bitty baby, and nobody ever knowing where that child is again, is disgusting to all of us.

"But what are the odds that, as the state has said
here today, that the state, in their efforts to find the
culprit, the person that did this, they have a mass investigation. The FBI, the Saginaw police, the Tarrant County District Attorney's investigators, are all
involved in this mass effort. Thousands of man-hours,
about thirty-five agents involved. Everybody was trying
to find Opal Jennings's abductor."

Haley looked toward the prosecutors' table and
pointed.

"One day a lead is passed off to a group of investigators with this office. And in a rush to judgment, they
try to do the right thing. They take the lead they got
on Ricky, who I anticipate the evidence will show has
an IQ of about sixty-five, a young man with a child's
mentality of about ten to twelve years old. They follow
the young man around. And what are the odds that
you are not doing anything but minding your business, going to the store, being with your wife or your
other family members? And what are the odds that
one day you are abducted by seven people from the
Tarrant County District Attorney's Office and told you
have a traffic warrant? But what are the odds that
somebody would snatch somebody over a traffic ticket

and, instead of taking them to jail so they can make bond and their family can get them out of jail, they take them to the Tarrant County District Attorney's Office and lock them in a room?"

Haley had the full attention of the jurors. They were following his scenario, captivated by the story. He told them that his client had been interrogated by a person trained to manipulate the minds of individuals. A person trained to "mess with you," to "screw with your head." He stated that investigators hadn't allowed his client to sleep, had only given him soft drinks and some chips in the twelve hours he had been held for questioning. Haley then emphasized in an accusatory fashion that investigators had gotten what they had worked for, a statement from Ricky Franks indicating his role in Opal Jennings's disappearance.

"And I anticipate the evidence will show that he steadily kept crying, that he steadily kept telling them, 'No, no, no, I didn't do this. You're confusing me, you're manipulating me. Can I go home?' That's what the evidence is going to show," Haley announced.

The experienced trial attorney lastly stated with outward confidence that the evidence would show that Ricky Franks was a scapegoat, that the DA's investigators made a very serious error they couldn't rectify. Haley informed the jury that there was no physical evidence that tied his client to the offense. No blood, no fingerprints, no saliva.

"I'm going to ask you, and I'm going to expect from you, a not guilty [verdict] when this is over," Haley stated. "We are tired of this. Thank you."

As Haley sat down, Miller mentally agreed with Haley. He, too, was tired of the Franks case. The Sanderfords were tired of it. The Frankses were tired of it. But they all realized the case wouldn't go away until Ricky Franks was definitively found guilty or not guilty of abducting Opal Jennings.

Before the first state's witness was called to testify, Judge Gill invoked the rule of sequestration, commonly known as "the rule." Sequestration of witnesses was frequently ordered by the court at the request of the parties to insure that in-court testimony of each witness not be colored by what another witness said.

Greg Miller had other witness concerns.

"Is the court going to instruct them to not watch TV, the TV monitors? How do you want to handle that, Judge?" Miller asked.

Reporters and cameramen from all four local news channels had positioned themselves right outside Judge Gill's courtroom. In order to keep an eye on the events of the trial, each station had a monitor that was fed by one pool camera located inside the courtroom. The state, as well as the defense, wanted to make certain that scheduled witnesses were not privy to the proceedings.

"They have subpoenaed one of the Frankses and that was a problem before," Haley stated. "He's out there griping right now. But it's up to Greg, it's his witness, but we really don't want him out in the hall. He caused a disturbance last time. It needs to be dealt with somehow."

Judge Gill agreed. He didn't want any potential hallway ruckus to run over into his courtroom. The judge ordered that Harold Hemphill be told to leave and he would be contacted when it was time for him to testify.

"Okay. I would like one of you to go with me to tell him," Miller remarked to Haley.

The two attorneys left the court momentarily to

speak to the hostile witness. When they returned, Lisa Callahan called the first of the state's witnesses.

Teresa Ann Sanderford walked from her seat on the bench next to her husband to take her place in the witness chair. She appeared more confident than when she took the stand in the first of Ricky Franks's trials. Although her voice quavered only slightly at first, she soon projected self-assurance as she spoke of her family. Teresa knew what would be asked of her and she was ready to tell the story. She only hoped this would be the last time she would have to take the stand.

As before, Callahan guided Teresa through identifying photos of her Saginaw neighborhood and its connecting streets. She spoke of Austin and Spencer, Opal's playmates, and she told them about Opal.

The savvy assistant DA had Opal's aunt paint a picture of a child who was a good student, mischievously fun-loving, and adored by everyone. Teresa brought to life a child whom the jury wouldn't meet personally, but would never forget. Callahan presented a photo of Opal. It had been taken at her school only about a month before her kidnapping. Crooked bangs and dark hair framed her bright, happy face.

Callahan walked slowly down the double row of jurors, showing them the photo of Opal Jennings. She was putting a face to the victim. It was a face of innocence and hope, a face that had been tragically snatched from her family with no warning. The picture of the smiling child made the crime personal. The jury was being asked to convict a man of aggravated kidnapping, not of an unknown, unseen child, but of Opal Jennings, the girl with the captivating smile and deep blue eyes that stared out of the photo as Callahan passed by.

As she had done in Franks's earlier trial, Teresa told about the kids playing in the yard, the grandparents checking on them periodically, and of hearing Austin crying on the porch. A terrifying cry she would never forget.

Ricky Franks stared at Teresa Sanderford with blank indifference. He showed no emotion.

Teresa described the steps she had taken to find Opal and the fear at not being able to locate the child.

When Teresa recalled the description of the car and the man who had snatched Opal away, Ricky Franks's eyes began to flutter. He blinked them tightly as if he were afflicted with an uncontrollable twitch that occurred twenty times a minute. As he blinked, he moved restlessly in his chair.

Callahan ended her direct examination by asking, "Mrs. Sanderford, since March 26, 1999, have you ever heard from Opal again?"

"No," Teresa said softly.

"Have you ever seen her again?" Callahan pursued.

"No," Teresa said, bowing her head slightly.

"Pass the witness," Callahan announced.

Teresa Sanderford took in a deep, long breath as Edward Jones, attorney for Ricky Franks, approached the witness stand. Teresa exhaled and waited for Jones's questioning to begin.

"Now, you have testified before, haven't you?" Jones asked.

"Yes."

"You testified at the last trial back in June of 1999," Jones stated.

"Yes."

"And in June of '99, correct me if I'm wrong, nowhere on that date did you testify to the fact that

Spencer Williams told you that and pointed to a black car that went by and said it was a Chrysler or Cougar-type product and that's the car that got Opal. Did you ever testify to that the last time you were here?" Jones asked, repeating testimony Teresa had given to Callahan.

"No, sir, no one asked me," Teresa responded calmly.

"They didn't ask you that last time?" Jones asked.

"I don't believe so, no," Teresa stated.

"Okay. But you didn't tell the last jury that, did you? But you told them that today; is that right?" Jones asked.

"Yes," Teresa responded calmly.

Jones continued with his questioning concerning the car, going over other cars seen in the neighborhood near the time of Opal's abduction. When he was finished, Jones had accomplished his objective. Although Teresa was certain the car in the photo, Ricky Franks's car, was very much like the car she had seen cruising their neighborhood in the weeks prior to Opal's disappearance, she couldn't swear they were one and the same. Again she couldn't place Ricky Franks in that car, or that specific car in the neighborhood.

Jones was creating doubt, just as he had in the minds of jury number one. He naturally hoped for a verdict of not guilty, but even another hung jury would be acceptable. If only one juror out of the twelve was convinced that Ricky Franks hadn't been in his car watching Opal Jennings for weeks, hadn't snatched her from her playmates on the day of her disappearance, Jones would have enough to see Ricky Franks go home.

After several additional questions concerning the automobile seen in Opal's Saginaw neighborhood, Jones's tone softened as he changed his line of questioning. "Let's be fair, ma'am. You want this over with, don't you? It's been a horror for your family, hasn't it?"

Teresa took a long, deep breath. Opal's disappearance had been a nightmare. The grief they had all felt, the fear for Opal, the anxious moments each time the phone rang, hoping, praying that it was good news about their precious Opal. Yes, it had been a horror, a terror that no one who has never lost a child would know, and one Teresa wished on no one.

She released her breath and stared at Ed Jones. "It has been very hard on our family and, of course, we would like it to be drawn to a conclusion," she said in a controlled voice.

"You want closure, right?" Jones asked, moving closer to the witness-box. "You and your family want it over with, right? Everybody wants it over with, don't they?"

"I would assume so. Our family, of course, would like for everything to end, but, you know, we just have to wait and see what happens," Teresa said with little emotion in her voice.

"Right, but if Ricky didn't do this, you don't want him to be convicted, do you?" Jones questioned.

"No," Teresa answered honestly. She and the family wanted Opal's abductor punished. If that be Ricky Franks, fine; if not, then they wanted the real perpetrator caught and dealt with. But multiple law enforcement agencies believed they had the right man; she could only trust their judgment.

Bessie, Ricky's mother, and Judy, his wife, wiped tears from their eyes as Ed Jones asked his final questions of Teresa Sanderford. The women both wore T-shirts that read: WHEN GOD CLOSES A DOOR HE OPENS A WINDOW. They believed Ricky had not kidnapped

Opal Jennings. They wanted a not guilty verdict. They wanted Ricky home.

After completing his questioning, the defense passed Teresa to the prosecution for additional questioning.

Lisa Callahan pushed her glasses onto the bridge of her nose as she approached the witness-box. After a number of follow-up queries, Callahan turned to Jones's final line of questioning. Callahan asked Teresa if she wanted Ricky Franks convicted if he was not the person that had abducted Opal. If she had put any pressure on the prosecution to convict just any person of the crime, or if she had been breathing down their necks to get someone responsible for the act.

Teresa assured Callahan, and the jury, that was not the case.

"If he is the person that has taken Opal, then I want him to get what he—what the law allows for him to get, jail time or whatever. If he is not the person, then he needs to go home. I'm seeking justice."

Judy Franks wiped tears from her eyes, coated with dark blue eye shadow, as her mother-in-law put her face in her hands and wept. The two women, connected by one man, both hoped that Ricky would be going home soon.

But Teresa Sanderford was only the first state's witness to take the stand. There would be many to follow who, convinced of his guilt, would testify that Ricky Franks was the man who had abducted Opal. As much as his family wanted Ricky Franks to go home, there were others that wanted nothing more than to see him spend his life behind bars.

The stage had been set with the testimony of Teresa Sanderford. The initial witnesses called by the defense would be those heard during the first trial. Many of the questions would remain the same and much of the cross-examination by the defense would be similar. If anything appeared noticeably different, it was the determination with which each side approached the tasks of proving guilt or innocence.

On the first day of trial, thirteen witnesses took the stand, including two of Opal's aunts, two former jail inmates, and five-year-old Spencer Williams. Their testimonies remained the same, with the defense taking a more aggressive approach in cross-examination than they had in the previous trial. Some jurors appeared to give their undivided attention to the testimony of each state's witness, while at least one gray-haired man seemed bored by the proceedings.

The addition of state's witness Myra Stevenson, manager of the Decatur, Texas, Golden Fried Chicken, which had once employed Ricky Franks, was presented to show that Franks, unlike the man whom defense attorneys categorized as mentally comparable to a child, was fully competent of holding a job.

Stevenson, her black jeans and blue shirt accented by a black-and-white-striped headband, told the court that in the three to four months Franks had worked for her, he cooked and waited on customers. According to Stevenson, while waiting on customers, Franks had taken orders, made change, and run the cash register. She emphasized that the register was not computerized but did have food dots affixed to help employees with ordering. Giving an example, Stevenson stated Franks would have to know to press four chicken tenders, rather than four tender dinners in order to complete the transaction correctly.

While manning the drive-up window, Franks had also been able to take the order, remember it, and give it to the appropriate customer, in addition to completing the monetary transaction. Stevenson insisted the task could not be completed by a twelve-year-old child, as the defense had suggested. For his efforts Franks had been paid $5.50 an hour.

Franks's former boss described Franks's general appearance as "somewhat clean." He had worn his hair in a ponytail and was sometimes clean shaven, but at other times not. Stevenson admitted Franks hadn't been fired because he was incapable of doing the work, but because he showed up for work dirty, had been sent home to clean up, and had never returned.

Myra Stevenson's testimony ended with Greg Miller asking, "What was your opinion of his intellectual level?"

"If he didn't do something right, I'd say, 'Ricky, you know better than that.' He'd grin. Ricky wasn't dumb."

As Stevenson left the witness chair, Ricky Franks watched her cross the courtroom, a smirk across his face.

A man donning a blue striped Western shirt, blue jeans, and leather belt, with GENE tooled on the back, strolled to the witness-box. Gene Morrison, a retired truck driver, had been asked to testify by the state that he had resided in Saginaw for more than thirty-five years. Many of those years Morrison lived only a few houses from Danny Doyle, Ricky Franks's half brother. Morrison stated he had seen Franks at his brother's house on many occasions. In addition, Doyle had worked on Morrison's plumbing several times, and Franks had been in Morrison's home at least once, helping his brother.

The defense had few questions for Morrison, the state had made their point—Ricky Franks was familiar with the Saginaw neighborhood where Opal Jennings's abduction had taken place.

The jury was excused to return to the jury room while the next witness was questioned outside their presence. Judge Gill would decide if Robert Wood, a Mansfield policeman and former Tarrant County jailer, would be permitted to testify in front of jurors.

Wood, at the time of Franks's arrest and indictment for the kidnapping of Opal Jennings, oversaw Franks at the county jail. Wood had overheard Franks on a couple of occasions tell other inmates that he wouldn't be indicted, because they couldn't find a body. Franks didn't think he would be caught because there was no body. He also had said he picked Opal up, but took her to the store, then dropped her off back at her house. Wood admitted that Franks hadn't told him personally; he had only overheard the conversations between Franks and other inmates. At the time Wood not only overheard the conversations, but he also observed Franks crying in his cell.

"He didn't want to be convicted. He wanted to go home to his family." That was how Wood explained Franks's weeping.

Wood had written up the incidents and given them to his supervisor, as instructed.

Roger Polson, a member of the Mansfield Independent School District (ISD) Police Department, and former Tarrant County jailer, also testified outside the presence of the jury.

Polson, a large man, stated that he, too, had been assigned to the section of the county jail that Ricky Franks was housed in prior to and after his indictment for Opal Jennings's kidnapping. Polson had overheard Franks telling Chris Freeman, aka Andrew Bouyer, who had testified in Franks's first trial, that he had picked Opal up, took her to a convenience store, got a pack of cigarettes—and that's all. Like Wood, Polson insisted he hadn't interrogated Franks, only listened to him talk.

"After he was indicted, I heard him say, 'They can't

indict me, they don't have a body. If they found the body, I'll probably fry—but they'll never find her body.'"

Polson stated that Franks and Freeman would yell back and forth between their cells, indicating that Franks liked to talk a lot, with conversations going on from morning till night.

On Polson's cross-examination Ed Jones stated to the court that the defense would like to present evidence that Ricky Franks was on medication at the time Polson claimed Franks had the discussions with Freeman. Jones requested time to go get the jail records to present at that point in his cross-examination. Judge Gill denied the request.

Jones then asked for time to be given to the defense for supplemental discovery in the form of a motion for a continuance. The motion was denied. Jones requested that the personnel records of Wood and Polson be allowed into evidence by the defense. Judge Gill denied that request. Judge Gill announced that following a recess, both Wood and Polson would be allowed to testify before the jury.

The court broke for the noon recess. Greg Miller, as always, returned to his office to review trial notes. Judy Franks sat on a bench outside the courtroom and waited for permission to take her husband his lunch: two burritos, a Dr Pepper, and two bags of M&M's.

After the recess Greg Miller called Wood to the stand. Ed Jones rose and announced that the defense would like a running objection, as presented outside the presence of the jury.

Both Wood and Polson reiterated statements each had made before the court while the jury was out. Leon Haley took an antagonistic approach in an attempt to discredit the officers.

"When guys are up there charged with offenses

like Ricky Franks, you don't like them much; isn't that fair?" Haley asked Wood.

"No, that's not fair," Wood responded.

Polson reported that Franks had conflicts with several of the men in his area, and although he and Freeman were friends, Franks and Freeman would have occasional tiffs over cigarettes or commissary. The Mansfield ISD officer also stated that if Franks didn't get his way about things, he would get upset.

Most in the courtroom were captivated by the former jailers' accounts of Ricky Franks's life in jail, with the exception of one white-haired bailiff, who snoozed at his post at the front of the courtroom.

The expression on Ricky Franks's face was one of contempt as the second of the two officers was excused. Franks, like most jail inmates, was unaware that everything he said, everything he did, had been closely scrutinized by jailers on each shift.

As in the first trial, James Blackburn, a former jail inmate, testified for the state.

"He said he'd been stalking her for a year and went over to get her to get satisfaction," Blackburn told the second jury.

A male juror, wearing a crisp white shirt, was visibly disturbed by Blackburn's words. He placed his hand over his mouth, his expression angry.

"I took it he meant to have sex with her," Blackburn said.

Lisa Callahan, anticipating the defense's strategy of discrediting the state's witness, presented a chart that indicated that Blackburn had been arrested for unauthorized use of a motor vehicle. Probated and back home by June 26, 2000, he'd seen the news of Franks's arrest. Likewise, Greg Miller presented a similar chart when he called Chris Freeman to the stand.

As Ed Jones cross-examined Freeman, he, too, reviewed the record of the former Tarrant County inmate.

"You are a criminal; don't you agree?" Jones asked.

"No, I don't agree," Freeman replied.

While Jones cited Freeman's past record, Freeman interrupted Jones by saying, "I object."

"You can't object," Jones said. Jones, Franks, his codefense attorneys, and the prosecution all joined in laughter.

Psychologist Lawrin Dean and Special Crimes Assistant Assistant Chief Mike Adair rounded out the first day of testimony, with Adair to continue the following day.

As promised, the prosecution had presented new witnesses not called in the first Franks trial. It was anticipated that even more new witnesses would be called on day two.

CHAPTER 17

Mike Adair, looking as cool and confident as he had the previous day, sat in the witness-box to complete his testimony. He had little left to convey but made one lasting impression with jurors.

Adair informed the men and women of the new panel that initially there had been a number of other suspects in the abduction of Opal Jennings, including her father. Through the investigation these suspects had been cleared, and the case against Richard Franks was the one that stuck. He felt certain Richard Lee Franks was responsible for Opal Jennings's disappearance.

Forensic scientist Max Courtney's testimony may have left confusion in jurors' minds when he stated he was certain of Franks's guilt, even though no DNA evidence linked Franks to the six-year-old's abduction. Courtney confirmed that there was no physical evidence found in Franks's car linking Opal to the vehicle, but Courtney explained he based his conclusion on the vast amount of circumstantial evidence compiled prior to Franks's arrest. He, as others involved in the investigation, considered Franks's past history as a sex offender, his familiarity with the area, his car closely matching the description of the car taking Opal away, his altered appearance soon after the kidnapping, and Franks's own statement given to investigators.

The witness following Courtney was familiar to anyone who had followed the first Franks trial. Jesse Herrera had once served as Ricky Franks's probation officer. Herrera seemed to have lost the tenseness he showed during the June trial. Throughout the aggressive cross-examination by Ed Jones concerning the exact date he had turned over a tip to the FBI, Herrera maintained his composure. Several jurors rolled their eyes, while others visibly drew in deep breaths, obviously turned off by Jones's perceived harassment of the witness.

With the exit of Jesse Herrera, Judge Gill announced a welcome midmorning break. As everyone in the courtroom stood to watch the jury retire to the jury room, Greg Miller picked up a large black plastic binder with a white sheet of paper taped to the outside bearing the name of Richard Franks.

After flipping through more than one of the tabbed indexed sections of the binder, Miller rested his glasses on the table and rubbed his eyes. Those sitting behind Miller saw the wide neck and broad shoulders of the prosecutor, but the weariness on his face was hidden from their view.

After the break Eric Holden spoke of his interview with Franks the night of Franks's arrest for the minor traffic violation. Holden testified until a lunch break was taken, and he was back on the stand after the noon recess. Jurors appeared to listen closely while Miller questioned the witness, but during the defense's cross-examination they appeared disinterested, their eyes heavy and their shoulders slumped.

Lisa Callahan next interviewed Kathy Manning,

leading the investigator through obtaining the traffic warrant for Franks and his arrest. The crowd laughed as Manning explained she had enlarged the Miranda green card on the Xerox machine because she "had trouble with the small print." They chuckled again, giving a break from the intense detail-oriented testimony, when she explained that Charlie Johnson typed Franks's statement because "he was the only typist in the office."

Humor was abandoned when Greg Miller set up an easel in front of the jury box and placed an enlarged copy of Franks's confession on it. Even before Manning began reading Franks's statement, it was apparent jurors were reading it silently to themselves. Faces furrowed; one juror shook his head; another put her hand up to her mouth; while still another folded her arms across her stomach—all visibly shaken by the words of the accused. As Manning read the statement, Franks looked down at the table, avoiding the stares of jurors. When Manning completed the reading, Franks's eyes lifted to look angrily at the female investigator.

Mannings's testimony ended with Ed Jones asking, "In your opinion, don't you think Opal and her family deserve a better investigation?"

"I believe it was a good investigation," Manning replied with assurance. She was excused.

The second day's testimony ended with Danny McCormick. As in the first trial the seasoned investigator was direct in his answers, displaying a no-nonsense manner while explaining the procedures taken by the Special Crimes Unit after apprehending Franks. Judge Gill announced the trial would continue the following morning.

* * *

As day three of Franks's second kidnapping trial began, the defense requested permission to introduce a witness out of order. With permission granted, Dr. Richard Leo took the stand.

A tall, thin man with a short beard and black hair, Dr. Leo held a Ph.D. from UCLA and was in private practice specializing in police interrogations. Dr. Leo's specific expertise was in police interrogation practices, police procedures, and false confessions.

Dr. Leo stated that interviewers always want to verify a suspect's statement, determining if it is true or false, by using four specific criteria:

1. No crime had occurred.
2. A physical impossibility that the suspect could have committed the crime.
3. Scientific exoneration (the DNA doesn't match).
4. The suspect confesses; then someone else comes forward and confesses.

Lisa Callahan scribbled a note on a piece of paper, then turned and handed it to Bill Parker, seated behind her. The note read: "None of his four areas fit this case." Parker, a noted expert himself, nodded slightly. Callahan looked satisfied and turned her attention back to Dr. Leo's testimony.

Dr. Leo stated that according to a 1996 publication by the Department of Justice, in the twenty-nine DNA exonerations cited, 20 percent had false confessions.

According to Dr. Leo, it was first important to find out if the suspect possessed knowledge only the killer could know. He added that, too often, the suspect would feed back what they were told by the police. Dr. Leo stated he believed this feeding of information could be eliminated if all confessions were tape-recorded.

"Alaska and Minnesota require by law that all interrogations be videotaped. It becomes an objective record of the interrogation. It answers 'he said/she said' allegations," Dr. Leo stated.

Dr. Leo added that when a suspect gives a false confession, typically they recant it.

Judge Gill called for a much-needed recess. Jurors, as well as spectators, were growing weary during the doctor's lecture-type testimony.

After the break Lisa Callahan challenged the study cited by Dr. Leo.

"You cite twenty-nine cases mentioned in the article, but there were approximately three hundred eighty-nine thousand interrogations nationwide during that period; is that correct?" Callahan asked.

"Yes."

"The twenty-nine you talk about were only .0007571 percent of all those interrogated. Wouldn't you say the vast majority of confessions are true?"

"Yes."

Dr. Leo left the courtroom en route to his previously scheduled lecture at Claremont College, then on to Cypress the following day for a teaching assignment. He walked with an air of self-importance.

Following the interruption of the state's witnesses by the inclusion of Dr. Leo for the defense, Greg Miller called the next prosecution witness.

Vivian Largent, her brown hair slicked back in a tight bun, told the jury that she had known Judy and Ricky Franks for about two years and had visited their home on many occasions.

"We had normal conversations," Largent stated. "In my opinion he has a lot of common sense."

The witness identified photos of Ricky Franks when

he had a mustache, long hair, and pimples on his face. She told jurors he often wore a red ball cap and had surmised it must have been his favorite.

"I saw Ricky and Judy at noon on March twenty-seventh at my house. He seemed distant, and I asked him what was wrong. He said he had a lot on his mind," Largent stated.

"Did you notice anything unusual about him?" Miller asked.

"His hair, he was almost bald. He had told me he wanted to let it grow until he was thirty-one or thirty-two years old. It was considerably shorter than it is today," Largent remarked.

Everyone in the courtroom turned their attention toward Ricky Franks. His expression remained stoic.

"I saw him off and on until his arrest, but I never saw him wear the red ball cap again," Largent added.

Ed Jones then asked for the defense if Largent had cut Franks's hair for him the week before March 27.

"Yes, I often cut it. I cut it for free," Largent responded. But she insisted she hadn't cut it as short as she had seen it on March 27, 1999, the day after Opal Jennings was abducted.

Next on the state's witness list was Special Agent Lori Keefer. She told the twelve men and women of the jury that she had been with the FBI for 11½ years. She was assigned to the Fort Worth agency in the Violent Crimes squad, dealing with kidnappings, bank robberies, and fugitive matters.

It was difficult for some to believe the soft-spoken, petite, and attractive young woman on the stand was an FBI agent assigned to such criminal activities.

Agent Keefer explained that in July 1999 she had been involved in the O. J. Simpson case, and in August 1999 she had met with Ricky Franks.

As in Franks's first trial Keefer told the jury about

the false scenario given to Franks on the evening of his arrest, and his response.

"He said angrily, 'I knew when I admitted having Opal, I'd get blamed for every crime like it,'" Keefer said.

The statement passed on by Keefer gave rise to conjecture by spectators. Franks had admitted in his statement he'd taken Opal and he admitted it once again when given the false scenario. Why, then, wouldn't the jury believe he had been responsible for her kidnapping?

When the defense had no questions for Keefer, the state called Special Agent Andy Farrell to the stand. Farrell told of his role in heading up the task force for the FBI and the progression of the case. When Farrell was passed to the defense for cross-examination, Judge Gill called for a welcome noon recess.

At 1:20 P.M., Ed Jones began his cross-examination. The senior FBI agent explained that Randy Crawford, Opal's father, had been scrutinized closely as an initial suspect. Although Crawford was living in Nashville at the time, he had once stated if he ever came and picked up Opal, he would take her to East Texas and they would never see her again. Leola Sanderford had believed it was possible that Crawford had taken their daughter, just to get back at her. He had had Opal's name tattooed on his body and professed his love for her, although he hadn't spent much time with Opal during her six years. But Crawford had been eliminated as a person of interest when his alibi in Tennessee had proved credible.

Farrell's long testimony covered all of the points made in the previous Franks trial, and although repetitive for the prosecution, defense, and those spectators who had endured both trials, it was the first time the second jury had heard the evidence. Neither the prosecution nor the defense intended to let anything of evidentiary value go unsaid.

After two hours of cross-examination, the defense passed Andy Farrell for redirect back to the prosecution. At that point in the trial, Judge Gill called for an afternoon recess.

While Ricky Franks rested in the holding cell adjacent to the courtroom, his family milled around outside. Twenty minutes later, they were back in the courtroom.

Farrell spent another long hour on the stand before Greg Miller announced that the state rested its case.

Everyone in the courtroom let out a sigh of relief. The testimonies had been long and tedious. With the defense calling only two witnesses in the previous trial, the courtroom audience anticipated a brief presentation before the judge adjourned the jury and they began deliberations.

But the defense had reviewed their strategy and decided to present expert testimony as to the mental integrity of their client. If the jury believed that Ricky Franks was truly retarded, Haley and Jones hoped they would see the confession as one coerced from a childlike adult and disregard the statement during deliberations. Dr. Daniel Lowrance, Ph.D., was called to testify.

Dr. Lowrance had met with Ricky Franks, reviewed previous IQ tests taken by him prior to Franks's first trial, and evaluated his school records. Dr. Lowrance stated that his best guess of Franks's overall performance, based on three IQ scores, was an IQ ranking of 64. The score placed the thirty-year-old defendant in the mildly retarded range. Dr. Lowrance stated Franks read on a fourth-grade level.

The measurements, assessments, and determinations presented by Dr. Lowrance seemed to catch the attention of the jury, although many in the gallery fought to keep their eyes open.

The witness told the packed courtroom that Franks had been in special education since he was in the first grade, and was presently on the level of a functioning adult in a sheltered workshop.

"Mr. Franks is on the lower end of minimum-wage earners," Dr. Lowrance stated. "If he managed a store, they'd be bankrupt. He can perform labor-intensive work with supervision, but they would have to stay on him even if the work level is low."

"Could he fake the mental tests?" Leon Haley asked.

"I guess anyone could fake it. He would have had to do so from the first grade forward," Dr. Lowrance answered.

"Do you know his mental age now?" Haley asked.

"I can guess, I didn't calculate it, but probably about a ten-year-old. The lowest would be a seven- or eight-year-old," Dr. Lowrance stated.

When Greg Miller stood to address the witness, he concentrated on Franks's abilities to adapt, rather than on Franks's test scores.

Dr. Lowrance admitted he hadn't talked to any of Franks's teachers, nor had he asked Franks how he had been able to function on his own. He had asked about jobs Franks had performed, but he hadn't asked about specific job skills. Dr. Lowrance admitted he had not seen the statement Franks had made to investigators.

It had been a long day. A couple of the jurors rested their elbows on the arms of their chairs and put their heads on their hands. They, as well as almost everyone in the courtroom, were weary. The dry testimony concerning IQ scores, personality tests, and mental evaluations did little to eliminate their drowsiness.

As long as the day had seemed, Judge Gill was determined to squeeze every moment out of it, instructing the defense to call their next witness.

Colleen Vincent lived next door to Spencer Williams and his grandmother on North Hampshire in Saginaw. She sat in the witness chair, dressed in a lime green pantsuit, her red hair a blaze under the harsh fluorescent lights. While chewing gum, Colleen explained that she had been present in Spencer Williams's house the night that he had first seen a photo of Richard Franks on television.

"What did Spencer say?" Ed Jones asked.

"I asked if that was the man who got Opal," Colleen began. "He said, 'No.'"

Having made his point, Jones passed the witness.

After Lisa Callahan asked Colleen to go over the description of the man Spencer had told her had abducted Opal—including the red ball cap, long hair in a ponytail, and rough face—she asked if the photo Spencer saw on television revealed a clean-shaven, short-haired Franks.

"I believe so," Colleen replied.

Lisa Callahan returned to the prosecution table, pleased that Colleen had given a reasonable explanation of why Spencer hadn't recognized Ricky Franks as the man he saw snatch Opal.

The defense's last witness was Billy Carl Strine. Strine had spoken in the first trial of seeing a little girl and her grandmother at the grocery store next to the pawnshop in Saginaw. Again he explained he had seen a man looking at the little girl—a girl he believed to be Opal—in an inappropriate way.

"Is my client the man you saw?" Jones asked.

"No."

After a few brief questions Leon Haley announced that the defense rested.

Judge Gill excused the jury for the night and requested they be back in the jury room at nine o'clock the following morning to begin another day.

Greg Miller would use the evening to prepare questions for his rebuttal witnesses. He intended to have his experts counter the defense's, and to come out with a guilty verdict.

CHAPTER 18

William Parker was a former police detective who had begun Parker/Jones, Inc., an investigations company, in 1985. His expertise was in interviewing and interrogations, in particular with crimes against children. Well known by both the defense and prosecution, Parker was respected by both.

Greg Miller made a point of having Parker tell the jury he had real-world experience, not just academic theory like Dr. Leo, who had testified earlier. Parker had not spoken to Franks personally, but had conferred with Eric Holden, who had obtained Franks's statement, and he had read the defendant's statement.

Placing a chart on an easel in front of the jury box, Miller pointed out the four types of false confessions introduced by Dr. Leo. One by one, Miller read each of the confession types and asked Parker if they fit Ricky Franks's statement. Parker stated they did not.

Parker—who had interviewed people such as Darlie Routier, a mother convicted of killing her two young sons—reported to jurors that Eric Holden had reached a critical point during his meeting with Franks. When Franks was given the false scenario and had angrily insisted he hadn't committed the crime, Parker explained that was a significant indicator that Franks had told the truth when he admitted taking Opal.

"If you have someone who will admit to anything to make you happy, then when given a false scenario, they will admit to that as well, to make you happy," Parker explained.

"Is it common to blame the victim?" Miller asked.

"Yes, it's common."

"Are they trying to minimize their actions?" Miller inquired.

"Absolutely," Parker responded.

Leon Haley rose to address Parker on cross-examination.

"When we talk academia and practical experience, academia is what teaches us," Haley stated, smiling.

"Yes, sometimes," Parker said.

"You went to classes to learn to be a detective," Haley said.

"Yes, of course," Parker concurred.

Haley's smile faded and his words turned biting. "Why should these people believe anything you say when you have a bias because you're a detective?"

"You're making an assumption. I have no bias here," Parker said calmly.

Audrey Sanderford, who was late for the beginning of the morning session, slipped into the back of the courtroom, hand in hand, with Amber Hagerman's mother, Donna. Donna hadn't had the opportunity to attend the trial of the man who had taken Amber, he had never been identified, but she wanted to be there for Audrey. Donna wanted to give her support to Audrey through yet another emotional time.

Audrey and Donna, along with others in the courtroom, heard Parker state that it was very rare for a person to confess to a crime he didn't commit, and then Parker admitted that under certain conditions there could come a breaking point where a false confession might be made.

"In my experience I've placed a tremendous amount of pressure on people who never confessed," Parker stated.

"You have to be careful. The weaker the mind, the easier the confession," Haley said.

"Not necessarily. I have interrogated lawyers and gotten confessions," Parker said, smiling.

"You haven't gotten one from me, have you?" Haley rebuked.

"Not yet," Parker said with a grin.

Laughter broke out in the courtroom.

The attorney and witness began to banter back and forth as speculative questions were answered with flip responses.

"You know how to mislead people, don't you?" Haley asked.

"Define 'mislead.'"

"The law allows you to lie to people, to trick them, doesn't it?" Haley asked accusingly.

"I don't think so," Parker said calmly.

"They lied to him," Haley stated, pointing to Franks.

"It gets down to the definition of 'lie.'"

"Oh, now you're getting down to Clinton," Haley said as the courtroom again burst into laughter at the reference to the former president.

After a few more questions concerning the difference between interviews and interrogations, Haley asked, "Someone other than my client could have taken Opal; is that not right?"

"Not in my estimation," Parker replied.

When asked why a video or a tape recording hadn't been made of Franks's interview, Parker explained that they were seldom used because suspects were often reluctant to talk in front of the electronic devices. Parker reminded the court that a statement had been taken from Franks and signed by him.

With one last effort to impart to jurors that psychological abuse was rendered on his client during the time he spent with Eric Holden, Haley then passed Parker back to Miller for further questioning.

"Texas is the only state in the United States that requires a written confession," Miller stated.

"That's right," Parker agreed.

"When you told him you thought he had killed Opal Jennings, his reaction was to get up and move to the corner. Was that significant to you?" Miller asked.

"Yes, it was."

"Do you think Ricky Franks killed Opal Jennings?" Miller questioned.

"Yes, I do."

Parker left the stand and took his seat in the section of the courtroom reserved for law enforcement. There he waited, along with courtroom spectators, for the next witness.

Like Parker, Dr. Randy Price, a Dallas clinical and forensic psychologist, was well known to both prosecution and defense attorneys. During his career he had testified for both defense attorneys and district attorneys alike.

The primary objective of Dr. Price's testimony was to present his analysis of Franks's confession. In forming his opinions, Price had read thousands of pages of documents, school files, defense documents, and psychological studies.

On a color-coded chart analyzing Franks's statement,

Price pointed out the overwhelming majority of words used by Franks were one-syllable words, some two-syllable, 5 to 6 three-syllables, and none with more than three.

Dr. Price agreed with Dr. Lowrance's assessment and testing of Franks's IQ, but he noted that in Texas three factors must be present in determining mental retardation: the IQ must be below seventy; there must be evidence of defects in adaptive abilities or life skills; they both must have started in childhood. In Dr. Price's opinion Ricky Franks did not meet all three criteria.

"Is the content of the statement consistent with the statement of a person who would commit this type of crime?" Miller asked.

"Yes, the rationalization, blaming of the victim, minimization of his own culpability, raising the child to a pseudoadult status, and in some way being protective of her, are all similar characteristics," Dr. Price stated.

In discussion of Dr. Lowrance's estimated age of Ricky Franks being that of seven to ten, Dr. Price stated that the mental age idea is an outdated concept that was never intended to apply to adults, and shouldn't be used. Dr. Price insisted it was misleading to use a mental-age estimate.

"Can you give a true mental age?" Miller asked.

Using the chart Miller had set up, Dr. Price began his calculations determining that, in his opinion, Franks's mental age was nineteen years, two months.

"Different than ten or eleven, isn't it?" Miller asked.

"And certainly different than seven," Price responded.

Defense attorney Ed Jones attempted to reaffirm Dr. Lowrance's estimations of Franks's IQ and his inability to understand what was happening to him on the night he was arrested. But Dr. Price was confident in his own professional assessment. He remained convinced that Franks was aware of what he told investigators and that he comprehended the implications of his statement.

By 1:30 P.M., on the afternoon of day four of the second trial, both sides rested. All four attorneys were exhausted from the preparations and executions of two trials. None of them wanted to be back in court for a third. They all hoped, some prayed, for a conclusive verdict of guilty or not guilty.

Judge Robert Gill read the charge to the jury and counseled them not to consider all "possible" doubt but, rather, all "reasonable" doubt. As Judge Gill addressed the jury, Ricky Franks sat motionless, devoid of his often-present twitch. He stared straight ahead. Judge Gill then called for closing statements.

Lisa Callahan slowly walked to the center of the courtroom, placing the familiar confession on an easel before the jury.

"In all of the old Western movies, you see a group of men seated around a campfire," Callahan began. "They are seated in a circle of light and around them is nothing but darkness. And there are predators in the darkness. You hear them and you can see the shining of their eyes. You are that circle of light.

"You are people who go to work, who pay your taxes, who care for your children, who try to do what is right. But there are others in our community, others who stand outside, who wait for a moment of opportunity, for a second of lack of attention. Like foxes outside the henhouse, they wait for a moment to steal a chick. What are the odds that this defendant is just such a predator?"

Callahan pointed out the written confession she had set before them and the confessions Franks made in the county jail to four different people. She told the jury they could convict on the statements Franks made in jail alone. Even if they believed the written confession was improperly obtained, they had the evidence the prosecution had introduced.

The assistant district attorney pointed out that Spencer Williams had described events that were basically just like those contained in Franks's statement.

"What are the odds that a person who wasn't present, doesn't know anything about it, would be able to describe that series of events so completely, would be able to describe how many children were playing in a field?" Callahan asked.

Callahan continued with what she termed "incredible coincidence," including that Franks's statement indicated Opal lived in the house near the field. She asked the jury how the defendant would know that.

"There is no question about it. This is one and the same individual that committed the offense. Not only beyond a reasonable doubt, but beyond any doubt," Callahan stated.

In closing, Callahan tugged on the jurors' emotions.

"Ladies, at the heart of who and what we are as women is the idea that we protect life—and not just all life, but particularly new life. And, gentlemen, at the heart and the core of what you are is the idea that you will protect those who cannot protect themselves.

"It is too late for this little one," Callahan said, tears filling her eyes, her voice cracking from emotion as she pointed to the photo of Opal Jennings. "It is too late for her, and we grieve for that as a community. But it's not too late for others. Convict this defendant because he is guilty. Because he committed the crime. Because he did it.

"The state of Texas, the people of Tarrant

County, and the family of Opal Jennings will await your verdict."

Callahan's participation in the second trial was over. She could only sit back and hope that her words had touched the jury, had helped to convince them that Richard Lee Franks was responsible for the disappearance of Opal Jennings.

Edward Jones rose, momentarily placed a hand on the shoulder of his client, and then walked to the jury box. Jones told jurors he was tired, as were all the other attorneys whom they had seen in the past days, as he knew they were. "Everybody wants this over with," Jones said.

"It's a horror. It's a horror that this little girl is gone. It's a horror, but—just like Ms. Sanderford said—if Ricky didn't do it, they need to let him go home," Jones remarked.

The young attorney recapped witnesses' testimony that Ricky Franks was not the man they saw on the afternoon of Opal's kidnapping, including that of young Spencer.

"The state is going to rely on sympathy and bias. And they are relying on that, not evidence. Is it so astronomical to believe that maybe he didn't do it? Where there is absolutely no evidence to show you that he did?"

Like Callahan, Ed Jones had completed his portion of the trial. It was Leon Haley's turn to talk to the jury, to convince them Ricky Franks should be sent home.

Haley began by asking the jury to hear him out, informing them he didn't have much time to speak to them.

"Ricky is on trial because the investigators for the state had a theory. They had a theory based upon information that they received. And you know what is unfortunate about the whole thing is that it all started out, not because Ricky did it, but because somebody said Ricky had a red hat on, a red cap that everybody runs around town wearing. My kids, your kids, people with young minds, have red caps," Haley stated.

The defense continued by admitting that Franks had made the written statement, but pointed out that just because his client had made the statement didn't make it true. Over and over again Haley implied that Ricky Franks was like a child, easily manipulated and confused.

"He didn't do it," Haley stated. "There is no evidence to support it. No physical evidence. No scientific evidence. Absolutely nothing. And you don't come in here and convict somebody because they said they did something and there is nothing to corroborate it, absolutely nothing."

After accusing investigators of conducing an improper arrest and interrogation, Haley walked to his client, stood behind him with his hands on Franks's shoulders, and continued to address the jury.

"I intend to take him home. Let's join hands and do it right. Let's make them go back out there; let's make them find Opal, which is what they say they want to do. I promise you, when they find Opal, wherever she is, they will be sick and looking really silly when they realize it wasn't him.

"When a system overreaches and puts one of our citizens on trial, only you, *only you*, can stand there and say stop it. You can do it. You told me during voir dire you had the courage to do it. Now do it. Tell me that I can take my client home."

Ricky Franks wiped tears from his cheeks while his brother Rodney brushed away his own tears.

Greg Miller stood, a fire burning within him. He began a spirited final statement, which had a cutting edge intended to pierce the defense's pleas for acquittal.

"Mr. Haley asked you to take a look at Ricky Franks. I'm counting on the fact that when Ms. Manning was reading Franks's statement, some of you were looking at Ricky Franks.

"All through the trial, Ricky Franks has sat over there, head up, held high, laughs when everybody laughs, smiles when everybody else smiles, shows the appropriate reaction. But when Kathy Manning read this statement to you," Miller said, pointing to the enlarged statement on the easel, "[you] didn't hold your head up so high, did you, Ricky? You had it down in shame because you knew you took her."

Without notes to assist him, Miller fervently ran through the witnesses and the evidence the defense rejected as valid.

"When you add it all up, there is only one conclusion that you can come to: Richard Franks is guilty of aggravated kidnapping.

"And there is a reason why Richard Franks hasn't told us where the body is. And it didn't come from any of the officers, any of the other witnesses. Andrew Bouyer (Tarrant County inmate) summed it up perfectly when he said to Richard Franks, 'If they find her body, you will fry.'

"There is a world of difference between an aggravated kidnapping conviction and a capital murder conviction.

"When you add up all the evidence, you're going to come to the same conclusion that some of these people told you about, that Richard Franks is guilty of aggravated kidnapping.

"Mr. Haley says he wants to take him home. Well, I want him to go to a new home. I want him out of Tarrant County in another home, in the prison system. Don't turn Richard Franks loose for someone else's young child.

"Good luck with your deliberations."

As in the first trial, anyone in the courtroom waiting for a "smoking gun" to be presented in the final moments of the trial was disappointed. There would be no *Perry Mason* moment, when someone would come forward to convince jurors and spectators alike that without a doubt Ricky Franks kidnapped Opal Jennings. The state's case was strictly circumstantial. No blood evidence, no DNA evidence, no fingerprints. Just a strong case built on glaring circumstantial evidence and Franks's own vile statement.

At 2:25 P.M., deliberations began for the twelve jurors contemplating Franks's guilt or innocence.

Sometime later, the jury sent out a note asking for certain testimony. The first of the inquiries was Mike Adair's question to Franks regarding Saginaw and Ricky's response to Adair concerning his knowledge of the area.

By late evening, after deliberating for eight hours, the jury hadn't reached a decision. Judge Gill released them for the night, instructing them to return at nine o'clock the next morning to continue their discussions.

The court gallery had dwindled considerably the following morning. It was a Saturday and most of those not required to be present had gone about their normal routines.

Ricky Franks walked into the courtroom with his shoulders thrown back and a smile across his face. His eyes met his wife's and his smile broadened.

Judy Franks and Ricky's mother, Bessie, were dressed in identical T-shirts. Judy had donned her familiar heavy blue eye shadow and her hair was slicked back. One of her front teeth was missing.

Again the jury asked for testimony to be read to them for clarification. They wanted to know if Eric Holden had asked open-ended questions or closed questions during his interview with Franks. The third inquiry was about Dr. Leo's testimony regarding testing the validity of a statement. However, Judge Gill believed the inquiry too general and that the question should be more specific. The panel later wanted to hear the description of the person and the car seen by a number of people who had testified.

At 2:20 P.M., testimony of Jesse Herrera about Franks's haircut and the tip he had passed on to the task force was requested. Then at 2:52 P.M., jurors asked for Agent Lori Keefer's statement about the false scenario told to Franks on the night of his arrest.

Greg Miller sat in the jury box talking with another assistant district attorney. From his location he could hear loud voices coming from the jury room. Miller suspected there was a lively, even argumentative discussion taking place. He wondered how the jury was leaning. Then the buzzer from the jury room again sounded. The bailiff went to the jury room door, took a piece of paper handed to him, and gave Judge Gill the note.

"The jury has just sent a note saying that they are unable to render a unanimous verdict." Greg Miller's eyes closed momentarily. He let out an exhausted sigh. *Not again,* he thought. *Not again.*

"At this point I intend to read the jury an Allen charge and tell them to continue their deliberations," Judge Gill announced.

An Allen charge is an instruction by the court to a jury that is having difficulty rendering a verdict in a criminal case. It encourages the jury to make a renewed effort to arrive at a decision. Some judges no longer permit the instruction to be given after the jury reports it is deadlocked because it may have a coercive effect upon the jury. Judge Gill thought it necessary in this case, with this the second jury to hear the Franks kidnapping case.

Leon Haley stood to address the court. Haley asked for a mistrial and objected to the Allen charge being given to the jury.

Judge Gill made note of Haley's objection, then called in the jury.

"Mr. Foreman, without telling me what the numbers mean, could you tell me numerically what the split of the jury is at this point?" Judge Gill asked.

"Ten to two," the jury foreman replied.

Judge Gill rendered the Allen charge and instructed the jury to continue deliberations, informing them that if they were unable to reach a unanimous verdict, it would be necessary to declare a mistrial.

Once the jury was back in the jury room, Leon Haley again addressed the court.

"Your Honor, I would like for the record to reflect that one of the jurors is crying and I submit that with that Allen charge being submitted to them, with all that coercing, that one juror is being intimidated by at least ten of the other jurors. I'd ask the court for a mistrial."

"Denied," Judge Gill responded.

Nearly eight hours after beginning a second day of deliberations and sixteen total hours of debating the guilt or innocence of Richard Franks, the jury came in with a verdict.

"I expect the jury's verdict to be received by you with the proper courtroom decorum," Judge Gill announced to everyone present in the courtroom.

"Has the jury reached a verdict?" Judge Gill asked.

"Yes, we have," the foreman stated.

"We, the jury, find the defendant guilty of the offense of aggravated kidnapping as charged in the indictment," the foreman said.

Judy Franks sobbed loudly, sucking in deep, painful breaths. Blue eye shadow and black mascara streamed down her face as her body shook from intense weeping. Bessie Franks held her hands to her face, hiding the tears she shed for her youngest son. Rodney Hemphill clung to his girlfriend, his face buried in her hair. Richard Franks pursed his lips and narrowed his eyes in an angry scowl directed at the jury.

Lisa Callahan allowed a smile to cross her lips as Greg Miller simply heaved a sigh of relief.

The Sanderford family sat quietly. There was no celebration of victory for justice. No triumphant smiles. They hoped, as Greg Miller had assured them, that the person responsible for Opal's disappearance had been held accountable. But the verdict still left them hollow. Opal was still gone.

Judge Gill announced October 2, 2000, as the date he would sentence Richard Lee Franks.

On October 2, 2000, the defense for Richard Franks asked for a mistrial. Judge Gill denied the motion. It was then on to the punishment phase of the hearing.

Greg Miller called Angela Weaver, a twenty-year-old woman who had first met Ricky Franks when she was about five years old. Franks was fourteen or fifteen at the time. Weaver had met Franks at his mother's home in Newark, Texas.

"Did Franks ever touch you?" Miller asked.

"He would touch me in my vagina area," Weaver stated.

She explained that Franks would also make her perform oral sex on him, and he would perform oral sex on her. Franks told her it was a game they were playing and they would both be in trouble if anyone found out. Weaver told the court that she finally told her mother when she was thirteen years old. Franks had never been prosecuted for the abuse.

The disclosure of the abuse suffered by Weaver was just one more indication that Ricky Franks was a sexual predator. His deviant behavior was known to have begun by age thirteen or fourteen, although it could have been even earlier, and continued until age thirty when he abducted Opal Jennings. The chances were that there were dozens of other victims who had never told.

Cassie Bishop was called to the stand. Bishop, a probation officer for Wise County in 1991, was in court when Richard Lee Franks entered a plea of guilty to the offense of indecency with a child, the victim being his eight-year-old niece. He'd been assessed a seven-year probated sentence. Miller presented the witness to show that Franks had been convicted of a sex crime against a child previously, thus enhancing his sentence and mandating a life sentence.

Judge Gill spoke to the defendant. "Mr. Franks, the jury having convicted you upon your plea of not guilty of the offense of aggravated kidnapping, and having made an affirmative finding that the offense was committed with the intent to violate the victim sexually, and having found that the sex offender notice in the indictment is true, it will be the order, judgment, and decree of this court that you be sentenced to life confinement in the Institutional Division of the Texas Department of Criminal Justice."

Flanked by Tarrant County sheriff's deputies, Richard Lee Franks was led from the courtroom without incident to begin his life sentence at his prison home.

CHAPTER 19

Nearly five years had passed since Opal Jennings had been playing with her friends in the yard of her grandparents' Saginaw, Texas, home. The trees along North Hampshire Street had grown a little taller, but little else had changed.

Teresa and Clay Sanderford, along with grandson Austin, had bought the house across the street from Audrey and Robert. Austin participated in play therapy in order for him to deal with Opal's abduction, and Teresa listened whenever Austin felt a need to talk.

"Opal's gone. That bad man got her, put her in a car, and made her cry," Austin would say.

Patricia Barrett, Teresa's sister, and her family continued to live on the corner, only a couple of houses away. Spencer Williams and his grandmother were right next door. Spencer and Austin remained playmates.

With the passage of time Audrey seemed to have found strength through the tragedy of Opal's kidnapping. Although the physical and emotional strains had taken their toll, including the dissolution of her marriage to Robert, Audrey had found a purpose. She moved back to Clarksville, Arkansas, the place of Opal's birth, and began an association that supported the National Center for Missing and Exploited Children. Opal's great-aunt, Michelle Schmoker, set up projects to fingerprint and photograph more than five thousand children so parents would have proper identification. Michelle's "Project Kid Print" also included a kit for taking a DNA sample. Together Audrey Sanderford and Michelle Schmoker set up an "Opal Jennings Memorial Kid Print and Safety Fair" on March 26 of each year, the day Opal was kidnapped. They did it all in the name of Opal Jennings.

The people of Clarksville barely knew Opal, yet the newspapers had dubbed her an Arkansas "River Valley girl."

Arkansas became one of the first states to copy Texas's AMBER Plan child-abduction system. In 2001, even before the system had been adopted nationwide, fourteen Arkansas children were rescued, three from dangerous abductors, thanks to the early-warning plan.

Leola Sanderford moved back to Saginaw permanently. Teresa became her closest confidante. They often spoke of Opal, not with sadness but with the joy she had brought to their hearts in the few short years she had been with them.

Leola had "Opal" tattooed on her left ankle, not to remind her of her daughter, who was seldom out of her thoughts, but to show her unfading love for her.

Judy Franks returned to her parents' house in South Fort Worth, while Bessie, Ricky's mother, moved from Fort Worth to a small community less than one hundred miles west. Bessie had not only lost Ricky to the Texas prison system, but another son, Danny Doyle, had hanged himself while being held in the Bridgeport, Texas, jail.

Rodney Franks, although sympathetic to Opal's family, continued to believe in his brother's innocence.

He appeared on local programming to expound upon a biased investigation and an overzealous prosecution.

Edward Jones, Leon Haley, Greg Miller, and Lisa Callahan moved on to other cases, but their thoughts often returned to Ricky Franks and the missing Opal Jennings. Only Patrick Davis remained on the case, as Franks's appellate attorney. He filed motions with the courts on Franks's behalf, but he finally exhausted all legal avenues of relief. Franks's conviction and sentence were upheld, assuring that he would serve at least thirty-five years of his life sentence.

The years since Opal's abduction and the trial of Richard Lee Franks remained in the hearts and minds of, not only those close to them, but also the millions of people who populated the Dallas/Fort Worth metroplex. With Franks behind bars for life, the people of Saginaw felt a sense of relief, but Franks's incarceration failed to erase totally their sense of insecurity. The town would never be the same.

Everyone close to Opal had learned to cope with her loss, but the question of where she was always remained.

On December 30, 2003, a Tarrant County couple rode their horses along familiar terrain one hundred yards from Western Oaks Road, near the western shore of Lake Worth. The horses walked slowly through the rural, brushy area about seven miles from Saginaw.

Talking as they enjoyed their afternoon in the brisk December air, the couple suddenly pulled their horses up short. They had spotted what appeared to be a human skull in a rugged culvert. Nearby lay a faded pink Barbie tennis shoe. They immediately notified authorities.

Additional bone fragments were found in the area and speculation ran high that the bones belonged to Opal Jennings, but authorities refused to comment.

Citizens on Patrol members constructed a road-block at the entrance of Western Oaks Road the next day, preventing onlookers from driving down the dead-end street. A command post was set up for dozens of cadets from the Fort Worth Police Training Academy, Homicide detectives, Crime Scene officers, officials with the Tarrant County Medical Examiner's Office, and an anthropologist. The cadets, as well as cadaver-finding dogs, searched part of a 116-acre city-owned tract of land.

Opal's Saginaw family waited patiently for official notification. They had waited nearly five years for word of her whereabouts; they didn't want to get their hopes up.

"If it turns out it is Opal, that would be great," Teresa Sanderford told reporters. There would be some closure for the family.

Dr. Marc Krouse, deputy chief medical examiner, announced that the remains would have to be examined and compared to DNA profiles of missing persons. Krouse indicated the process of identification could take weeks.

As the second day of the search for skeletal remains resumed, the screeching sound of chain saws blared through the tranquil countryside. Searchers pushed back thick brush and foliage to see the ground better. Although a number of various tools were used to cut through the dense undergrowth, most of the search was by hand, in the dirt. Searchers wanted to make certain that no fragment of bone, no matter how small, was overlooked or damaged during the excavation process.

The area of discovery was in the opposite direction of that pointed out by Ricky Franks during the fruitless searches he led DA investigators on. It was within the ten-mile radius of Opal Jennings's home, as FBI profilers had suggested. And it was in the area that Assistant District Attorney Greg Miller had suggested searchers probe right after Opal's disappearance.

Texas EquuSearch had returned to the North Texas area ten months earlier to probe the region again for any sign of Opal. They had concentrated their efforts in the low-lying areas of the search grid, relying on Franks's initial comments that he had put her in or near the water. Texas EquuSearch hadn't looked at the higher elevated site where the bones were found, stating they had run out of time and daylight.

It appeared no one had searched the dense area of underbrush since Opal's disappearance.

Greg Miller had talked with Tarrant County medical examiner Dr. Nizam Peerwani personally, requesting that he not make any announcements concerning the identification of the bones until he had consulted with the district attorney's office. But on January 2, 2004, Peerwani told the press that the size-thirteen tennis shoes found with the remains were the same type that six-year-old Opal was wearing when she was abducted.

"Coupled with a forensic anthropologist's estimate that the skull is of a child, five to seven years old, suggest that the bones might be Opal's," the India-born medical examiner said. "I can't speculate whether or not this is Opal Jennings as of yet. We're only suspecting that. Certainly, if we do identify the remains as that of Opal Jennings, this will be a wonderful thing because it will bring a closure to the case."

The announcement was made before Miller and others in the district attorney's office had had time to decide if any further charges would be filed against Franks in the event the remains were indeed Opal's. They weren't prepared to answer questions concerning murder charges against Franks; they needed time to find evidence that tied Franks to the location or to the body. It was unlikely more charges would be filed. Considering Franks's mental disability, it was doubtful he would receive a death sentence. Franks was already serving a life sentence and it seemed a waste of the county's resources to try him for murder, even if conclusive proof was found.

A cause of death also would be needed to prove murder. Peerwani already had announced in a news conference that more bones were needed to determine how the child had died. The bones that had already been recovered were spread across an area of several hundred square yards. It was uncertain if enough bones could be found to garner a conclusive cause of death.

The scattering was not unusual, remains are frequently scattered because of scavengers or weather, human traffic or animal traffic in the area.

Opal's family just wanted the ordeal to be over. They had waited years to find Opal. If the remains were Opal's, it would be a relief after years of wondering.

"I just want it to be over with. I just want to bury her," Leola Sanderford told reporters tearfully as she was held close by Teresa.

Clay Sanderford, Opal's great-uncle, added, "There's never going to be closure. That's a word I just don't understand. I call it acceptance."

Meanwhile, the Sanderford family spent time attending holiday get-togethers at the Garden of Angels, a memorial to murdered children and young adults along the grassy roadside on Trinity Boulevard, near the Fort Worth and Euless border.

The Garden of Angels began with a single cross remembering Arlington teenager Amy Robinson, a mentally retarded girl killed by two men who were eventually sent to Texas's death row. From that single white cross eventually sprouted a two-block stand of crosses along the roadway from the original parklike setting. The area was further graced with an iron archway, a waterfall, a statue of a boy and girl playing gleefully, and concrete benches nestled among pink crape myrtle trees.

Gary Price, a Fort Worth carpenter, was known as the "Cross Man." He already had constructed one of the 3-by-4-feet white permanent crosses for Opal Jennings, and another eight for future youths taken under horrible circumstances before their time. If the bones found near Lake Worth were those of Opal Jennings, Price would paint Opal's name, date of birth, and date of death in black paint on a cross to be added to the seventy-six others already in place.

On January 12, 2004, Dr. Nizam Peerwani officially identified the remains found in the area near Lake Worth as those of Opal Jo Jennings. The Tarrant County Medical Examiner's Office had submitted a small bone fragment to the University of North Texas Health Science Center, DNA Identity Laboratory, in Fort Worth.

Texas is the only state to operate its own Missing Persons DNA Database as an additional tool for investigators trying to locate missing persons or identify remains.

The lab collected a family reference from Leola Sanderford. The mitochondrial DNA type demonstrated a likely maternal relationship between the sample from Leola and the mitochondrial DNA of the remains.

After further discussions with Dr. Peerwani, the lab was then provided with a tooth found in the skull for further DNA analysis. The DNA obtained from the tooth yielded conclusive DNA evidence, with a 99.99 percent probability that the remains were those of Opal Jennings.

Opal had been found. Finally the Sanderfords could put her to rest

CHAPTER 20

A light mist gently fell on motorists' windshields as they approached the Richland Hills Church of Christ. Cars filled with friends, relatives, and even strangers filed past the uniformed officers pointing the way to designated parking. Umbrellas in black, red, blue, or green shielded mourners as they made their way to the entrance of the large, impressive church.

The Sanderford family attended a smaller Methodist church not far from the imposing Church of Christ. But with the enormous outpouring of love, concern, and support they had received over the previous four-plus years, they felt a larger venue was needed. The family expected many of the hundreds of volunteers and lawmen who had worked on the case to be present. They wanted to make certain no one who wished to say their final farewell to Opal was turned away.

Audrey, Robert, Leola, Teresa, Clay, Patricia, Duane, and dozens of other family members had stood in the rainy drizzle of the cold January gray morning only hours earlier to mourn the loss of Opal privately. They had watched as the little girl that lit up their lives was eulogized and her small casket lowered into the ground. She was gone from their vision, but she would live in their hearts forever. At the close of the service, her mother lifted her arms toward the heavens and released a single white dove.

The Saginaw Cemetery, across from the elementary school where Opal loved learning, would provide a constant connection between the little girl who loved purple markers and the school that encouraged her creativity.

At the church, flowers that adorned the front of the sanctuary were nestled around the now-familiar picture of Opal. Balloons, teddy bears, and other mementos were scattered among the blossoms. Mourners sat in silence, staring at the larger-than-life dancing eyes of Opal Jennings staring back. For nearly five years people had searched for her and prayed for her safe return, but with the discovery of her small shattered body only weeks earlier, all hope of finding her alive had been lost.

Opal appeared to mourners in the form of an enormous full-length photo prominently projected on a screen above the cloth-covered altar. Her black blouse and black-and-white-checked skirt were accented by black patent leather Mary Jane shoes and white lace-trimmed socks. It was the last photo ever taken of Opal; as usual, she was smiling from ear to ear.

Attendees wearing pink ribbons affixed with white pearl-head pins silently watched the photo as if Opal would bound through the screen and laugh at them for their sadness. Mourners read the small two-page program that bore a sketch of praying hands on the front, with the words "In Loving Memory" under them. Inside, a verse by Helen Steiner Rice spoke of going on and living life. Across from the poignant poem was the name of Opal Jo Dace Jennings and the words: Opal was born November 24, 1991, in

Clarksville, Arkansas. She was abducted Friday, March 26, 1999, from her home in Saginaw, Texas, and her remains were found December 30, 2003, in Fort Worth, Texas.

The words threatened to shatter the sanctity of the moment. Then the faint sound of music drifted through the hall. Not the familiar solemn psalms of ordinary funeral services, but children's music.

"Twinkle, Twinkle, Little Star," "I'm a Little TeaPot," and "My Bonnie Lies Over the Ocean" played on a single piano rang through the church like a one-hundred-piece orchestra. Mourners dabbed their faces with tissue as tears filled their eyes, each visualizing Opal innocently playing in the yard with her two friends Austin and Spencer.

Tributes thoughtfully placed at the altar were in Opal's favorite colors. A pink-and-purple spray, pink carnations in the form of a heart, pot plants with pink and purple bows, and a sunburst of pink gladiolas filled the church with the fragrance of spring, shutting out the harshness of winter. The familiar sound of "London Bridge" hung in the air like a thick English fog and stirred feelings of sadness.

A contingent of women of varying ages walked in and took seats in the left front section of reserved pews. Wiping their eyes as they looked at the photos of young Opal, they listened to the songs so familiar to them all. All teachers at Saginaw Elementary, the women had played games to the tunes with their schoolchildren on the playground and recalled Opal as a gleeful participant.

Nearly fifty members of Opal's extended family made their way to the front of the church, taking their seats directly in front of Opal's images. After an invocation by Reverend Grady Brittian and a moving song, "Our Texas Rose," sung by Sara Martino to the tune of "A Candle in the Wind," Teresa Sanderford steadily walked to the podium and addressed the surprisingly sparse crowd.

Only about one hundred people had made their way to the Richland Hills Church of Christ. Many not in attendance could not face the finality that Opal was gone. Many felt frustration and heartbreak that their efforts had not brought Opal home alive. Assistant District Attorney Greg Miller had told the family in a private moment the evening before the scheduled memorial that he would not be attending. He feared the media would disrupt the services by asking him questions about pressing murder charges against Ricky Franks. Miller believed the focus of the day should be on remembering Opal, not her kidnapper and killer. Miller had said his own private goodbyes to the child he had never known but had passionately championed.

Teresa Sanderford spoke from her heart. She thanked the Saginaw Police Department, many of whom were in full dress and seated in the audience. She acknowledged the FBI for their help and Greg Miller for his compassion. She thanked Rod and Beverly Petty, the couple who found Opal's deteriorated body, for bringing their child home. Teresa read a poem one of Opal's aunts had written right after Opal was taken. Tears brimmed in everyone's eyes.

Teresa, an adoring aunt, announced that the family had put their "blue-eyed princess to rest" earlier that morning. She recalled the endearing things about Opal that family members remembered well.

"When she was two years old, Opal called every woman in the family 'mama,'" Teresa said with a smile. And it was appropriate since every female in Opal's family considered her their own.

"At six, Opal was allergic to soap," Teresa said with

chuckles from the family. "She would stand in the bathtub and splash water on her face." The memory of the shortened baths brought smiles to the audience.

"Opal loved her family. She would beg to go with her grandpa when she would hear his car start. She loved to eat at the El Sombrero restaurant, always ordering the number-five special, with chicken and a Sprite.

"Once, Opal decorated the seats of the school auditorium, works of art not appreciated by the teachers or the principal," Teresa said, laughing, revealing her niece's impish side.

"She had a one-hundred-watt smile," Teresa continued.

All eyes drifted to the photos of Opal at the front of the sanctuary. Her beautiful blue eyes and her radiant grin penetrated their hearts.

"If we could see her now, she'd be smiling with that mischievous twinkle in her eye. I urge you to remember the sweet little girl, not the victim," Teresa concluded.

As Teresa stepped down from the podium, sniffles resonated throughout the sanctuary and a flurry of white tissues were lifted to tear-filled eyes. For those who knew Opal well and loved her, the service was difficult, just as it was for those who never knew Opal but had come to cherish her.

Donna Whitson Norris, mother of Amber Hagerman, struggled to keep her composure. She wanted to bawl like a baby. Opal's photos, the memorials, the flowers, all brought back the loss of Donna's own little girl. Norris was one of only a few people at the service that knew, *really knew*, what the Sanderford family had endured. Amber Hagerman's mother understood the loss of a child was the saddest of all tragedies that could befall a family.

Norris had brought with her a gift for Audrey Sanderford. The two had forged a bond, Norris giving strength to Sanderford and the courage to go on. Norris had smiled as she watched Audrey file in with the family, clinging to the purple bear Donna had given her. The attached note read: "Opal, you will always be in our hearts." These were sentiments shared by all present at the service.

Gioia Jones was Opal Jennings's kindergarten teacher. She had only known Opal for six short months, but the spunky six-year-old quickly had become one of her favorite students. Jones spoke to the audience, not of lessons Opal had learned, but of lessons Opal had taught her.

"Opal taught me red is absolutely the best color, hugs are a really good thing, and smiles make a bad situation better," Jones said. "I also learned purple markers don't come off lockers or auditorium seats."

Jones shared with the others that Opal was loved by her school family. It wasn't difficult for anyone to believe. Even those who had never met the child believed they knew her. Opal Jennings had truly become everyone's little girl.

In closing, Jones reminded everyone, "Every child has worth. Children are our legacy."

Heads nodded in agreement as Gioia Jones returned to her seat in the midst of the other Saginaw Elementary School teachers. Both Teresa Sanderford and Gioia Jones had raised the moods of the mourners with playful depictions of Opal in their eulogies.

Reverend Grady Brittian focused on the Gospel, stating that Jesus loved the little children. Then, twisting the title of Hillary Clinton's popular book, Reverend Brittian remarked, "It takes a child to raise a village. Saginaw was Opal's village. And every village needs children to teach us to laugh and to play."

The preacher thanked those persons who never gave up, those who continued to search, to hope, and to pray for Opal's safe return. He thanked the media for making them more aware of Opal's plight and that of other missing children.

"A village needs children and it needs grace. Our natural feelings are to forgive, but I have war with those feelings," Reverend Brittian admitted.

Most of those in attendance understood the minister's words. They, too, had a war raging within them, a war of forgiveness versus revenge, but Reverend Brittian proclaimed his own vow. "I will not serve a god of retaliation, nor should you. A village needs comfort. It is over. Our hearts have been breaking for some time, but it's over. It's over.

"Jesus said, 'There will be no more death, dying, crying, and pain. The darkness will be no more.'

"The village needs peace, a place for children to grow up. Peace without violence.

"And a village needs hope," Reverend Brittian said. "He now waits for you. Opal belongs to God and always has."

Following Reverend Brittian's words, the beautiful, innocent voice of thirteen-year-old Michelle Mashburn, a seventh grader at Highland Middle School, filled the round sanctuary with the sweet sound of music. Michelle sang "My Little Girl," a song written by former Roanoke, Texas, police detective Ron Crawford after Amber Hagerman was abducted.

Tears streamed down the faces of those who loved Opal, as well as Donna Norris, who relived the loss of her own child as well as Opal.

The service was over. People embraced Leona, Teresa, Audrey, and other Sanderford family members. They had shed tears for nearly five years, it was time to smile and to laugh again. Audrey clung to the purple bear given to her by Donna Norris as she met with friends. She looked forward to moving on.

While well-wishers met with the Sanderfords in the Church of Christ foyer, one lone uniformed police officer remained inside the church. He had hung back, waiting for the others to pass by the picture of Opal and say their own farewells. The officer slowly walked forward and stood in front of Opal's smiling image. His head bowed, his shoulders stooped, the officer paused for several minutes. Before turning to go, he wiped a single tear from his cheek.

In memory of Opal Jo Dace Jennings
November 24, 1991–March 26, 1999

EPILOGUE

January 21, 2003, Senate Bill S. 121, the *National AMBER Alert Network Act of 2003*, was passed by the U.S. Senate in a ninety-two to zero vote. The measure was introduced by cosponsors Kay Bailey Hutchison (Republican from Texas) and Dianne Feinstein (Democrat from California).

The act expanded nationwide the AMBER Alert communications network that helps law enforcement find abducted children. It established an AMBER coordinator within the Department of Justice to enhance the operation of those communications. The act also established voluntary, minimum standards for coordination between various AMBER plans, particularly between states. It provided for a grant in the Department of Transportation to fund, on a fifty-fifty matching basis, AMBER Alert programs. Lastly the *AMBER Alert Act* provided for a grant in the Department of Justice to fund, on a fifty-fifty matching basis, education, training, and related equipment for AMBER Alert programs throughout the country.

"When a child is lost, the whole community grieves along with the family. An AMBER Alert channels this energy to a positive purpose. Tips from average citizens have resulted in the safe and rapid recovery of many children. We can spread the word about abducted children across county and state lines quickly, before the kidnappers have the chance to cover their tracks and get too far away," Senator Hutchison stated as she addressed the U.S. Senate prior to their historical vote.

PROTECTING CHILDREN
Provided by
TEXAS AMBER ALERT NETWORK

To help protect your child from stranger abduction:

- Know your neighbors and your child's friends, including their names, addresses, and phone numbers.
- Check the references and qualifications of day-care centers and baby sitters. Ask day-care centers if criminal background checks are conducted on staff members.
- Teach your child what to do if approached by a stranger. Common ruses are offering a ride, gifts or candy, asking the child to help look for a lost pet, or claiming that the child's parent has asked them to bring the child home because of an emergency.
- Listen to your child; don't disregard their fears. Instead, let them know that you take their fears and concerns seriously.

For more information and tips, download the "Personal Safety for Children: A Guide for Parents" publication from the National Center for Missing and Exploited Children at missingkids.org or the Polly Klaas Foundation Child Safety Kit at www.pollyklaas.org.

A child is too precious to lose.

Acknowledgments

There are always so many people to thank in the writing of a true story. In this tragic tale of an event that changed the lives of countless people, I must first thank Opal Jennings's family. Their loss has been overwhelming, yet they opened their hearts to reveal the tragic impact such an unthinkable experience has on those left behind by a lost child.

Teresa Sanderford is a strong, loving person who has the unique ability to comfort others in times of her own grief. She has been a rock to her family, especially her grandson Austin and Leola Sanderford. Teresa has held together a family that has suffered the greatest of losses. I thank Teresa for her honest, uncensored account of the events surrounding the abduction of Opal.

Leola Sanderford, often misunderstood, is without a doubt a loving, unselfish mother. I thank her for her willingness to open up old wounds that run deep. I wish her all the best as she attempts to build a new life in the shadow of her daughter's memory.

Thanks go to Audrey Sanderford for her assistance and her dedication to the cause of lost children.

This book would not have been possible without the tremendous support of Greg Miller. This case was one that no prosecutor would relish tackling, yet he persevered not once, but twice. I thank him for his insight and his candor.

Many thanks to Danny McCormick, of the Special Crimes Unit, for the time he shared during the preparation of this publication.

I regret both Ricky and Judy Franks's decisions to

decline all interviews. There are always two sides to every story. I expressed theirs the best I could.

Behind the scenes there are always those who continue to offer their expertise, support, and undoubting belief in me. A heartfelt thanks to Tina Church, Tina Church Investigations, and Jan Blankenship, LPC. Both women are fabulous resources, as well as great friends. To the gang at PSI, Carrolle Montgomery, Tami Russell, and Myra Rodriguez, I thank you for putting up with the endless mood swings and for your ever-present encouragement. And special kudos to Eddy Lynton, who always makes me smile and continually makes me believe in myself.

Thanks to Michaela Hamilton for tolerance that was stretched to the limit.

And finally much appreciation goes to LaRee Bryant, friend and editorial consultant extraordinaire. Without her my work would never be complete.

MORE MUST-READ TRUE CRIME FROM

M. William Phelps

MORE MUST-READ TRUE CRIME
FROM PINNACLE

Slow Death   0-7860-1199-8 $6.50US/$8.99CAN
By James Fielder

Fatal Journey   0-7860-1578-0 $6.50US/$8.99CAN
By Jack Gieck

Partners in Evil   0-7860-1521-7 $6.50US/$8.99CAN
By Steve Jackson

Dead and Buried   0-7860-1517-9 $6.50US/$8.99CAN
By Corey Mitchell

Perfect Poison   0-7860-1550-0 $6.50US/$8.99CAN
By M. William Phelps

Family Blood   0-7860-1551-9 $6.50US/$8.99CAN
By Lyn Riddle

Available Wherever Books Are Sold!

Visit our website at **www.kensingtonbooks.com**.